MW00583393

Irish Spirit

PAGAN * CELTIC * CHRISTIAN * GLOBAL

Edited by

Patricia Monaghan

WOLFHOUND PRESS

Published in 2001 by
Wolfhound Press Ltd
68 Mountjoy Square
Dublin 1, Ireland
Tel: (353-1) 874 0354
Fax: (353-1) 872 0207

© 2001 Patricia Monaghan as editor for her texts, and individual contributors for their texts

All rights reserved. No part of this book may be reproduced or utilised in any form or by any means digital, electronic or mechanical including photography, filming, video recording, photocopying, or by any information storage and retrieval system or shall not, by way of trade or otherwise, be lent, resold or otherwise circulated in any form of binding or cover other than that in which it is published without prior permission in writing from the publisher.

British Library Cataloguing in Publication Data
A catalogue record for this book is available from the British Library.

The publishers have made every reasonable effort to contact the copyright holders of text quoted in this book. If any involuntary infringement of copyright has occurred, sincere apologies are offered and the owners of such copyright are requested to contact the publishers.

ISBN 0-86327-875-2

5 4 3 2 1

Cover Image: Image File
Typesetting and book design: Wolfhound Press
Printed in the Republic of Ireland by ColourBooks, Dublin

Contents

Introduction

Stone circles. Spiral carvings on rock. Fairy kidnappings.

Tara's king, drinking from the cup of the goddess. Priestesses tending a perpetual flame. Supernatural heroes in deadly combat.

Monks illuminating gospels on vellum, their quills tracing intricate scrolling ornament. Nuns serving the poor, far from their green island home.

Holy wells. Pilgrims climbing sacred mountains.

A bomb blowing an infant from its mother's arms. Slurring slogans sprayed on slum walls.

Which of these most truly represents Irish spirituality?

By itself, none. For Irish spirituality is all of these, and more: visions and poetry, love of nature and of place, embodied passion and a call to service. Irish spirit is found in the piercing poignancy of the uillean pipes and the keening of a woman for a murdered love. It is online rituals and jazz fusion and New Age druids.

Ever since Ireland came into history, it has been renowned as a place of spirit. In ancient times, it was a land where the veil between the world and the other was thin, where divine races wrestled with each other for primacy. Later, Ireland became the land that kept the faith when it was in danger of being lost, a land that sent back the good word to light the continental darkness. Even later: a place of backward superstition and fanatic sectarianism. Since the beginning of history and probably before, the life of the spirit has not been taken lightly in Ireland.

Nor is it today, although Ireland has transformed itself into a secular state with unmatched speed. Globalisation and membership in the

European Union has helped propel the Irish economy from pre- to post-industrial without stopping in the middle. Social mores are shifting too as the residue of colonialism continues to fade, affecting everything from electoral politics to education. No institution, including religion, is untouched by these bedrock shifts. Church-based laws and customs have passed into history at the same time as scandals have brought about widespread disaffection with organised religion.

At the same time, the industrialised world looks towards Ireland as a beacon of spiritual wisdom against the darkness of materialism. Books on Irish spirituality (usually labelled 'Celtic' and published outside Ireland) crowd the bookstalls. American churches plan special services for ancient Irish holidays. Tourism to Ireland is booming, with visitors clogging the roads to passage graves. At a time when religion has been de-centred from the lives of Irish people, both individually and as a collective, the world looks to Ireland to save, if not civilisation, at least civilisation's spiritual component.

And Ireland is rising to the task. For an increasingly pluralistic world, Ireland's spirituality is a living example of how differing religious visions can illuminate and enliven one another. The Celts, coming to Ireland from continental Europe at the dawn of history, encountered an unknown culture and wrapped themselves in it. Christianity arrived and, unique in the ancient world, made no martyrs out of the indigenous pagans, who in turn killed none of Christ's followers. This exemplary history is scarred by the tragic continuing war in the North where economic prejudice cloaks itself in religion, but even that struggle offers lessons for those who would find a way towards peace.

Irish Spirit offers you the voices of dozens of writers from Ireland and the Irish diaspora. No one alone defines Irish spirituality. Indeed, even taken together they do not exhaust its possibilities. For Irish spirituality is like the Irish landscape, where nothing is ever utterly lost or destroyed. The most ancient spiritual truths are still discernible, like dolmens behind holiday homes. We begin with those dolmens, and the other stone monuments that dot the countryside, as we explore the continuing resonance of an unknown people's spirit. Then we examine the lasting influence of an historical people, the Celts. After looking at a few of the many ways in which Christianity influences the Irish spirit, we acknowledge some of the more destructive aspects of the Irish spiritual heritage. Finally we conclude with a journey through some of the surprising ways that Irish spirit makes itself felt in the present. This book is not a series of sermons, but a conversation, one that we hope continues beyond this work's ending.

Part One

The Time of Stones

*T*en thousand years ago, the great ice finally retreated from Europe's westernmost point. The land rebounded from its glacial burden, revealing immense stones strewn across a landscape that had been in many places scoured to bedrock, while piles of rock debris formed little rows of hills. Seeds of arctic plants carried in the glaciers' frozen hearts sprouted and soon — soon, at least, in geologic terms — the island was dark with great climax forests. Birds flew in to nest and breed. Animals followed, migrating across a land-bridge from what is now Scotland.

Humans readily found places like prehistoric Ireland, where animal and plant food was plentiful. It was a very new land — perhaps only a few thousand years old — to which the first humans arrived, probably from Scotland. Archaeological digs in Ulster have found vast middens of shellfish, suggesting that the rich beds of oysters, periwinkles and mussels were a mainstay for these first Irish. Other settlers soon followed, making their homes first around the rich river mouths, then slowly penetrating the forested interior where they carved small clearings in the forest and established tiny villages.

We have no way of knowing what these people believed, for they were prehistoric — literally, living before written history. Small implements, possibly for ritual purposes, have been found in archaeological digs from this period. In addition, we find names in unknown languages affixed to prominent aspects of the landscape. Thus the hooded crone, the Cailleach, whose non-Celtic name is found on many mountain peaks in Scotland and Ireland, may be Ireland's most ancient divinity. But only such faint traces are left of the Irish pioneers.

Then, some seven thousand years ago, something revolutionary happened in the Irish spiritual consciousness. It may have been the coming of a new people who worshipped in stone circles and artificial caves. Or those long resident in Ireland may have learned through trade and travel about the creative and spiritual explosion on the continent that resulted in the great stone monuments of Brittany and England. No temples or shrines are found before this megalithic ('big rock') period, which lasted perhaps a thousand years and left an astonishing number and variety of structures across the land. Built of stone, they include many of the most impressive and renowned of Ireland's spiritual sites.

The simplest, and possibly the oldest, is the dolmen or court-tomb, built of upright stones capped with a lintel. The feat of hoisting such massive stones into position — to say nothing of the engineering skill that has kept them standing for millennia — has given rise to many legends and speculations. Even more impressive is the astronomical acumen apparent in the construction of such structures as the Brug na Bóinne at Newgrange, surely Ireland's most famous megalithic structure. An immense mound of rock covering a corridor of trilithons or standing stones capped with the world's oldest corbelled arch, Newgrange is oriented precisely to the rising sun on the year's shortest day, the winter solstice. A beam of light shoots through the roofbox above the doorway into the small dark cave, a dramatic event whose spiritual significance seems unquestionable, though its meaning is fiercely debated. Similar alignments have been argued but not as dramatically confirmed for other megalithic structures in Ireland.

Because there are no written records from this period of Ireland's past, we lack the words of the builders themselves to interpret these grand and moving structures for us. But perhaps they did tell us — in the gorgeous expressive rock carvings found at so many of the megalithic structures. Best known today is undoubtedly the triple spiral from Newgrange, omnipresent in art and advertising. But other glyphs, like the star and the sunburst, are found graven into the hard granite, weathering away as they have on the collapsed stones around Loughcrew in Meath or protected from the elements as in the interior of the cairn at the same site.

Conservative archaeologists warn that we cannot decipher these carvings without some Irish equivalent of the Rosetta Stone to guide us, and no such ancient glossary in several languages has been unearthed. But imaginative scholars like Marija Gimbutas, and artists like Martin Brennan, boldly offer interpretations of the exuberant carvings, finding evidence of a great Mother Goddess, whose watchful eyes gaze out at us from the rock and whose ample body sustains us with food and fresh water. Such theories have made Ireland's megalithic sites required pilgrimages for those seeking a non-patriarchal spiritual worldview.

There are other ways in which the spiritual vision of the pioneer Irish has been carried forward to the present. Irish myth resembles that of many other indigenous and tribal people in imagining multiple settlements of the land by people with differing religions. Folklore, that highly conservative force, preserves fragments of those ancient beliefs but mixes them together so that it becomes impossible to know the origins. Irish lore, transcribed from oral sources in historical times, therefore may encode information about the pre-Celtic inhabitants of Ireland. These folkloric fragments suggest that the worldview of the time was animistic, seeing the divine not as separate from this world but as resident within it. Stones, birds, mountains, rivers and even people, in this view, are holy, for all are part of the great mystery.

The Long Circle Home

✤

Pete Hamill

Born in America to emigré parents from Belfast, Pete Hamill is one of New York's most beloved columnists. His books include the novel Snow in August *as well as the non-fiction books* Why Sinatra Matters *and* A Drinking Life: A Memoir. *He believes that even those who do not consider themselves religious or spiritual — even those, like him, who define themselves as agnostic — connect with the Irish Spirit.*

When I first went to see Ireland in the summer of 1963, I was not certain about what might await me. To be sure, I was not completely ignorant of Ireland. My parents, immigrants from Belfast who had met in New York, remained Irish in many ways. The tales of Fionn mac Cumhaill and Cúchulainn were part of my childhood, along with a potted version of Irish history and what I thought was Irish music. I was educated in the schools of a Brooklyn neighbourhood where the word 'Irish' was a synonym for 'Catholic'. I had marched in St Patrick's Day parades. I was delighted by the vision of Ireland presented in such films as John Ford's *The Quiet Man*. If that vision was a lie, it was a charming lie. Later, while learning the writing trade, I had read Yeats and Joyce, Wilde and Shaw and Swift, O'Casey and Frank O'Connor. All gave me an abiding curiosity about the land from which so many of the Irish had fled, including my mother and father and their friends.

But when I flew to Ireland that first time, I was no longer a boy and certainly not in search of my Irish roots. I was a newspaperman, trained by vigorous masters to a permanent secular scepticism. My newspaper teachers distrusted the abstract, the ideological and the mystical. Every day of the week, they subjected the events of the world to empirical proof. 'Trust your mother,' such men insisted, 'but count the cards.'

As a result, I was determined to try to see Ireland clearly, not through the hazy lenses of Irish-American sentimentality. That detachment was underlined by the character of my parents. As Belfast people, the Ireland of leprechauns and Blarney Stones was remote from their lives; they were city people, whose myths were about British soldiers, murder gangs and pogroms. Ulster put marks on them that would last all their lives. As a son of the Irish diaspora, I had my own uneasy feelings about Irishness. I was repelled by the figure of the 'shure-and-begorrah' stage Irishman; it was another version of the shuffling Stepin Fetchit stereotype that so enraged many of my black friends. I quickly wearied of the green beer and shamrocks of St Patrick's Day. And I could not imagine Yeats or Shaw breaking into some beery version of 'Danny Boy'.

In 1963, religion and the spiritual barely existed for me. I was not against religion, which at that time embodied the more glib notions of the spiritual; I just didn't get it. Even as an altar boy, when I enjoyed the secret codes of Latin and the dramatic structures of the rituals, I felt detached from the core of the Mass itself. The whole notion of a jealous, vindictive and narcissistic God, sitting in a place called Heaven, judging the flaws, failures and sins of his own creations, seemed even less plausible to me than Flash Gordon. As I grew older, I came to cherish the music and art of Catholicism, its grand sacred architecture, the kindness and compassion of its individual priests and nuns, the demand of its schools for human excellence. I just didn't believe in the central premise. I was not like the Dostoevsky character who passionately believed in atheism. I was more like E.M. Forster, who said, 'I do not believe in belief'.

And so I was unprepared for what happened that morning when I first glimpsed Ireland from a window seat in an aeroplane. After the long night's journey, I finally saw through shreds of cloud the green, rain-softened land. And I was astonished. My scalp tingled. My skin pebbled. I felt a sensation of something invisible rising towards me, like atomic particles. A kind of fine dust made up of a billion scrambled messages, directed at me from the green silent land. Transcending centuries. Or millennia. Rising from beyond the knowable world and its wretched histories, to speak to me.

Come, they seemed to whisper.

Come home. We've been waiting for you.

I recognise now what I did not understand all those years ago: I had been touched by an obscure feeling that most properly could be described as spiritual. I do not know if it is simply a proof of the power of the human imagination. It might be, in the broader sense that all gods are the inventions of men. But in my own case, I did not first imagine my reaction and then find a way to have it verified. The pebbling of skin and tingling of scalp had not truly happened to me before that day. Neither had the sense of being bombarded by primordial messages.

They did happen to me again in Ireland, in the years that followed. Once when looking at Newgrange. Another time when walking around the Hill of Tara. In each case, I was older and knew that the verifiable facts do not always lead to the truth. I knew more about Irish history and Irish myth but remained hopelessly secular. But at Newgrange and at Tara, my skin pebbled, my skin tingled, and I felt again that I was receiving messages from the congested earth.

With one major exception, these feelings never came upon me in Irish cities. Since I was a city man, and the son of city people, I loved those cities. Belfast, Dublin, Cork and Galway demand to be explored. When I'm there, I prowl bookshops and visit museums. I devour the newspapers. I stand in doorways and look at faces and the way people walk. I love listening to the jokes — the 'crack' in Belfast is a glorious cousin to the sardonic humour of the Jews. I have visited the grave of

Jonathan Swift and tried to find the house where Frank O'Connor grew up. I have resisted the Bloomsday celebrations, with their platoons of leather-elbowed academics, but I have gazed at the Martello tower in Sandycove. I have just never had a spiritual experience in an Irish city.

Except when I hear the music. The Irish music I heard as a child was only technically Irish. Much of it was a commercial concoction, created to exploit the sorrows of the millions who lived in the Irish diaspora that began with the Famine. Those songs — like Yiddish and Italian ballads of the day — were full of longing and grief and the finality of departure. Tin Pan Alley refined its own 'Irish' genre in the twentieth century for an audience that was primarily Irish-American, becoming essential to St Patrick's Day celebrations and to the repertoire of such singers as Bing Crosby and Dennis Day. But many twentieth-century songs also contained elements of English music-hall ballads, driven by the ongoing comedy of class, and were then expanded to include rebel songs, full of martyrs and defiance. My father loved to sing many of these songs. So did I.

But when I first heard true Irish music, originally made by men and women whose names were lost to history, I felt another one of those strange internal shifts. The pipes, flutes and drums touched a mysterious place in me, as if echoing through some deep cavern. I did not know the tunes but seemed to have always known the music. Images of bonfires, roasting carcasses, empty landscapes scribbled through me. I wanted at once to fight, sing, shout, make love, and howl at the moon.

Since then, I have heard more of the music that I suppose must be labelled 'pagan' and, no matter where I am, it moves me in some extra-rational way. In its presence, I feel utterly Irish. The dark power of those chords performs — at least in the moment of hearing — an extraordinary act of erasure. Gone are 'Galway Bay' and 'McNamara's Band', of course; but gone too are New York and baseball and the American language, along with most recorded history. I feel connected to a world that is virtually empty. In those moments, Christianity seems a mere latter-day parenthesis in Irish life. I am in a place where wolves move through Irish forests and whales can be seen from Irish shores. I speak a language that I no longer know. I feel the existence of the Otherworld, illuminated by the green glow of emeralds, harbouring the honoured dead.

Again, I do not know if such reactions are merely essays in the human imagination. I know I felt them (and feel them), but that old scepticism keeps nagging at me. Each time I have encountered New Age zealots, I have eased towards an exit, needing fresh air to rid me of the cheap incense of charlatanry. The books published by many of these people are intellectually slippery and mediocre, written in the style of salesmen. Add them all together, and they do not have the value — as literature or thought — of a single page of the King James Version of the Bible. Like many other people, I have no interest in adopting some pagan creed in reaction to the failures of organised religion or the complexities of the modern world. Cults appal me, because they entail a surrender of will and choice. We have seen in the Nazi cult and the Stalinist cult what can happen when true believers have guns.

And yet there are many cases of people firmly rooted in the world of reason who have had experiences similar to mine. Like me, they are not mystics, but they have felt emotions that could properly be called spiritual. Human intelligence is, no doubt, in a very early stage of its quest to understand why and how such experiences take place. But I have come to accept the intuitions (based on wide cultural and individual research) of Carl Gustav Jung. In 1936, the Swiss psychologist wrote, in explanation of his theory of the 'collective unconscious':

> While the personal unconscious is made up essentially of contents that have at one time been conscious but that have disappeared from consciousness through having been forgotten or repressed, the contents of the collective unconscious have never been in consciousness, and therefore have never been individually acquired, but owe their existence exclusively to heredity.

That seems true to me. If I am reading him correctly, Jung is insisting that there is a kind of genetic memory in human beings, passed down through all the generations — altered, refined, diffused, displaced, but alive. This seems to be true of cultures all over the world, Jung says, and Ireland is surely no exception. Somewhere in the Irish mists, things happened. Tales were told about those events. Music was made to express them, to defy them or to tame them. And both the events and their artful mirrors were so vivid that they became part of a general-ised, tribal memory. Somehow — and this is the place to which the investigations must go — they were deeply encoded in the people who shared the same portion of the earth. They were passed down, consciously or unconsciously, century after century. In my own case they became part of the consciousness (even if buried) of the Hamills and Devlins who passed them on to me.

Somehow, in Ireland, this enduring consciousness is also connected to the land. The Irish landscape has been denuded, abused, scarred, exploited. But in the land's empty places, an Irish visitor, even from the diaspora, can still feel the abiding presence of those men and women who came before, wearing the skins of animals, and shaping iron into pots and swords.

Listen to them whisper. Listen to their music. In that moment, you are home.

Soil and Myself

Liam Heneghan

Liam Heneghan, a Dubliner, has lived in the United States since 1994. A soil ecologist by training, he teaches and does research at DePaul University, Chicago, Illinois. His research topics have ranged from acid rain impacts on invertebrates in a Kilkenny spruce plantation, to tropical soil ecology in Costa Rica. Currently he is working on prairie and woodland ecosystem restoration projects in the Chicago area. The author of more than a dozen very dry research papers, published in international ecological journals, he finds spiritual sustenance in his scientific pursuits. He can be contacted at lhenegha@wppost.depaul.edu.

I am approaching the summit of Mount San Antonio. During the gold rush of the 1870s the mountain was prosaically renamed Mount Baldy. The bald one. Mount Male-Pattern Baldness, as Kaj, my wispy-haired Swedish-American hiking companion, calls it. The 10,064-foot pinnacle dominates the San Gabriel mountain chain and gives 'unrivaled views of desert, mountain and sea'. I have come here to complete my spiritual rejuvenation. I am very focused right now. I survey my physiological reactions to the extreme altitude. Lungs feeling good. I inhale deeply, being careful not to damage delicate intercostal muscles. The air is aromatic, scented by lodgepole pines and cedars. But my head pounds and I am dizzy. At this elevation an Irishman can afford to take no chances.

My pace is sluggish. My legs feel as massive as the granite constituting the peak. One foot in front of the next, interminable footfalls crunching the scree. My pasty skin is frying, but I am chilled by the sweat evaporating from my body in the brisk breeze that blows across the trail they call the Devil's Backbone, a narrow ledge separating Lytle Creek gorge and San Antonio canyon — a one-thousand-foot drop to either side. Fortunately, I am in better physical condition than I have been in for years. No more than twenty-five pounds overweight, thirty tops. I'm flabby but determined. Adipose and raw will-power propels me to the summit.

I have come to this place of wilderness to complete a journey that began on a smaller peak on another continent fifteen years before. A journey that began with a loss of faith.

✤

Shortly after I graduated from University College, Dublin, I journeyed with two friends to the Holy Land. It was my first extended trip away from Ireland. I had spent five days in London a year before, consulting with an entomologist in the British Museum about some unusual flies that I had collected in the National Parks in Donegal and Kerry while working on my zoology thesis. I now had two months of free time before starting graduate school in New York City. After twenty-one years living in my parents' home, with the occasional sojourn in national parks, I was about to leave Ireland for quite some time. The plan was to spend October and November of 1986 in Israel, return for Christmas, and then depart in January for the New World.

We chose Israel as our destination, anticipating that it would be exotic enough to be a complete break from Ireland, yet familiar enough culturally to be accessible to us. In addition to the mundane ambition of seeing another country — a dress rehearsal for any longer stay away from home — I hoped that a visit to Israel would help me resolve the religious questions that had troubled me at university.

I had jettisoned my Catholicism while still an undergraduate. It seems surprising now that as recently as the early 1980s many students were devout when they arrived at college. This was especially true of conservative science students. Despite the abandonment of Mass attendance, few had proclaimed atheism. I had. I had taken the leap of non-faith — a deliberate decision not to believe. Reconstructing my thoughts now, my atheism was motivated by a desire to force the hand of God. I would not have expressed it like this at the time, but I wanted God to take sufficient interest in my spiritual plight that He would intervene and somehow, through the workings of His universe, reveal Himself to me. I wanted a miracle.

I had been a very religious lad, more pious than most I suspect. I went to Mass every day during secondary school, attending the 5.40 p.m. service with the Carmelites in Terenure College. I prayed fervently. I read the *Lives of the Saints* and cultivated a devotion to Padre Pio. I was priest material; I had in fact contemplated a monastic vocation. What more must a boy do to expect a miracle?

I recall reading that George Bernard Shaw, as a party game, used to bellow: 'If there be a God, I challenge him to smite me.' There would be a pregnant hush as the company waited aghast for the Supreme Being to pound the supercilious playwright. And nothing would happen. After having snubbed God, I also paused and disappointedly observed the unaltered laws of the cosmos. After that I found that I couldn't easily turn back to my old devotions. My defection from faith had broken something. Religious muscles rapidly atrophied. I had this chunk of spiritual flesh, useless and unwieldy, that I lugged around with me. I could never forget it was there.

Although my experiment with the cosmos yielded no immediate results, my scientific training compelled me to reassess my expectations. I still hoped for a way back to spiritual wholeness. I needed to affirm that my childish religiosity was either being replaced by a mature understanding of God, one that was in accord with my new-found scientific outlook, or I needed confidence that my relation to the universe made sense without a creator. Thus I was in a state of spiritual free-fall. I had launched myself from the summit, but had not yet crashed upon the rocks below. When I sat with my travelling companions, Bill and Helena, in Bewley's Oriental Café discussing our upcoming trip to biblical lands, I did not burden them with the thought that my entire spiritual welfare, the fate of my immortal soul, was accompanying us on the trip.

We spent most of our visit in the Old City of Jerusalem, immured in an ardent world conducive to the sort of saturation that we desired. My companions were ideal, leaving me to my own purposes when I needed the time. More often than not, though, we travelled together. In 1986 the internecine tensions that were later to spill over so ferociously in Israel were palpable. While we were there, a Palestinian storeowner was stabbed in the marketplace and the culprit fled through the street unapprehended. Nevertheless, a variegated throng of visitors populated the city, undeterred by such events. They streamed through narrow streets, resembling erythrocytes surging through blood vessels, coagulating in the markets, flowing by some biblical marvel or another. The events of thousands of years are scattered throughout the city, the sacred and the profane co-mingled. People of diverse faiths congregate uneasily like oil and water, sharing the city, sharing shrines, but never coalescing. There is no careful segregation of tourist and resident, and there is a blending of holidaymaker and pilgrim. Jerusalem is a great city to be bewildered in, for you are surrounded by the bewildered of every nation.

What I recall most about the Old City is the hats. Jerusalem is a milliner's paradise. Black-hatted Eastern Orthodox priests, Arabic white, and the formal wear of Orthodox Jews. I had been cultivating an exotic look of my own. For at least a year, I had paid no attention to grooming, which had never been my strong point. Styling myself after a picture of Tolstoy in peasant garb, I elected to dress in rags. I cobbled together a rough aesthetic of neglect. In addition to the rags, the aesthetic required eating little more than rice and brown sauce. I was, I am told now, a little scary to meet. A flaming red spade beard flowed down my chest like that of a young prophet. In the absence of a good rain hat, in Jerusalem I wore an ill-fitting blue plastic bag. I fitted right in.

I visited every religious shrine on the map, all the while reading my Bible, attempting to reconcile the geography of the place with historical events. One morning I traipsed down deserted lanes to the Church of the Holy Sepulchre for Mass. The Franciscans flocked around the altar anterior to the tomb of Christ, after the Orthodox priests had beaten a retreat like a routed battalion. They said their Mass with concision. I was moved by circumstances — the Holy Sepulchre, the incantations. But despite tremendous efforts I could not say to myself, 'I believe in God, the Father Almighty'. I monitored myself, observing my reactions. But I failed to translate the historical realities that I encountered, that I felt I could now authenticate, into a firm commitment to the Christian story.

Although the city of Jerusalem was the centre of the fervid world that the three of us created for ourselves, we made several excursions throughout Israel. One of these trips brought us up to Tiberius, on the shores of the Sea of Galilee. In the Church of the Multiplication, I reflected on the gospel story relating Christ's teachings on the Mount and His miracle of provisioning the loaves and fishes. The chapel was cool, tranquil and dimly lit by a greyish light drizzling down upon the pews. Examining a set of mosaics elaborately reconstructed on the chapel floor — a delicately excavated past — I realised that I had travelled in pursuit of an objective that I had not been able to fully articulate.

I could not explain why this disengagement that I felt from the beliefs of my own past had occupied a central position in my life. Later I wandered out onto the small balcony at a chapel overlooking the Mount of Beatitudes and acknowledged that even here I could sense no re-awakening of faith. I felt, in the heat of an Israeli afternoon, the anti-climax of having had no substantial resurgence of religious fervour despite immersion in Christianity's geographical epicentre. The crush-ing weight of my phantom problems and my choking physical need for belief evaporated. I had nothing to show for years of religious devotion. Bill snapped a picture of me standing on a parapet staring down into an olive grove. I don't recall what I was thinking, but he has dubbed this picture 'Liam losing his faith in God'.

No Saturday morning sodality, no secondary-school religion classes presided over by bored Spiritan Fathers, no idle reading of Hans Küng can prepare you for this — the loss of faith that doesn't feel like anything at all. Atheism had become a viable worldview for everyone, not just jaded intellectuals, when I became reconciled to it. Atheism was consistent with so much of what I suspected about the world, resonant with so much of the science I had imbibed, that when I finally plunged in, I disappeared from sight without kicking or screaming, without troubling the murky surface waters at all. I expected this moment to feel like drowning. It did not. It felt like a first gasp of air after an interminable holding of breath.

✖

The night before I first came to the United States I had two dreams. In the first I dreamt that I was in a locked cell. Light streamed in from a small window far above me. With an ingenuity that I, who cannot change a light bulb, found immensely pleasing, I managed to train rays of light onto the lock. The lock sprang open and I was free. In a second dream I flew like a bird above the American prairie. The unploughed prairie, the sod thick, intact, pullulating with the seeds of unidentified plants. It was an exhilaration that I can still conjure up — gliding breathlessly, moved by the beauty of the tall grass. The next morning I left for New York City.

Although it would be easy to characterise the next few years of my life as secular ones and contrast them to the previous ones dominated by my Catholic preoccupations, few things have such circumscribed boundaries. I had escaped the untenable pieties of my childhood — my mumbled rosaries, my preposterous asceticism — on the Mount of Beatitudes. Growing simultaneously, inadvertent and unattended, was another set of preoccupations, spiritual ones I see now, that tapped into a primal tradition. It was largely to this other tradition that I escaped. Though I never became an exemplary pagan, I cobbled together an adequate connection with the organic world that allowed me to navigate myself through the next few years.

I was born into consciousness with my legs below the water-table and the base of my head — irregularly shaped in youth, like a celestial object spun too violently on its axis — flush with the surface of the soil. My father was beside me baling water from a sump and sloshing it into the drain to the side of the 'sunken studio' that he had built at the bottom of our back garden. The studio had been constructed on a meagre budget and without a waterproof course adequate to withstand the pressure of the bounteous Irish water-table. Repetitively leaning in and baling water from a hole in the bottom of a Dublin suburban garden with my father, neither of us talking, the winter chill ignored, was an enviable nativity. I achieved Zen clarity, a glimpse of eternity, an oceanic bliss in our aqueous pit. These, at age nine, are the first moments of a continuous memory of myself. I have some earlier fragments, but I can account for my life pretty much continuously from that submersion in the sump until the present.

Templeogue Village, where I grew up in the 1960s and early 1970s, was no pastoral paradise, though it did retain some touches of the rustic. It was one of the furthest southern suburbs of Dublin. Stretching between Templeogue and Old Bawn were acres of pasture. As kids we would clamber over the garden wall on a summer's morning and disappear into a less civilised domain. In this realm of well-grazed fields and overgrown hedgerows, children ruled, some despotically. Never an assertive child, I steered my own routes, avoiding the invisible borders of these principalities. The row of trees at the back of the first set of fields was my destination.

The trees in the hedgerows were personal friends; most had names and particular attributes that recommended them. There were trees for swinging out of, one rigged with a seat that swung on a frayed rope over a yawning abyss. Other trees were climbing challenges. Though the trees are long gone — bulldozed one summer morning without warning, making way for a new housing development — I remember the ascent of my favourite tree. A foot placed in the crotch at the base of the reiterated trunk, a foot purchase on a small nubbin to the rear of the bole, some precarious gambolling from branch to branch. I could climb no more than halfway up. Friends could climb the fifty feet to the crown, up to the tiniest tendrils, and there they could, with confidence, rotate the tree until it was set swaying like a skyscraper in a hurricane. I would embrace the trunk far below, vicariously thrilled by their physical self-assurance.

I was happiest on a tree we had christened the BBLO. There may be kids from Templeogue who can recall what the initials stood for, but I do not. The BBLO was for repose. It was a dead trunk that protruded at a forty-degree angle at the edge of the field. Shimmying out to its tip, a trek of no more than twenty feet, I would lie along the bark-stripped bleached wood. Not far above the ground, but securely above the fray — a respite perched in the empyrean.

But all the time while lying there I would, at the back of my mind, contemplate the descent. I was torn between the delicious pleasure of being in the tree and the distrust of my physical ability to extricate myself. This was the problem for me. From early on I sensed the allure of the organic — the pleasures of knee-deep submersion, the thrill of swaying in the breeze, the calm of lying along the grain on the trunk of a favourite tree. I loved wild places and felt kinship with nature. I was committed to a pagan ethic — wishing no harm on others while claiming for myself a right to discover my true nature.

A third element of a pagan belief triumvirate — sensing divinity in the natural world — was alien for me however. I could no more satisfy myself with the expectation that the trees I loved hosted a divinity than I could acknowledge a transcendent God, Creator of the Universe. Despite moments where, lying among grasses and sedges and bog cotton on a peatland, I wept from a fleeting sense of the beauty of the firmament to which I belonged, I could rarely satisfy myself that I was integral to the natural order. Part of this was that I was — I am — desperately physically incapable. I have a gracelessness that surprises all who encounter me. I cannot, for instance, use a revolving door without it smacking me on the heels. There have been more extreme manifestations in recent years. When I walk, my feet take a little longer to reach the ground than I am expecting. It is as if the world spins away from my footfall, as if I am less attractive to gravity than another body of equivalent mass. My physical ineptitude has divorced me from a deep engagement with the world. It has meant that most of my transactions with the natural world have been quiet, methodical ones, or academic ones. Having discovered the joy of being both aloft in the trees and below the soil's surface, I have also recognised my alienation on the flat surface of the Earth. These peculiarities have drained my potential for a druidic life.

Thus, at the dawn of my departure from Ireland, I was an avowed non-believer, an imperfect pagan. I have now spent many years away from Ireland. I have felt myself to be part emigrant and part exile in the United States. The urgency of developing an ironclad set of beliefs, the necessity of faith, has become less insistent during these years. Living away from Ireland for so long made everything that characterised me — my Hibernian epigenesis, so commonplace before — appear outlandish compared with the childhoods of my US brethren. My brand of piety, my devotions, my struggles amuse my friends.

There was a time when being native to a place was important to me. It was important to me to return home to Ireland after my peregrinations. I also thought that I would inevitably return to Catholicism. But I have not. I will not return to Ireland to live, and I am no longer Catholic. That which I thought was authentic, native, natural, was no more than a mirage. An Irishman born in the 1960s in Dublin, influenced by pop music, by post-enlightenment science, by tree climbing, by baling water from a hole in the ground, is tenuously connected to an Irish past. Looking back now, I sense how things were unravelling for many of us then. There was no religious instruction in things that mattered. There were no lessons on prayer, no preparation for the dark night of the soul. Nor were there lessons on developing kinship with the natural world. The only education I had was my education in science. And if science has a faith, it is faith in a method. For the scientist, all belief is provisional. As a scientist, I believe until the evidence tells me not to.

There is a small patch of prairie about fifteen miles north of Chicago, the city where I now work. As far as anyone can tell, it has never been ploughed. In the summer, it blooms with compass plants, prairie blazing star, purple cornflower — highly conservative species, plants that grow only in areas that have not been disturbed. It is part of a network of sites that I now study. These sites are along a transect from city blocks to pristine remnant prairies, from urban to suburban forests, from trees on streets to tangled undergrowth in the forest preserves. Among the questions I want to answer: what sort of nature emerges when people are not paying attention, when nature is out of place? Do ecosystems with no firm roots in the past differ fundamentally from 'authentic' natural ecosystems?

The topics that scientists choose for research are rarely chosen at random. We follow the funding. Generally though, we have a measure of control over the arenas we choose. The things I have studied are the codicil of my struggles. Decomposition, nutrient cycling, the ecology of soil organisms that toil away in the mouldering litterlayer. More recently, I have studied the impact of species introduced from Europe on the soils of ecosystems surrounding Chicago. In decomposition a sloughed-off leaf is reincarnated — it loses its identity, breaks down into its constituent parts, slowly incorporates into a vast organic matrix that connects all parts of the forest — soil organisms, more diverse and numerous than we have even been able to dream of, many still nameless, given no tidy binomials, working away in the dark, providing for the world's renewal. Without them, plant growth would cease. We would cease. Redemption emerges from below.

Exotics, pests, aliens, invaders. These are the pejoratives used to label those audacious species that find themselves growing far away from home. Transported, often passively, over long distances, they grow alongside plants they have not co-evolved with. Some grow so spectacularly well that they dominate their new abode. Freed from the influence of their long-term competitors and the constraints of their aboriginal herbivores, they can spectacularly achieve their biological imperative — they reproduce and spread.

How could I, an exile, a transplant, an escapee from my own history, not be drawn to them? I am not, however, fully sympathetic to their plight. They should not be here; they deplete the diversity of native systems. As I walk through small woodlands of the Chicago Wilderness that are choked with European buckthorn, before emerging into wet meadows that are smothered in purple loosestrife — another European invader — I ask myself, an exotic in that landscape: should these robust survivors, this human legacy, be expunged from the land?

From the summit of Mount Baldy, if the weather is clear, you can see ocean, desert, and mountain, and if the marine layer has not cast a translucent mask over the southland, you can see the sprawl of Los Angeles. A few arcs of rock provide windbreaks at the summit. There is no new insight up here for me. There is no stunning realisation about my path ahead. It is no more a point of departure for me than the Mount of Beatitudes was the site of a fall from grace. But there are times when decisions have to be made, and linking decisions to particular moments in time, to special localities, makes them more easy to account for.

I am now husband, father, ecologist, teacher — all vocations that call for good ethical tools. I have derived these navigational devices from a variety of sources, all of which seemed to be religious ones, the remnants of my Christianity and my sense of the essential correctness of my place in this universe. I realise that the ad hoc rules that have helped me along the way are no more pointing true north than a compass does. Although I have kept off the rocks of perdition, once again I feel the need to find something less functional, more comprehensive in my dealings with the world; the old pain of separation from something personal and reassuring has awoken in me. I am in my mid-thirties, balanced precariously in the smack-bang centre of my biblical allotment of life span. There is little time for poor choices.

Chaos Theory is Irish

❈

Ed Hagan

Edward A. Hagan is Professor of English at Western Connecticut State University. He is currently working on a book about contemporary Irish and Irish-American fiction and autobiography. His most recent publication is an essay on Frank McCourt in New Hibernia Review. Hagan's father is from Dungannon, County Tyrone; his mother is from Cloonkeelane, Enniscrone, County Sligo. He can be reached at hagan@wcsub.ctstateu.edu.

Once upon a time in the 1980s, the American Conference for Irish Studies (ACIS) was looking for a logo. A graphic artist offered three designs for the consideration of the members, mostly Irish Studies professors in American universities. One design imaged the dome of the US Capitol garlanded in shamrocks. All three, in fact, made use of shamrocks. Begorrah!

The membership went nuts; the artist must have been chastised and threatened with fostering and other Irish benefits. The artist buried the shamrock, like the old Orange flute of the Ulster ballad, and adopted a La Tène motif — a design with orderly entanglements, webs of lines that fascinate while they puzzle. A bit of real Celticism, you know. None of that Irish-American, Bing Crosby, Danny Boy, Irish Eyes Are Smilin', gimcrackery that shamrocks represent in America. That the La Tène design derives principally from Celts who lived in what is now France troubled not the purifying professorate. So I thought the sin of 'shamrocking' had been banished from respectable Irish company, and

Real Irishism was to be preserved, precursing Michael Flatley's restoration of the black mini-skirt to Irish dancing. You know Flatley, the lad from Chicago, isn't it?

So what am I to do when I find myself on the tour at prehistoric Newgrange during the summer of the year 2000, and I realise that a professor from Cork has unearthed 5,000-year-old whorls on stone that seem to represent some idea like the Trinity? Other scratchings on stones resemble entangled webs in the *Book of Kells*, which, in turn, resemble the La Tène design. Surely, I thought, these pre-Celtic pre-Christians must have been the avatars of ACIS; they too had the good sense to bury their three-in-one doodles deep beneath a mound. But then I remembered that Protestant song about the flute that wouldn't play Papish music despite an exorcism. Some patterns, ideas, beliefs won't stay buried.

Newgrange's three-in-one fingerprint-like whorls and the shamrock are similar but not identical. The whorls register a human imprint on cold, hard rock, while Saint Patrick apparently used nature's shamrock to explain the Trinity. Human consciousness has rather permanently altered the stone; individual shamrocks die in the temporal world, but the shamrock species is likely to outlive the human imprints on the Newgrange rocks. The rocks and the plant do it differently, but both express a fundamental unity of the one and the many.

We have here a physics, the material shapes of the whorls and the shamrock, indistinguishable from a metaphysics, the three-in-one idea. This odd recurrence of the shapes as human concept and natural phenomenon suggests an implicate order in sheer randomness — a strange attraction fundamental to Chaos Theory. Is the coincidence mere accident, to be dismissed without serious consideration? Or glibly attributed to social and economic forces that we'll eventually understand? We're left to figure out our random, post-modern, chaotic lives for ourselves, by ourselves. We're oppressed by fragmentation; we doubt we can find continuity. But that bit of continuity between 3000 BCE and Saint Patrick, who arrived in Ireland c. 432 CE, offered me some solace in the summer of the new millennium, fresh as I was from wondering what had 'slouched toward Bethlehem to be born'.

It is a tough life, it is, I know. Many of my fellow professors are convinced that the spiritual life I seek is delusion and weakness. I will confess to fascination with a little roadside shrine in Culleens, County Sligo, a few miles from Cloonkeelane, my mother's home townland. Local teenage girls said Mary visited them there a few years ago, and I like to believe them.

I have some peculiar ideas about spirituality, and I may have learned them from my Tyrone-born father. He attended Mass in the neighbouring parish because the pastor of the New York City parish in which we lived once tried to tell him about his 'duties'. Every Sunday he would walk an extra six blocks to find the anonymity 'his parish' offered him. He suspected Roman collars as a general principle, so he rarely went to communion, although he never missed Mass on a Sunday and said his prayers daily. I'm not quite sure what he believed, but I suspect he felt embarrassed and guilty about his unorthodox Catholicism. He seems to have taken transubstantiation seriously. If he didn't believe in it, he could have looked good by hitting the communion rails regularly. Somehow that communion wafer just might be the body of Christ, so he wasn't going to be sacrilegious about it.

I quite agree. Transubstantiation is not about the actuality of the hocus-pocus; it's about recognising the identity of the material with the spiritual, the unity of physics and metaphysics implicit in Chaos Theory.

As I became a young adult, James Joyce helped me to see transubstantiation as broadly applicable to the artist's task. Joyce put it this way: 'I found a certain resemblance between the mystery of the Mass and what I am trying to do — to give people a kind of intellectual pleasure or spiritual enjoyment by converting the bread of everyday life into something that has a permanent artistic life of its own — for their mental, moral, and spiritual uplift.' Joyce did not dwell in the world of the remotely spiritual; his art was conditioned by the life of ordinary sense experience, just as the communion wafer does not lose the properties of bread once it becomes the body of Christ. *A Portrait of the Artist as a Young Man* convinced me that I should try to attune my senses to those moments of sudden spiritual insight that Joyce called epiphanies. The material world is not alien to this sense of spirituality; it's just hard to see. The ancients arranged Newgrange so that once a year they could see the power and regularity of the sun in the grey wetness of winter — apparent undifferentiated chaos, lacking power or system.

At such moments objects realise (or we realise) their full 'thingness' and become utterly luminous, sacred, pregnant with meaning, insight and, most of all, connection. All of this quite literally happens inside the passage tomb at Newgrange at the winter solstice and only then. Though planned at Newgrange, such moments surprise us daily. Spirituality sees that connectedness, while at the same time it maintains its awe at the mystery of virtually every facet of our existence. Spirituality catches the order at moments, and then respects, even enjoys, the chaos of everyday existence. The spiritual person tries to live every moment as if it were outside temporality, while at the same time remaining keenly aware of the pain of temporality. A chaos theoretician would say that such epiphanies result from accidents that are really self-organised order. Accident is order although it also appears to be chaos. Epiphanies occur suddenly, just like accidents.

But note: the thing remains a thing, except that I now see it as a part of other things. Joyce convicts Stephen Dedalus in *A Portrait of the Artist as a Young Man* for precisely this flaw in his aesthetic theory: Stephen does not see the art object in relationship with other objects. I too convict myself of spiritual blindness for my habit of failing to see. That failure is altogether normal, and I am tempted to both complacency and scepticism by it at all times. Spirituality is open both to the believer and to the agnostic. (That usually leaves out fundamentalists and atheists.)

So here I am, trying to explain how Chaos Theory offers me spiritual light, and I begin by telling stories that degenerate into essays or what they call meta-fiction these days. Let me complete the turn to literary critic and point out some underlying ideas in my stories:

- Categorising is a normal human weakness: because we're weak we develop needs to ensure the purity of our categories. (Shamrocks offend the category of Real Irishism.)

- Categories create a false sense of control over the world by claiming for it an order that it does not necessarily possess in any absolute sense. (Shamrocks do image the Trinity, but 'three persons, one god' remains mysterious.)

- Smug dismissals of apparitions of Mary in the west of Ireland are rash, evidence of falsely sophisticated thinking. I don't care that the social and behavioural scientists have plausible, materialist explanations (such as the instability of the contemporary Catholic Church) for apparition eruptions. I like to think that Mary just might be disturbed by crass materialism, or perhaps she doesn't like using the excuse of corrupt clergy to indulge the self. Although the social and behavioural scientists think they start from scientific premises, they actually start from the un-acknowledged position of many scientists — belief in their ability to explain phenomena completely, their premise being that the world is ordered according to categories known or discoverable. They differ little from religious fundamentalists, who act as if their beliefs are really bodies of knowledge.

- Miracles should not be dismissed even when they seem like delusions. Think of them as eruptions of order amidst chaos or chaos within order. (The Culleens phenomenon organises the local faithful whose faith is simultaneously disorganised by the eruption of the unusual.)

- Similarity attracts our attention; it fascinates because it offers hope of a connectedness that otherwise seems elusive, even foolish. And similarity is just that: resemblance but not identity. Patterns, ideas, phenomena resemble one another but not completely. The match is never complete. (Shamrocks are not identical with Newgrange's whorls.)

- Paradox and irony are the stuff of good stories. They reveal sur-prising, synonymous and simultaneous order and chaos. (La Tène possesses dubious Irish roots.)

- A pattern of thought (the futile burying of the shamrock) has its parallel in the natural world (the burying and exhumation of

Newgrange). Metaphysics and physics are immanent in one another.

- In Ireland physical objects have embodied the spiritual, regardless of the religion. Shamrocks and rocks are sacral objects that embody the spiritual. They don't represent the spiritual; they are spiritual in and of themselves. Newgrange unites the spiritual idea of rebirth with its nearly exact orientation to the winter solstice. Light enters its inner chamber and reveals a larger order that the bleakness of winter seems to make impossible. This activity suggests sexual intercourse of the sun and human-imprinted earth. The Newgrange people directly apprehended their metaphysics with their physics.

Chaos Theory shows why Yeats's question in 'Among School Children' — 'How can we know the dancer from the dance?' — is blessedly unanswerable. While we can talk theoretically or abstractly about the dance and we can break down the dancer's bodily movements into parts, we cannot really distinguish choreography from dancer's interpretation, nor can we find exact identity of one performance with another. Since the dance can only be perceived or realised in the dancer's movements, we cannot separate one from the other. Chaos Theory sees a similar dynamic in nature: order is implicate in chaos, chaos implicate in order. They are inseparable dancer and dance. Here are some salient features of the dancing that we find frequently in Irish art and literature:

- The part resembles the whole. Chaos Theory finds this resemblance in what it calls fractals. Fractal geometry, through the feedback created by repeated iterations of non-linear equations, creates beautiful and elaborate designs when represented visually. Parts of the designs resemble the whole design. This resemblance is called self-similarity. In 'Among School Children' Yeats's speaker asks the chestnut tree rhetorically, 'Are you the leaf, the blossom or the bole?'

- Science is no longer a matter of Euclidean exactitude. Shapes of interest are no longer geometrical in the traditional sense. I particularly like the fact that non-linear equations were required to calculate gravitational effects when more than two celestial bodies interact with one another. And then everything becomes wonderfully unpredictable in detail. (There's something to that threeness.)

- Nature is messy, but it is also orderly. More accurately, its messiness is, in fact, its orderliness. Simply put, we have hurricanes, but we also have the regularity of the seasons. Small differences, nuances, can lead to major differences; conversely major differences can develop resemblance. Thus simplicity and complexity are not divorced from one another. Emptiness and fullness exist in paradoxical relationship to one another, like the one and the many. Chance is respected, and judgement is withheld about its apparent randomness. Conversely, coincidence is not necessarily proof of design. In fact, order often seems accidental.

- No final theory that will explain all the natural forces of the universe is possible, because there is no fixed place from which to observe the dynamical world we are part of. Chaos Theory undermines the mechanistic, Newtonian view of the world as a clock, the workings of which scientists are slowly recording. When a system is dynamical, change is constant; truth is dynamic, not static, and therefore does not yield its secrets to precise measurement.

We can find these features of Chaos Theory everywhere in Irish literature and art. In fact, it's hard not to call Chaos Theory an aesthetic theory as much as it is a scientific theory. Chaos Theory heals the Enlightenment split of the scientific from the aesthetic. In his preface to *The Playboy of the Western World*, John Millington Synge claimed exemption for Ireland from this disease. (And to think the British have been saying for years that the Irish aren't enlightened.) He recognised the failure of 'the intellectual modern drama' and the 'false joy of the musical comedy'. Instead, the Irish artist of Synge's time had the ability to illuminate the 'rich joy found only in what is superb and wild in reality'; it could be found in the barren landscapes of Aran 'among the country people of Ireland'. He knew that 'All art is a collaboration', for his Ireland was a country 'where the imagination of the people, and the language they use, is rich and living, [and] it is possible for a writer to be rich and copious in his words, and at the same time to give the reality, which is the root of all poetry, in a comprehensive and natural form'.

In Aran and the west of Ireland generally, Synge could not help but collaborate with the 'comprehensive and natural' non-Euclidean geometry of rocks and ocean, their dynamism, the fractal nature of tragic resignation on Aran, its resemblance to the idea of fate in Greek drama, and the utter difference that perspective makes to a blow to the head in *The Playboy*. Synge knew that creativity was insight into what is, not invention of the new. In Ireland writers had 'a chance that is not given to writers in places where the springtime of the local life has been forgotten, and the harvest is a memory only, and the straw has been turned into bricks'.

'Saint Patrick's Breastplate', a poem attributed to Patrick, identifies its speaker with a similar physical and metaphysical intimacy:

I arise today
Through the strength of heaven:
Light of sun,
Radiance of moon,
Splendour of fire,
Speed of lightning,
Swiftness of wind,
Depth of sea,
Stability of earth,
Firmness of rock.

Patrick goes on to find himself suffused with an all-encompassing physical presence of Christ:

Christ with me, Christ beneath me, Christ above me,
Christ on my right, Christ on my left,
Christ when I lie down, Christ when I sit down, Christ
    when I arise,
Christ in the heart of every man who thinks of me,
Christ in the mouth of every one who speaks of me,
Christ in every eye that sees me,
Christ in every ear that hears me.

Patrick obviously has no Manichaean view of divided realms of good spirit and evil body, no binary oppositions of the natural and the supernatural, no privileging of speech over writing, but a perception of the unity of all: heaven is immanent in all, in the here and now, in the forever. Christ is not just a figure of history; he is a current presence, to be perceived viscerally.

Such physical intimacy finds its parallel in a traditional Irish unwillingness to separate the numinous from the mundane. There is no separation in tales; thousands of years of Irish spirituality did not distinguish between the sacred and the profane. In *Gods and Heroes of the Celts*, Marie-Louise Sjoestedt makes this point most clearly: 'Every strange feature of the soil of Ireland is the witness of a myth, and, as it were, its crystallisation. The supernatural and the natural penetrate and continue each other, and constant communication between them ensures their organic unity.'

It is all the fashion among contemporary Irish materialist intellectuals to demythologise, but a critique of that fashion I'll save for another time. Instead I have an Aran story for you, of the ninth-century church called Cill Ghobnait on Inisheer. The church is tiny, barely the size of a living room. A stone slab still stands on the altar, in front of a narrow slit window that widens inwardly to spread light as it enters the room. The stone slab bears the engraved imprint of human work — the cross and the alpha and omega. Go there and genuflect as the priest once did. Do so when the sun is expected to shine through the slit window. Imagine the darkness of the room with a roof overhead. Then see the sun enter the room and cast the stone slab's shadow. When you're on your knee, you'll only be able to see the stone silhouetted against the sky. You'll find how a ninth-century spiritual man, like his predecessors at Newgrange, found order in the obvious chaos of rock and the eternal mutability of crashing seas. It is a fractal place. If you do as I recommend, you'll live happily ever after (or maybe just for a few moments).

Following the Black Dog

Cynthia Lamb

Cynthia Lamb is a part Irish-American pagan eclectic with a special interest in legends and otherworldly animals. Her novel Brigid's Charge *(Bay Island Books) is based on the life of her ancestor who was accused of birthing the Jersey Devil, a dragon-like creature still said to haunt the Pine Barrens of New Jersey. She collects worldwide sightings of the Black Dog through her website at www.cynthialamb.com.*

While visiting Ireland in the summer of 1994, my friend and I were doing our own standing-stone tour, travelling from one sacred site to the next, appreciating the access even to those monuments on private land. It's surprising that I didn't see the dog at one of those isolated sites where we felt like trespassers as we clambered up hillsides, our feet and legs soaked by the high grass; but no, we were at Droumbeg in County Cork, where we passed a dozen folks on the path in and out. We had been there for about a half hour, dressed in heavy wool sweaters, jeans, and hiking boots. The moist air was cold. In a state of grace that I often feel in nature, I stood inside the circle, hands on hips, admiring the lush green expanse, when something caught my eye. A few yards in front of me a young dog, resembling a Labrador retriever, leapt out of a standing stone, then disappeared into its neighbouring stone. I turned to my friend to learn if she also had seen the dog, but she was facing the other direction. Hoping the dog would reappear, I gazed back at the stones, wondering what in the world I had seen.

Later we visited a woodcarver, who started whittling and telling stories as soon as we entered his studio, a converted butcher shop. His hands, the knife and the wood co-created his tale as we watched. Within minutes he produced, then gave me, a carving of a hound. I stared at it, absorbing the coincidence, then told him that I had just seen a black dog disappear into a standing stone. His eyebrows raised as he casually suggested I might have seen the púca, a sinister creature, he explained, that takes people on unbidden adventures or portends death. When I said that the dog was not frightening — indeed, it appeared playful, even joyful — he shrugged, then grinned. Perhaps 'sinister' is just the Christian interpretation, he said; the púca is pagan, for sure.

I am inclined to agree on both accounts. Dermot MacManus, a collector of sightings in Ireland, says the púca is an animal spirit — some say fairy — that takes on different forms: bull, goat, pony, ass, horse, eagle, as well as dog. But everyone he met outside Ulster who saw the púca described it as a great black dog. According to both his and Lady Augusta Gregory's collections, the black dog may walk beside you calmly, as Margo Ryan reported in 1952; sometimes it fights with a flesh-and-bones dog; it may gaze at you with red, fiery eyes, or not regard you at all; and frequently it vanishes while you watch. In none of the stories I've heard or read has the dog leapt joyfully.

Like others who have seen the black dog, I wonder why I saw it. One answer is simple: It was there to be seen, and I was lucky enough to be looking at the right moment. While I appreciate the way that explanation normalises spiritual experience, it remains unsatisfactory. Didn't the dog choose to materialise and then disappear? And why is my experience of it different from others I've read or heard? Perhaps it had some message for me. Yet I don't want to impose artificial meaning on the appearance simply because of my need for it to make sense.

Lady Gregory's book *Visions and Beliefs in the West of Ireland* reports multiple sightings around her home in Coole: at Ballinderreen, Coole, Kinvara, Lissatiraheely, Ballinamantange, Loughrea, Gort and Lismara. One man witnessed his dog fighting something invisible in the road; another time, a black dog the size of a calf with huge paws and eyes as big as saucers came into a woman's house and stared at her. A man swung at the dog, and it magically reappeared a few yards away. Another woman saw the black dog first when she was a child and later as an adult; she fled both times. A priest claimed to have banished the black dog from a spot in the road that it frequented, although a regular driver in the area was said to have seen it in the same place every night.

MacManus's *The Middle Kingdom* describes how a friend of his, fishing in Derry, saw a huge black animal approaching him through shallow water. Frightened, the man climbed the nearest tree, which bent dangerously with his weight. As the animal passed, it looked up at him with almost human intelligence and bared its teeth, its eyes blazing red. Later the man saw a picture of the púca on a card that came with a pack of cigarettes and recognised the creature he had seen. After reading that story, I thought it shrewd of the púca to show itself to those like us. Someone who had heard of the creature might be able to push it off as a product of suggestion, but that man and I will never forget or dismiss our experiences.

MacManus also reported that a woman near Ballaghadereen, as a teenager, encountered a black dog as high as her shoulder that looked at her with interest as it walked close to her. She didn't think it supernatural until it passed through a closed iron gate. Meanwhile, in Pontoon, the púca apparently was seen almost every night. MacManus reported that locals said a bridge there was haunted by a black dog that glowered at anyone crossing after midnight.

Ephemeral black dogs have been seen all over the world. One of the most universal interpretations of a sighting is as a portent of death, which seems to have its roots in the ancient myths of the dog as psychopomp, a guardian of the Underworld. Maria Leach's comprehensive book *God Had a Dog* lists such myths from nearly every continent. In Central American Zapotec mythology, a white dog and a black dog await the soul on the bank of the great river that rushes between this world and the Otherworld; and in Tepustepec, the Mixte

Indians believe that a black dog carries the soul safely over a big lake. In Egypt, the jackal-headed god of the dead Anubis leads the soul from this world to the next. In Greece, we find Cerberus, the three-headed hound who guards the entrance to Hades. In Icelandic mythology, Garm is the dog of Hel, goddess of the dead, whose name also designates her domain. In modern folklore the Cwn Annwfn, the hounds of Annwfn — the Welsh Otherworld — becomes a pack of spectral hounds that chases the souls of the dead through the air. One of Greek Hecate's three aspects is a dog, and she also had a pack of hell hounds, as did the ancient Semitic Underworld goddesses, Nikarawas and Ninkarrak.

The Irish black dog may have been an ancient death deity as well. The pagan holiday Samhain, antecedent of Hallowe'en — when the veil between the worlds is believed thin and contact can be made between the living and the dead — was said to be sacred to the púca. When nations change religions, when Hel becomes Hell, old beliefs don't disappear; distorted, they become legends. Death hounds may no longer escort us to the Underworld; now they warn of an upcoming death.

Since no one close to me died after I saw the black dog, apparently that was not the meaning of my sighting. So what was? Archaeologist Marija Gimbutas states that the dog, as a howler by night, was the Goddess's principal animal in Old Europe; it was a double of the moon goddess who, like the later Hecate, was worshipped by dogs barking at the moon. One of the painted vases that Gimbutas cites as evidence — showing two leaping black dogs — resembles what I saw. Could that spirit have been a manifestation of this moon goddess or her canine companion? Scholars suggest that the word 'púca' likely derives from *puc*, a buck goat, while Gimbutas states that goats and dogs, synonymous as stimulators of the life-force, were both associated with death and regeneration.

Archaeological findings, literature, and lore suggest that ancient cultures had contact through trade, emigration, and raids. John Manley says the earliest people in Ireland had settlements around 8000 BCE.

Those early Irish may have had dogs. Manley says the bones of a tame dog found in a British settlement, c. 9000 BCE, suggests that the dog could have been used for hunting much as it is today. Farmers probably joined the Irish hunter/gatherers after 5000 BCE. Barry Cunliffe documents the westward advance of the neolithic people, and their farming way of life, from Greece and the Balkans area across Europe and around the northern shores of the Mediterranean, and finally to Ireland in the fourth millennium BCE. Robert Graves said the Irish believed that the Tuatha Dé Danann, the people of the goddess Danu, came from Greece in the second millennium BCE. Exactly when the Celts arrived in Ireland is subject to debate, but the dog was important to them and their heroes, who were designated by the prefix Cú, 'hound of'.

Graves says the Celtic hero Cúchulainn, Hound of Culann, was a reincarnation of the Irish god Lugh. Cunliffe equates the Roman Diana, the huntress and moon goddess, with Flidais, the Irish goddess of the forest, both of whom had a dog. The Irish god Nuadu had a dog as well. Miranda Green notes that at a healing sanctuary of Nuadu's British counterpart, Nodons, no human images of the god have been found, yet nine representations of dogs were found, indicating that dogs were sacred to Nodons.

I imagine an ancient Great Dog, remembered in diverse ways: the bitch Hecate, the jackal-headed Anubis, the Hell Hounds, the black dog who helps the native Central Americans cross the lake to the Otherworld, and now the black dog, who outside Ireland is often called the devil. That the dog fell from grace, from deity to devil, doesn't surprise me. Throughout history, new religions attempting to supplant older religions demonised what deities they could, then incorporated the rest. What is notable is that Ireland seems to have resisted in the case of the black dog, which may be feared but is rarely called demonic.

Leach states that the black dog always carried a sinister connotation almost everywhere in Europe. Furthermore, in most European manifestations, the devil appears in the form of a dog, cat, or goat — often black. But in Ireland, where the individual dog is beloved, the Devil seldom appears as a dog. Barbara Allen Woods's *The Devil in Dog Form* testifies to the pervasiveness of Devil Dog by citing 600 sources in the Western world. Of the dozens of citations from Ireland, only two refer to the dog as the devil and one other as an evil spirit. The rest call it a spook or ghost dog. One notable exception occurs in one of the few witch trials in Ireland. In the fourteenth century, Dame Alice Kyteler was charged with having sex with the devil in the form of a black dog.

In response to the demonisation of black dogs, MacManus asserted that the púca is unique to Ireland and that black dogs from other lands bear at best a distant relationship. But rather than disclaim the púca's connection to other black dogs, it seems more to the point to respect the Irish for a high tolerance and appreciation for mystery, for embracing the black dog rather than demonising it, for supporting it with a rich habitat of belief and story and access to standing stones.

It seems appropriate to the ephemeral nature of the black dog that the line drawn from contemporary sightings back to ancient dog deities is itself gossamer — suggestive but not conclusive. I have sought to understand the meaning of my own sighting, which now seems clearer. Ireland is alive in spirit and magic. The moment I am on the land, I feel it. In America I have interactions with the spirit world, but I usually have to work at it; in Ireland it happens by itself. I just look and, like the black dog, spirit is there.

One interpretation of the Garden of Eden story is that it tells of the point — perhaps at birth, perhaps historically — when mortals were cut off from direct connection with the divine, and that existential angst reflects our desire to return to union with divinity. Sightings of the black dog seem to promise that return; they remind us that spirit exists, however cut off we feel. The black dog reminds me that connection is not a function of effort, but a natural part of life. And even though there seems not to be as much habitat for spirit in America as in Ireland, it remains my birthright as a being.

Spirit of the Drum

❉

Layne Redmond

Layne Redmond (www.LayneRedmond.com) is descended from Irish as well as Scottish, English and French settlers in Florida. She has released four CDs: Chanting the Chakras, Being in Rhythm, Since the Beginning, *and the newest recording with Tommy Brunjes,* Trance Union. *She was the first woman to have a Signature Series of world percussion instruments with Remo, Inc., one of the world's largest manufacturers of percussion instruments and drumheads. She is the author of* When the Drummers Were Women: A Spiritual History of Rhythm.

*M*y name is Redmond, and my inherited identity is as a seventh-generation descendant of tough Florida pioneers. My green eyes, reddish-brown hair and fair, freckled skin were not evolved for this climate. Yet I love this bright land with a fierceness that I cannot describe, as I see its fragile environment destroyed by the greed of over-development and unconcern for the natural world. For twenty-five years I was away from Florida, pursuing my career as a musician and artist in New York City. Finally the sandy soil, the blinding sun, the primordial swamps and the beautiful springs and rivers called me home. I squint as I tend my five acres near the Suwannee River, drip with sweat in the unrelenting humid heat while I fight off the biting and stinging bugs, and am amazed that my ancestors ever settled and survived here.

Recent generations of my family were much more identified as warriors of the southern Confederacy against the northern Yankees than as Irish. The tiny bit I know of our Irish ancestor is that he fought against Cromwell and ended up in prison. From there he was deported to the colonies in southern America as an indentured servant. Once here, all connections to his Irish history or spiritual traditions were lost to his descendants as he worked his way out of slavery to begin the tough life of homesteading. This Redmond's descendants married Scottish women who followed the only churches available, becoming Baptists or Methodists.

These pioneers were fiercely effective at clearing out the native people who were in the last stages of clinging to their lands. A native American teacher once told me that the English perfected tribal warfare on the Scottish and Irish, and that the survivors became ferocious in wiping out the indigenous people in America. Violence, sorrow and loss beget more of the same.

My ancestors migrated into Florida under the Armed Occupation Act of 1842, which gave them a chance at a large parcel of land that would be theirs once the remaining Indians were dispatched. This Act, the beginning of the large-scale settlement of Florida, provided for the depopulation of most of Florida's native Americans. Missouri Senator Thomas Hart Benton presented a bill before Congress in 1840 that allowed settlers to have 160 acres, if in exchange they would build a house, cultivate at least five acres of land, and live there for five years while protecting it from Indians. Part of the Act said that settlers were to receive guns, ammunition and food, but the government did not follow through on this promise. Nothing but the fight for survival was forthcoming.

When the first settlers came into west central Florida by covered wagon and on horseback, the only roads through the wilderness were Indian trails. The Second Seminole War had been ended by treaty, but the native people were resisting. The Seminole Indian nation, led by the great warrior chief Osceola, occupied the area in its last major defiance of the resettlement plans. My family settled near the Chassahowitzka River, and some died fighting for their piece of land. Soon the native cause was lost and the surviving Seminoles were deported west to land no one wanted — yet.

The Indians were gone, but the anger and sorrow were not. Nothing fills the black hole left by destroyed culture, loss of family, loved ones and homeland, followed by the experience of slavery in a strange land. Not even the destruction of another people. Even when by sheer force of will one survives, the anger and sense of outraged loss run deep through the generations that follow.

The only recognisable Irish traits preserved in my family are charismatic storytelling, love of drinking and an ancient anger that can flare at the smallest slight. No spiritual path or simple feeling of happiness in being alive was passed on to me. Only a sense of emptiness, a nameless anxiety and discontent kept at bay by constant hard work. In my mother's and grandmother's generations, the men had professional careers, while the women stayed home and had children. They were the first generations of women to escape from the unrelenting physical labour of farming, but they had no financial independence. They belonged to their husbands, and their lives were bounded by their children's needs. None were happy.

By the time I came along, my family attended the Episcopal church sporadically, purely for social reasons. No one conveyed to me a sense of faith in the sacred or divine. They worked, drank, took prescription drugs, escaped into reading or watching television, fought with each other. I entered young adulthood depressed. Yet it was the 1960s, when an optimistic sense of expanding cultural consciousness was everywhere. I left my small hometown in rural Florida far behind, knowing I would not marry, have children and bury my dreams as my mother had.

I wanted to be an artist. Deep within me was the whispering dream of a way of life filled with inspiration and creativity. I headed for New York City and studied painting, sculpture and photography, living the romantic myth of the starving artist in a tenement in the old Irish Hell's Kitchen on the west side of Manhattan. I made my living as a waitress and had no intention of looking for a real job. Creating art would be my life. As I write this, I realise I am the first woman descendant of that Irish Redmond who has had the freedom to do this.

My work as a performance artist evolved out of my immersion in the works of scholars such as Joseph Campbell, Robert Graves and Carl Sagan. Mythology from all cultures fascinated me. Using my training in photography and film-making, I created multimedia installations within which I enacted archetypal images of the World Tree, the Cosmic Egg and Medusa against a backdrop of deep space. As my interest in alternative music grew, I included unusual, obscure recordings of traditional music from around the world.

Through these performances, I explored ways of awakening some forgotten connection or recollection that could replace an indefinable 'something' I felt was missing from my life, something I believed related to ancient cultures, forgotten gods and goddesses of places lost forever. I wanted to present audiences with scenes they had never seen or heard but which reminded them of something infinitely familiar.

Although I loved the life I was leading, I sensed a lack of spiritual meaning. I was burning out on the ego-driven purposelessness, nihilism and self-indulgence of much of the contemporary art scene in New York. The intuition that art could have a deeper purpose drove me to search for the sacred. I became a student of spiritual practices and techniques of expanded consciousness — yoga, Buddhism, Hinduism, Gnostic Christianity, Japanese Tea Ceremony, Chi Gung and Ericksonian Hypnosis.

Then in 1980, on a whim, I joined an Afro-Cuban drumming class. Perhaps I was fulfilling an old wish: I had asked for a drum set once as a teenager, but my mother had told me to stick with my dance lessons — drumming was for boys. When I was growing up, women played the piano or maybe the flute. They didn't drum. In the drum class, I experienced for the first time the trance-union of a drum ensemble. I had an ecstatic sense of connecting, of being one with the other players. Even more, I felt at one with drummers throughout all time.

Soon afterwards I attended a concert where about twenty people sat in a circle around a man named Glen Velez as he played one type of frame drum after another. I was enchanted by the power and beauty of these ancient instruments. The sound of the frame drum seemed to lead me closer to what I was searching for than anything else I had experienced. I knew I had to learn to play these drums myself — a reaction I've since witnessed over and over again in many women and men.

A frame drum is defined by the diameter of the drumhead being much larger than the depth of its shell. The shells range in depth from two inches to six inches, and in diameter from four to thirty inches. Most of these drums are portable and can be held in one hand. The smallest is the kanjira from South India and the largest is the Irish bodhrán.

The frame drum most often has a skin on only one side, but sometimes it may have skins stretched across both sides. Bells or jingling and rattling implements may be attached to the inside rim, which in ancient times were believed to add to the drum's power to purify, dispel and summon. Often the drums were painted red, the colour of blood, or sometimes green, the colour of vegetation — primordial colours of life. Mystical designs and symbols might also be painted on the skin head or the wooden frame. Threads or ribbons knotted with ritual prayers or chanting often hung from them.

I convinced Glen to take me on as a student, and I started on a disciplined regime of learning to play the frame drum. It changed my life completely. Once a week, I went for a lesson, tape-recorded it and used it to practise with every day at home. I quickly realised that, with no prior musical training, I had embarked on the study of a very complex instrument. Yet I was an eager student and — I now realise — a talented one.

After a couple of years, Glen and I began performing together in the new music scene in New York and Europe. We earned some serious attention and good press. We started to record for several different labels in Europe and the US and spent nine years performing together. Although I had never planned on making a career of playing the frame drum, it soon became the centre of my life.

During this period I began studying the history of the frame drum. Its place of origin appears to be the ancient Mediterranean world where, for at least 3,500 years (c. 3000 BCE to 500 CE), it was the primary percussive instrument. There are occasional representations of hourglass-shaped drums or kettle drums, but the frame drum is by far the most prominent.

Glen had collected hundreds of images of frame drummers and, to my surprise, almost all of these drummers were women. From the civilisations of Anatolia (Old Turkey), Mesopotamia, Egypt, Greece and Rome, the goddess/priestess and the frame drum emerge as the core trance and mystical religious traditions. I found the frame drum at the centre of the oldest rave-like gatherings — mystery rites lasting for days at a time with non-stop drumming and dancing.

In every ancient Mediterranean civilisation that I studied, a goddess transmitted the gift of making music to humans. In Sumer and Mesopotamia it was Inanna and Ishtar; in Egypt it was Hathor; in Greece, the ninefold goddess called the Muse. Musical, artistic and poetic inspiration was always thought to spring from the divine feminine. One of the main techniques for connecting to this power of inspiration was drumming.

The drum was the means our ancestors used to summon the goddess and the instrument through which she spoke. The drumming priestess was the intermediary between divine and human realms. Aligning herself with sacred rhythms, she acted as summoner and transformer, invoking divine energy and transmitting it to the community.

From 3000 to 2500 BCE, the Sumerians describe the goddess Inanna as the creator of the frame drum. They tell of Inanna's priest-esses who sang and chanted to the rhythms of frame drums, which had arrived from Egypt, where women controlled sacred music and dance, somewhere between 2000 and 1500 BCE. The biblical lands also yield numerous images of women playing the frame drum. Old Testament texts refer to the tambourine as the toph, which has been translated as the timbrel and the tabret.

In Greece, the frame drum entered from several different directions — from Cyprus, one of the main centres of the cult of Aphrodite, where the frame drum was prominent from at least 1000 BCE, and from Minoan Crete where it was used in the rituals of Ariadne, Rhea and Dionysos. Preclassical Greece also saw the introduction of the cult of the goddess Cybele from Western Anatolia. The frame drum was the main instrument of the maenads, women initiates in the worship of Cybele and Dionysos; frame drums were also played by the priestesses of Artemis, Demeter and Aphrodite. A Greek text calls the goddess's drums 'the leathern clamorous sieves, played at Bacchic orgies'.

The bodhrán, the large frame drum still used by traditional Irish musicians, was closely associated with folk ritual, and was played in religious and festival processions. It is identical to the skin sieve of the Celtic goddess Brigit, ritually filled with sprouting grain; at Greek Eleusis in the rites of Demeter and Persephone, purification involved a liknon, or winnowing basket, a kind of grain sieve associated with the frame drum in ritual contexts from neolithic times. Robert Graves suggests that Brigit might be a descendant of the ancient Minoan goddess Rhea, who was associated with the frame drum.

In the ancient world, prayer was an active, trance-inducing combination of chanting, music and dance, and initiates often danced the sacred spiral into the labyrinth. The classic labyrinth is a single path meant for meditative circling. To enter was to experience a ritual death; to escape was to be resurrected. The danced line into the labyrinth was a sacred path into the inner realm of knowing. Dancers holding a rope signifying Ariadne's thread (allowing one to find the way in and out of the maze) followed a leader into the labyrinth, spiralling right to left, the direction of death. At the centre they turned, dancing out in the direction of evolution and birth, all to the driving rhythms of the frame drums.

Another function of the frame drum was to create a prophetic trance state. The most dramatic mode of prophecy was uttered in inspired rhythmic speech. In the depths of ecstatic trance, the oracle was possessed by the goddess, who rapped in powerful rhymes directly through the oracle's lips. The Greek word for this state of transfigured consciousness is *enthusiasmos* — 'within is a god' — the root of our word 'enthusiasm'.

Ecstatic prophecy has many parallels with shamanism. Prophetesses sought inspiration through a number of external stimuli, including fasting, ingesting honey, inhalation of burning herbs or essential oils, and intoxication through alcohol or psychotropic plants. Cybele's priestesses relied most heavily on the trance-inducing properties of music and dance. Their aim was the ecstatic transformation of consciousness through rhythmic movement of the body. The rhythms of frame drums, cymbals and flutes moved them towards the consecrated, concentrated state of divine revelation.

With the ascendancy of Christianity, Cybele's great temple in Rome was destroyed, the Vatican was built on the site and the new priesthood banned the priestesses and the instruments and music associated with Cybele's rites. Not only was the frame drum banned from Christian religious rituals, its use in secular contexts was also frowned upon by the Church, in particular its use by women. The Catholic synod of 576 CE decreed that 'Christians are not allowed to teach their daughters singing, the playing of instruments or similar things because, according to their religion, it is neither good nor becoming'. For three thousand years women had been the primary percussionists in the ancient world. As Europe pursued a policy of not allowing the teaching of music to women, they were effectively barred from the professions of composing, teaching or performing.

Ancient sources tell us that the frame drum was not just a powerful symbol of spiritual presence, it was an important tool for many spiritual experiences. Priestesses of the goddess were skilled technicians who knew which rhythms quickened the life in freshly planted seeds, which rhythms facilitated childbirth, and which rhythms induced the ecstatic trance of spiritual transcendence. Scientific research from astrophysics to biology supports the idea that rhythm is a fundamental force. Neurological studies suggest that drumming and other spiritual practices of our ancestors could indeed bring about a transformation of ordinary consciousness. By banning her drum, the patriarchal religions that suppressed the goddess cut off our access to significant parts of our own psyches, destroying psychological and spiritual techniques that had been used for many thousands of years.

In the late 1980s, I began speaking about the frame drum's incredible history. The response was overwhelming. Women would approach me to ask if I would teach them to drum. Although most of them had never seen a frame drum before, they felt an overwhelming urge to learn its rhythms. I soon found myself conducting five classes a week, teaching more than fifty women. Although some had studied music at some point in their lives, the majority had never played any musical instrument before. They shared a conviction that drumming could lead them back to something essential within themselves. As one student expressed it, 'When I heard you play, I realised I was thirsty for something I didn't even know existed.'

I made up my mind that I would discover a system of conveying the primordial feminine energy I felt when I drummed. I combined Yogic and Taoist practices of connecting to the earth and being a conduit for its energy. As I entrained with the beat of the drum — as I became the pulse itself — I felt that I was letting the force of gravity draw my essence down, down through the layers of the earth to the fire at its centre.

These were not images I thought up consciously. They seemed to arise spontaneously out of the trance-like state that my drumming engendered. Later, I realised that the concept of creative fire at the earth's core was a very old religious image. Before it became the Christians' hell, it was the fire of the goddess. As Campbell says, 'between Virgil and Dante too there was a difference, inasmuch as for the Roman the intelligence in the centre of the earth was not satanic but divine'. Teaching women to drum provided a context for all the practices that I had studied to coalesce. When teaching women, I felt I was really listened to for the first time in my life. I was honoured for who I was and what I had accomplished.

With my students I formed a drumming group called The Mob of Angels. We set out to revive the ancient tradition of women's ceremonial drumming. Our aim was to create a contemporary new music that is non-traditional but pulses with the rhythms of an archaic language. Drawing on images from paleolithic times to the present, we studied the goddesses, priestesses and laywomen who played the frame drum. We grounded ourselves in the energy of the earth and focused on the relationship of the different strokes to the elements — earth, water, fire and air. We learned the ancient technology for synchronising our minds and bodies. Our goal was to release the primordial archetype of feminine energy through the power of our drums.

When we began to develop ritual performances, the Mob chose to perform in a circle, a context that promotes wholeness and inclusion. Our rituals almost always include processions of drummers. The ancient ritual procession towards a shrine or holy place mirrored the archetypal journey to the centre of the self. We created our public rituals at seasonally important times of the year, the solstices and equinoxes.

The Widow Jane Mine, a large cave in rural New York, seemed a perfect setting to celebrate the autumnal equinox of 1993. The equinox is the magical moment when the days and nights are of equal length and the magnetic fields of earth and sun are aligned — a time of renewal and balance. More than 700 people from all over the United States arrived to participate in the ritual.

We began by playing in a field above the cave. Then we asked people to form a circle around us, and I led them in a pulse meditation, everyone moving and breathing in rhythm together. The Mob led the guests to the mouth of the cave. Everyone entered in ritual fashion, through rows of drummers, past people burning sage and incense. We descended into the sacred enclosure of the earth, the oldest known temple, and experienced the ancient tradition of ritual drumming. After the ceremonies we found that our guests came from all walks of life, from all religions and none, and were of all ages.

The appeal of this event speaks of our loss of connectedness to the rhythms of nature and our need for meaningful ritual. Today as in ancient times, collective rituals that recreate the origins of the world renew the community by reconnecting people with the rhythmic source of their being. Our rituals function as a gateway — an 'in-trance-way' — into deeper realms of consciousness. The rhythms of our drums have the power to draw listeners away from the constraints of clock time back to the cyclical time of mythology.

Following the trail of the frame drum has forced me to explore the very fabric of mind, to trace the patterns of mythological thought and to define the nature of divinity as it relates to myself. My curiosity about the female drummers of the ancient world unexpectedly opened up a door to a forgotten spiritual technology. And through the drum I have begun to heal the inherited wounds of people torn from their land and cast upon foreign but beautiful shores.

We are All Natives of Somewhere

❧

Barbara Flaherty

Barbara Flaherty, born in Boston to an Irish-American couple with roots in Connacht and Ulster, is the founder of the Fourth Order of Francis and Clare, an interfaith intertribal order of madmen, troubadours, fools and mystics (www.fourthorder.net). A performance poet, she is the author of Holy Madness *(Fourth Order Press). She is a counsellor and teacher who facilitates ecospiritual tours of Alaska and other sacred places through the Land and People Tours (www.fourthorder.net, www.landandpeopletours.com).*

I was sitting alone in a California café. A man and two women asked if they could join me. I was happy for the company.

They spoke with Irish accents and asked me where I was from. I told them, 'Anchorage, Alaska'.

'No, no,' they said. 'Where are you from?'

'Oh,' I said, 'I am originally from Boston.'

'No, no,' they said. 'Where are you from?'

I remember this moment clearly. It disoriented me and created a space of silence before I could answer. Their question was a hand rising out of the dark sea, reclaiming me. I remember looking at the smiling faces of these strangers who over the course of the next year would become my friends.

'My grandfather was Lawrence Flaherty from the Aran Islands. My grandmother was Bridget DeCourcey from Roundstone. How did you know I'm Irish?'

This caused all manner of laughter between them. 'How do we know she's Irish? Maybe it's the way she holds her cup. Maybe it's the way she holds her head. Maybe it's the way she casts her eyes down and about. Maybe it's her face that is walking all over Ireland even as she sits here today. It's not that you're Irish that is a surprise. It is that you're an American.'

They laughed at the things I did as if I were a joke out of place. I felt at home with them, comfortable but somewhat disjointed, always bumping into that strange silence.

I had never heard the Irish language, had no idea I even wanted to hear it, until they brought me to a Mass said entirely in Irish. I cried silently through the whole thing, disturbed to find reactions within me that had no conscious referent. The longing that accompanied my tears was even more disturbing. Through my Irish friends I experienced a part of myself that was deeply connected to the land and people of my genetic origins.

I became aware that my genes and physical makeup had been formed through the collision of races and invasions in a land I did not consciously know, whose animal and sea life, vegetation and minerals were parts of my being. This land I did not know knew me intimately like a mysterious hidden lover. Even more disconcerting was the knowledge that I bore the cultural traits and the personal mannerisms of the people of that land.

I was born in the largest Irish Catholic community outside of Ireland. Ireland itself was to me a faraway place, an ancient antecedent that belonged to my grandparents. My father's parents, rural people who came to America in the 1890s, never talked of Ireland with the eleven children they raised in the city tenements of South Boston. When they spoke of Ireland it was to each other in Irish, so no one could understand, which was exactly what they wanted.

My mother's people first emigrated in 1628, Yankee Puritans who intermarried generation after generation with the Presbyterian Scots-Irish immigrants from the north. I have Viking blue eyes and Traveller names within my family. In America I became the full catastrophe of Irish history.

My friends returned to Ireland. I returned to Alaska, to a city plunked into a vast wilderness, with its own stories, its own harsh and fragile teachings, its own native peoples. The day before I had left for California, a goose wing had come in the mail, ensuring safe flight and return with the summer season. In midwinter a sealskin had arrived with the note. 'A cure for your homesickness. You are not far from our thoughts.' This was the spiritual life of Alaska, communicating relationship with all that is. It moved slowly in me like the arctic flowers whose seeds work in the dark of the soil for years only to burst without warning in fabulous flashes of colour on the tundra. My first years in Alaska had been like that dark seed, a slow steady inner movement into relationship with the spirit in the natural world.

Alaska is not human yet. I loved Alaska's living system, her intricacies, her wildness, with an intimate passion and respect. The land was so big and humanity so small. I sensed a rightness in this relationship. Her grand impersonal self made me more human. I had been thirty years old when Alaska initiated me into the experience of cosmic wonder. I believe I saw the sky for the first time, saw the sky with eyes pierced by the expansive beauty of the land. My first Alaskan summers, I alternated the long-distance stare of a watchman at sea with the ass-up posture of a botanist in love with what grows from the ground.

I was also very homesick for family, friends, and familiar customs — an understandable grief. But a new grief emerged that disoriented me. I could write only one line about it in my journal that year, 'Grieving the land is new to me.' I missed the great trees of New England, the smell of the soil in the changing seasons, the thickening of the air before thunderstorms. I thought I would die if I did not taste the Atlantic brine on my lips, touch her, be upheld by her waves. I never knew until then that I possessed such depth of feeling for the land that had nurtured me from my birth. I was struck dumb, plunged into an inarticulate silence.

Healing started when a friend gave me the Inuit poem of the Baffin Island shaman, Uvavnuk.

The great sea has set me in motion,
Set me adrift
And I move as a weed in the river.
The arch of the sky
And the mightiness of storms
Encompasses me,
And I am left
Trembling with joy.

Many times I followed the thread of that poem out to the healing presence of the sea to smell the brine and taste it. I learned how to follow the flight of an eagle, the howl of a wolf, and the light on a leaf into the silent presence and nourishing communion with life.

To be sent that sealskin while in California was a powerful experience for me. If Christ were the Lamb of God for people in the Middle East, he would be the Seal of God for the peoples of the Arctic. The seal offers its life to give life: its oil for light, its meat and oil for food, its fur for warmth and beauty, its guts for protection from the wet and rain. Yup'ik peoples have always acknowledged the seal wisdom with their great give-away. At the outlawed midwinter Seal Bladder Festival the spirits of seals were returned to the sea in thanksgiving, in acknowledgement of the gift of their lives so that the people might live.

Every Alaskan tribe has its own customs regarding the hunt. All share the understanding that animals are not taken but offer themselves. In return the people offer respect and follow different hunting rules for each species, because each animal has its own wisdom and power. Individuals who give respect are accompanied by the wisdom, power and guidance of the animals appropriate to their being.

Plants, rocks, waters, the land itself with its sacred sites, circles and directions participate in this reciprocity. If you take something from the land — a herb, a rock, a moment's rest in a quiet spot — you must leave something. In the great round of being, all bring wisdom and support one another's life. Maniilaq, the great nineteenth-century Inupiaq prophet, taught that everything is relationship, like stars in a constellation, constellations within constellations.

Mountain ranges endure the passing of many generations. Braided rivers run blue with the blood of glaciers. The land is audacious with many coloured varieties of arctic flowers, berries, mushrooms and herbs. The soil is only inches deep, resting upon permanently frozen underground. Fragile layers of lichen, moss, and alpine flowers make their way through the difficulties of a harsh world.

So it was with me. I became ill with breathing problems. No medicine, no doctor could cure me. In order to breathe, I slept sitting up. I dreamed of Saint Lawrence Island in the middle of the Bering Sea, and an ancient stone circle with three rocks out of place. People were weakly crawling on the ground toward it, unable to get there until the stones were moved back in place. In these dreams I tried in vain to move the stones back into place. Awake I tried to will the dream stones back with the power of my mind. But the stones kept falling out of their place in the circle. A Yup'ik woman came to me and said I must go immediately to Saint Lawrence Island. If I did not, she felt I might die.

I went to the island on an airline coupon with eighteen dollars in my pocket, a sleeping bag and a guaranteed place to stay in the old church. The flight out of Nome was rough. Headwinds off the sea and shore jostled the small six-seater from side to side and up and down. The island woman in front of me turned to laugh as I grabbed her seatback in a vain effort to steady myself.

Once almost five thousand people lived on the island. Now there are fewer than one thousand. In the village of Kiyaligag on the south of the island an epidemic struck after contact with whaling ships. The people were all found dead in their beds and buried simply by caving in the roofs of their homes. Such epidemics struck all the villages. Only two remain. Gambel, the oldest island village, is closest to the Siberian coast. I was going to the only other living village, Savoonga, in the north.

Savoonga in its current location is a new village founded at the site of an old fishing camp less than one century ago after the terrible deaths in the old village, Kukulek. It is said that the people of Kukulek brought about their own end by slicing pieces of muktuk from living whales as they rose out of the waters to breathe. The whole village mysteriously died in their sleep shortly after that. Only a small child less then a year old was left alive. The people were buried in the same manner they were buried in Kiyaligag. The roofs were caved in.

In Savoonga they haul water, haul sewage, treasure soda and fresh fruit. Young and old go to the dead village to dig for tools and art made by ancestors. They sell these to buy heating oil and other practicalities in a cash economy. Fresh polar bear skins are cleaned in the river and draped on houses to dry. Walrus and seal flippers dry in the sun. Woolly mammoth tusks and whalebones lie next to houses. Bones are everywhere. They rise out of earth, flow with the river. Some are dragged up by the sea. In Savoonga waves shape stone into sea animal forms, huge rocks in the shape of walrus or seal.

I walk the edge of the wildest ocean I had ever seen. An old man follows me. I walk the boardwalks to ford the river. He leaps easily from stone to stone with no struggle. I tramp the shore. He stands in the grass above me.

At night I go to the Indian Relocation Act Hall where the men drum on walrus gut drums, and people gather to dance. The drummers warm up. They joke, check drums, synchronise their rhythm, and get coffee. The old women sit in a corner. The young women gather with children, babies, noise and teasing. The boys come in and join the men to tend the drums as men do. Many people dance. But I am shy, not knowing how. I sit and watch, feel the drums and songs run through my body.

A woman who looks older than the sea rises from her seat. The drummers falter. All step aside and are silent. The drums begin again as she shifts shoulders slightly, holding space like the first sound holds space. Her head rises. Knotted sticks of fingers pat the air like the first word in the space before the first breath. Her tattooed face smiles. She looks like a bird. Her thin limbs move within her kuspuk, shifting its shape. She is a bird. No, a young woman. No, a bird.

She is a bird rising. Yes, a bird rising.

She is a thin frail old woman who has stopped dancing. The old man sits beside me. They all look at me. Did you see? Did you really see? See how the young men move, heads turn from side to side, arms move up and down with power, legs stomp the floor in the Walrus Dance. Drummers sing out in strong voices. The old man pounds the floor with his feet like a drum. His arms snap up, snap down. He slaps me on my arm, motions me to move. He hits my knee. He moves in his seat entrancing me into my body that moves in waves of sound, of voices riding the drums like the sea. My shoulders and neck are free. My legs push the earth and carry me.

I dreamed that night — a walrus sucks me up. A polar bear eats the walrus and spits out my bones. I see them under the sea, the walrus people. They are drumming. They are waiting for the dancer.

I left that island free in my breath, free in my being, more comfortable with myself.

On a recent fall day, the moon hung heavy over the mountains surrounding Anchorage. My living-room furniture was rearranged for a ceremony. Not the ceremony that my Celtic ancestors enacted on their own feasts, but the ceremony of the Pipe of White Buffalo Calf Woman of the Lakota Nation from great Turtle Island called North America. This Pipe is an immigrant to Alaska, like me, although the Pipe Carrier is an elder of the Inupiaq people.

In the circle of nine people, one is full-blood Siberian Yup'ik. Three are full-blood Inupiaq. One is Alutiq and Athabascan. Some are mixed blood, a topic that comes up in the ceremony. Two are mixed Inupiaq and Irish. One is Creek Indian and Scot. I am the only one not of native American descent. We come from different trades — schoolteacher, administrative assistant, mechanic, counsellor, traditional healer, truck driver. We have done this before in the prescribed way and will do it again.

The Pipe Carrier passes a bowl of burning sage. In its smoke we cleanse ourselves. He says, 'The bones of the ancestors are every-where in the land. Honour them. Honour the land that graciously holds them. The spirits of your ancestors are with you to strengthen you and give you wisdom and skill. Listen to them. Some need prayers for healing or forgiveness so they can go on to the Creator. Pray for them. When we gather they are with us. Acknowledge them. At ceremonies or special circles introduce yourself and your ancestors. Know who you are.' The round begins.

I have had many spiritual teachers from different cultures. I am related to their lineages by teachings. I also have the spiritual ancestors of my faith who I feel guide me like Francis of Assisi. But now is not the time to name them. I am to name my own blood lineage and claim its history, challenges and its wisdom. My ancestors are invited to the Pipe.

I am Barbara Flaherty. My mother is Mary Murdock of Maine, daughter of Teresa Grant, granddaughter of Annie Colbert, great granddaughter of Mary Jane Watters. My mother's father is Guy Murdock, son of James Shearer Murdock, grandson of John Murdock of Ireland. My father is Martin Flaherty, son of Lawrence Flaherty of the Aran Islands, Ireland. My father's mother is Bridgit DeCourcey of Roundstone, Ireland, daughter of Nora King.

The Pipe Carrier passes a stick. Each one of us prays in thanksgiving, for wisdom, healing, forgiveness for ourselves, others, and our ancestors.

The Pipe Carrier loads the Pipe with sacred tobacco and begins the great prayer, the honouring of all our relatives; the four-legged ones, the ones that swim, the crawling ones, the ones that fly, the green and growing ones, the rock nations and minerals, the air we breathe, the fire that burns in the smudge bowl, the waters of the ocean, rivers, rain and the water in the glass we will pass at the end of the ceremony. He honours the star nations, the ancestors, his teachers and the medicine people who have carried the traditions through the centuries.

He lights the Pipe and begins a prayer that is all motion and silence. He lifts the Pipe up and blows smoke towards the heavens to acknowledge the Spirit of Grandfather, the Creator. He lowers the Pipe and blows smoke on the ground to honour Mother Earth who sustains us. He holds the Pipe in front of him and blows smoke to the front, the right, behind him and to the left to honour the four directions of the medicine wheel. This is sacred geometry, the acknowledging of relationship.

The Pipe is passed in silence. The circle is all breath and incense as each one offers this prayer on behalf of all our relations. In silence we listen as our ancestors speak to us.

In the silence and the silence of my heart I hear, 'I arise today by the grace of Heaven, Light of the Sun, Radiance of the Moon, Splendour of Stars, Quickness of Lightning, Swiftness of Wind, Depths of Sea, Firmness of Rock, Stability of Earth. Christ be before me. Christ be behind me. Christ be above me. Christ be below me. Christ on my right side. Christ on my left. Christ all around me, never to part. I am a wind of the sea. I am a wave of the sea. I am a sound of the sea. I am a wonder among flowers, a hawk on a cliff, a salmon in a pool, a hill where poets walk.' We are all connected. Nothing can separate us. We pass the glass of water, share a communal cup in the presence of our ancestors and all our relations.

Alaska is a land of silence punctuated by life sounds. The passage and meaning of each day is pregnant with the change of light, the play of ravens, the stillness of mountains, the movement of moose, the ice on branches of aspen turned pink in alpenglow. Everything is infused with communicating spirit in a great round of relationship. The silence itself cultivates the awareness of communication and nurtures the relationship. All things communicate spirit, power and wisdom, the great generosity.

My father was a city boy not used to rural woodland or pasture. Yet summer night after night, after working long days on the docks of Boston, he would come home and take us to the beach. I loved to swim. I loved the sea. He joked that I could ride the Gulf Stream off the shore of Boston like a river straight to my grandfather's island on the other side of the sea. He often told me, 'The sea has the power to heal you of just about anything. Go to her when you feel badly.' For him this was plain common sense that everyone knew. My father would have shaken his head at the use of the word 'spirituality' in this context. I never heard him use the word. That was something that belonged to religion and to the church, which he rarely attended. Yet this way of seeing, of sensing the world as alive and in relationship was a common sense part of his being, that his ancestors knew to be sacred, the oldest and most ancient spirituality, and he gave it to me.

I did not know of this gift or that he gave it to me until I came to Alaska. Nor do I know how that gift will unfold when I finally go to Ireland. I long to go to the sea and land that graciously hold the bones of my people. I will walk the shore on the yellow strand at Ballyconneely above Roundstone, where seals play. I will listen for my ancestors' voices and their wisdom. I will make my way into the salty wet of the life-giving sea. Riding the waves, I will sing out gratefully in a strong voice, 'I am Diaspora, a seed carried to far-away lands. I am a wave of the sea.'

Holy Ground

❋

Jessie Lendennie

An immigrant to Ireland from Arkansas by way of London, poet Jessie Lendennie founded a small magazine more than two decades ago in Galway to publish the exciting new work coming from the west of Ireland. That magazine, The Salmon, *grew into Salmon Poetry (www.salmonpoetry.com), one of Ireland's major publishers of poetry and considered its most innovative. Jessie lives near the Cliffs of Moher in Clare.*

*T*he major changes in society are often changes involving land, from demographic movements of people to shifts and changes as the earth remakes itself. Our battles are fought on, and over, land. We participate in what's done on the land and what's done to the land. In recent years many western cultures have polarised the debate into land as commodity vs. land as gift; baldly speaking, to use up or to replenish. Irish society, prizing what has long been the image of home for millions of people and still close to its own struggle for nationhood, has been slow to move away from the ideal of land as the essence of home. An awareness of the value of beauty has focused attention on the unique landscapes of this country; as an agrarian society, consciousness of land as sustainer is part of the fabric of society.

The power invested in ownership conveys identity, and the struggle for identity begins and ends with place. The way in which we define and claim ownership — whether fields, boundaries, borders, territory

— defines the scope of our influence. The most intense struggles are not for man-made structures, but for the very way of the earth. Irish myth is woven from rituals — pagan and early Christian — of the land.

The value of land is greatest to the people who take their identity from it, and Ireland's history is a history of the land. Colonisation, which Ireland has known so bitterly, aims to erase indigenous rights to the land and therefore obstruct the very life force of the colonised culture. Yet the people of Ireland, with a rich heritage and reverence for nature, could never truly lose the knowledge of themselves that the land bestows.

The twentieth century saw many major changes for Ireland, both inward and outward, and in the last decade the green of Ireland has become gold-edged. This gem of Europe draws investors from abroad, and Irish people increasingly feel deprived of the right to home ownership because of high prices. As place becomes commodity, we move from consideration of the spiritual wealth of our culture to the all-consuming aspects of material wealth. We come back to the question of what the land stands for and, closely related to this, what we want our lives to be.

The spirit of land and the life of the imagination are inextricably linked for agrarian cultures. This link runs through much of the poetry and scholarship of Ireland. It is its strength and its weakness. The tendency to exploit what is desirable is always a danger for the beautiful. We export our images — the afternoon sun on the hill of Tara; morning at Poulnabrone dolmen; sunset on the Burren; evening on the quiet river Boyne; sunrise over Mullaghmore. We respect rituals of blessing for the land. The honey smell of heather in Connemara; spring rain at Brigid's well. Are these places where time stands still, or projections that resonate with the need to feel connected? Irish society has not, as yet, moved so far that the sacredness of place is taken for granted. If reverence and awe of the land is lost to the tameness of golf courses and tourist conveniences, where will we find the timeless beauty and where will the land find those to care for it?

Irish exiles returning home expect their green isle to house them. Indeed, these lost children, these prodigals, are welcomed by the mother without question. But what will they bring to their homeland? What new knowledge of identity will be gained as the questions of what is our land and what is home are asked in the new united Europe. We are part of the land, but we own it, rent it, see it as a house with acres, see it as a condo. Our 'space' — the notion of space in living — becomes jargon as we see living areas dwindling in size.

For so long it has been the fate of countless Irish people to take on new identities in foreign lands. Now Ireland is seeing refugees on its own shores, stripped of home and stripped of identity. Certainly the experience of foreign cultures is not new to Ireland, but never has there been the expectation that Ireland must make a place for displaced peoples, and this new experience has provoked much soul-searching for Irish society. As Ireland connects more closely with its European neighbours, questions of identity will again be raised. Ireland's uniqueness as mythic homeland for millions of its displaced children — the Ireland of song and longing — has a new role. What this will mean in years to come, what the land will become, will depend on evolving perceptions of Irishness and will be very closely connected to the development of land and natural resources.

In a country with a history of suffering and struggle for identity, an intense and unsettled period of adjustment to prosperity is inevitable. An adjustment, also, to a growing, rather than shrinking, population. Dublin, it is projected, will double in size within thirty years. It is already a cosmopolitan centre and anyone spending even a short time there will feel caught up in the busyness of a city going places. Galway City, just fifteen short years ago, was a sleepy coastal town, with much derelict property and few amenities. It is now a sparkling European city of the west. A cultural capital, with booming population, and traffic problems that were simply unimaginable in the 1980s. Alongside physical change, there is much discussion about Ireland's new pluralism. How representative of the future are these examples of twenty-first century Ireland?

The rapid changes in Irish society would spur even the most disinterested observer to pause and reflect on what is gained and lost.

While the necessity of cultivation of the land is taken for granted, the sense of land as nurturing spirit is tamed more and more for tourism and monetary advantage. Yet, with the eroding of dominant structures, particularly the Church, many people are looking inward, as well as embracing past knowledge for guidance — revisiting old truths in a search for what is lost.

Our ancestors' acknowledgement of the earth as sustainer and source of power is something that we recognise intuitively; it almost seems as if such knowledge runs through bloodlines. The mystical conception of landscape as gateway to the unseen is a strong force in much work by Irish artists and writers.

I sit now looking down a valley to Liscannor Bay, and the sweep of the stone walls, the patchwork green, is calming and wonderful. This is what I do when I have work to concentrate on, and I know why I chose this landscape. When I was a child in the Mississippi Delta area of Arkansas, I sat for hours looking across the flat sweep of cotton fields — looking to the horizon. To me this was a place where everything was possible — a magic world based on thought and wishes. I've always felt the landscape dictated this; that everything was possible because the world was big enough. Growing up I began to place a fervent emphasis on freedom (which I equated with physical freedom), and I developed a need to move freely and a deep need for wide land-scapes. I equated them with that moment of timeless potential. The mind resting on emptiness — all things possible — the landscape of creation (creative readiness). This is an issue now in modern Ireland, the life of the imagination and freedom of place, set against economic needs and economic identity. For the artist, the visionary, a new way of seeing must acknowledge the first and transcend the latter.

As a child, I had a recurring mental image of a woman standing on a cliff-top dressed in nineteenth-century clothes, the wind blowing her hair and lifting the ends of her long dress. She was searching, and I knew that what she was searching for would never be in sight. This image fixed in my mind as a symbol of Ireland, although as third-generation Irish I had no close ties and knew little about the country at that time. That melancholy figure, recognisable to me even as a child as symbolic of the loss of home and land, was a marker for me of my own loss of my mother and of suffering — a solitary figure in a landscape — the pain of loss that struck so deeply and formed so markedly much of the nineteenth and early twentieth century in Ireland. This is not to say that I believe anyone in Ireland now wishes to return to loss and struggle, but it is crucial that the spirit of a nation, its history and the wisdom that has sustained it, blend with and enhance a society's evolving consciousness.

We are all born to the land in a way totally other than our received history. Our place on the earth is the same for us as it was for countless others — we, as they, must make our own understanding. We are, in fact, connected not to the past, but to life. Our inherited rituals of the land are now self-discovery — involving looking to the earth for wisdom and finding a core response within ourselves.

Part Two

The Cup of Sovereignty

The word 'Celtic', omnipresent in literature on Irish spirituality of late, is not in fact a synonym for 'Irish'. Folklorist Padraigín Clancy has suggested that the word's sudden popularity grows from a desire to claim something uniquely Irish in a time of increasing Europeanisation (and perhaps Americanisation). Yet the word does not distinguish Ireland, but ties its spirituality more closely to the continent, for Celtic cultures are found there and on the island of Britain as well as in Ireland. Irish spirituality is not purely Celtic but a melding of Celtic religion with that mysterious indigenous spirituality that preceded it, the culture of stone circles and a goddess in the Irish land itself.

We do not know who the prehistoric Irish were, and we know little about the Celts. Most of what we do know comes from their enemies, especially the Romans, who were battered by the 'barbarian' invaders (whose alien language sounded like barking: *bar-bar*) for more than two hundred years. That Europe became a holy Roman empire and the church Roman Catholic can be blamed on a flock of geese who warned the Senate, holed up in the city centre, that the surrounding Celts were about to cap their siege of Rome with a victory. But the geese of Juno screamed. The Romans were alerted, the Celts turned back, and history was written by those who barely escaped.

This episode, stirringly decoded from Roman sources by historian Peter Berresford Ellis, shows the Celts near the top of their military and political might. They had spread from a small original base somewhere in Austria in the early years of the first millennium BCE, moving westward into Spain and France, and southwards until they came into contact with the Greeks and Romans. It was through the eyes of these Mediterranean peoples that we catch our first glimpse of the Celts. Naturally enough, we hear mostly about their demeanour in war. Men and women alike entered battle so charged with manic energy that their enemies cowered in fear. But the Celts preferred the combat of single warrior heroes to organised soldiery, and the methodically murderous legions of Rome ultimately won the day. Because the Celts were politically decentralised, the legions had to individually conquer each group, but Roman rule finally extended across most of the Celtic world. France, Spanish Galicia, the Netherlands, Britain and Wales all became part of the Empire.

Once political rule had been established, the Romans applied their *interpretatio Romano* — a theory that all religions were forms of their own — to the conquered. Got a goddess of healing? Why, Rome has one too. Thus Roman names were slapped on divinities across Celtic lands, Roman-style altars and temples were erected, and Celtic gods and goddesses were sculpted wearing the non-Celtic toga (although sometimes with a torc around the neck). Celtic religion, practised outdoors in nemetons or sacred woods, was tamed and brought indoors. The power of the priest-poet-prophet class was smashed, most horrifically on the isle of Anglesey (Mona) where the last Druid stronghold was overthrown and the holy men and women massacred.

Although what we know of Celtic religion on the continent is corrupted by the *interpretatio Romano*, even through that distorting mirror, some commonalities can be traced. Celtic religion mirrored Celtic political organisation in being radically decentralised; only a few Celtic divine names are found more than once. Thus it appears that each group worshipped its own ancestral divinities and honoured the spirits of their place of residence, the so-called *Genii Loci*. Commonly, these divinities included goddesses of the land's fertility and of the watersheds, a god of the forge and a lord of the animals. Many Celtic divinities are found in double or triple form, sometimes in male–female couples, sometimes in multiples of the same sex, which has led some scholars to theorise a greater gender equality than in patriarchal Rome. While that cannot be proven or disproven, the great prominence and power of Celtic goddesses has attracted considerable attention of late.

There was one Celtic land the Romans did not subdue, and that was Ireland. But the land was no stranger to invasions. It is telling that there is no Irish creation myth; the story of Ireland begins with invasion, as the ancient text called the *Lebor Gabála*, the Book of Invasions, tells us. In it, history and myth are indistinguishable, although we can assume that the first Irish invader — a supposed granddaughter of the biblical Noah — was mythic. After her came a steady stream of others — the Partholonians, the Fir Bolg, the Fomorians. What history do these mythic texts encode? We can be certain that, as the *Lebor Gabála* claims, many groups found their way to Ireland, among them the Celts, who probably arrived in several stages. Some scholars argue that the Tuatha Dé Danann, the people of the goddess Danu, were early Celtic settlers conquered by later ones who moved the early deities into an Otherworld, nearby but no longer reached.

The Celtic era overlapped with the Christian one; put another way, Ireland's oral period flowed into its literate era. Early writers and scribes were Christian monks, who transcribed the great spoken literature of the Celts so that today we have such works as the *Táin Bó Cuailgne* (Cattle Raid of Cuailgne) and the *Tochmarc Étaíne* — although we have no way of knowing whether or where the god-fearing monks interpolated Christian themes into the old stories. Without the influence of Rome, we have no sculpted portraits of the ancient Irish gods and goddesses, so we are free to imagine Medb and Brigit, Nuada and Bres and Goibniu as we will, drawing from the vivid word-portraits composed aloud by the druidical bards, or filidh, and captured in writing by their descendents in Ireland's monasteries.

The Celtic Ireland of these epics and adventures, these vision quests and voyages and elopements, is a world in which the king was beholden to his people through an inaugural ceremony in which he drank from the cup of the goddess of the land. In doing so, the king did not so much acquire power as responsibility, including the responsibility to follow the required vows or *geasa*. Doing so would assure prosperity, while breaking the *geasa* — as we learn in the terrifying vision of doom called *Da Derga's Hostel* — would bring barrenness to the land and ultimately death to the king. This marriage of masculine heroism and feminine prosperity is a mark of Irish myth, although whether it is purely Celtic or whether it results from the mixing of Celtic and indigenous religion is debatable. This apparent balance, together with the vision of the inspired bard who travels to a magical Otherworld to gain inspiration and healing, attracts contemporary spiritual seekers to the Irish Celtic past.

The Pledge to the Elements

Tom Cowan

Tom Cowan (www.riverdrum.com) is an American of Scots-Irish descent from the Clan Colquhoun. His publications include Fire in the Head: Shamanism and the Celtic Spirit *(Harper San Francisco),* The Way of the Saints: Prayers, Practices, and Meditations *(G.P. Putnam's), and other works on shamanism and spirituality. He is an ordained minister in the Circle of the Sacred Earth, a church of animism dedicated to shamanic principles and practices.*

I swear by the gods my people swear by!

Leave it to the Celts to say things a bit sly and slanted. Does this oath sound slightly ambiguous? Or merely half-said? This old Celtic formula for attesting to the truth of one's word may sound somewhat disingenuous, a good ploy perhaps to avoid naming any specific deity to sit in judgement and thereby avoid making any sort of substantive vow you would have to answer for. And yet, there is more here than meets the ear. Rather than verbally sidestepping a direct plea to a supernatural witness to one's promise, this oath clearly links the speaker to the whole panoply of tribal deities and to the entire community of the tribe itself. It even suggests that the ancestors are listening and witnessing the vow.

Truth — and the promise of truth — have been primal features of the Celtic moral code from earliest times. In an ancient text known as the Colloquy of the Sages, Saint Patrick asks Caílte, a member of the Fianna of Fionn mac Cumhaill, who has returned unexpectedly from the Otherworld, how the forest warriors found meaning in life before Christianity, as if the old missionary couldn't imagine anyone leading a moral life before the coming of Christ. Caílte responded, 'We had truth in our hearts, promise on our lips, and strength in our arms.' In other words, inner truth, the promise of that truth, and the physical strength to live up to it sustained the Celts during the heroic age.

The Celts took truth seriously. In addition to calling upon all the gods of one's people, early Celtic warriors also called upon the forces of nature to witness their vows and pass judgement on the fulfilment of them. Consider this common oath formula, dating back to pre-Roman times: 'If I break my pledge, may the sky fall upon me, the sea rise up to drown me, and the earth crack open to swallow me.' Failure to live up to a promise could elicit retribution in the form of this triple death from fire, water, and earth.

A story that may go back as far as the ninth century relates the dire consequences of making a Pledge to the Elements and not living up to it. Lóegaire, a king of Tara, went into the province of Leinster to receive cattle as royal tribute. The people of Leinster defied him, battle resulted, and Lóegaire was defeated. While held captive, Lóegaire was offered a deal. If he promised never to demand cattle as tribute in his lifetime, he would be released. Lóegaire accepted and made his pledge, calling on the elements of nature to witness it. He promised 'the sun and the moon, water and air, day and night, sea and land' that he would never again demand tribute from Leinster as long as he lived. Whereupon he was released. And whereupon he forgot his vow. He later went 'on a hosting' to demand cattle from Leinster.

The story explains what happened: 'He did not however bear the pledges in mind — and he died there of the sun and of the wind and of the other pledges; for at that time no one dared break faith with them.' Later the poets would say, 'The elements of God that he invoked as pledge brought the fatal encounter to the king. The just sanction of the elements of God, it is this that killed Lóegaire.'

This was a heroic age. Feuds were settled by mortal combat. Warriors fought to the death. The merest slight or insult of today would have turned men to duelling in the past. We don't live in such heroic times; we are not as quick to lay our lives on the line for broken promises. Yet I believe that calling upon the elements is still a valid spiritual exercise, perhaps even more so given the era we do live in.

Today words are cheap. Our culture is so glutted with words, both spoken and printed, that we become discouraged at ever determining the truth or falsehood of them. Advertising come-ons, deceptive political promises, ambiguous sound-bites, scare headlines, facts purposely stated out of context, outrageous statements geared solely for self-aggrandisement, all the slogans and cover-ups of spin doctors and media-masters leave us feeling cynical about the notion that truth and the promise to be true should be the moral centre of our lives. The belief that a person is as good as his or her word sounds quaint, old-fashioned, no longer applicable to the modern world, and frankly, just too elusive to take seriously. Today people are too ready to repudiate their promises in both written and verbal contracts. We give up trying to discern the truth from the half-truth from the outright lie.

The ancient Pledge to the Elements can be a corrective to this kind of moral conduct and to our standing as human beings in the cosmos itself. In doing so we call upon nature to witness our promises, and we acknowledge the vital role we, as humans, play in maintaining the health and well-being of the universe.

It is quite clear from the mythological lore of Ireland and other Celtic lands that Truth is the vital glue holding the cosmos together. A ninth-century Irish text highlights the importance of the King's Truth:

By the King's Truth, great clans are ruled.

By the King's Truth, great death is warded off.

By the King's Truth, great battles

    are driven off into the enemies' country.

By the King's Truth, every right prevails.

By the King's Truth, fair weather comes in each fitting season:

> winter fine and frosty,
>
> spring dry and windy,
>
> summer warm with showers of rain,
>
> autumn heavy with dews and fruitful.
>
> By the King's Truth, the land is fruitful
>
> and every child born is worthy.
>
> By the King's Truth, there is abundance of tall corn.

The king holds the centre in the Wheel of Life, and his authority comes from his ritual marriage to the Goddess of Sovereignty and the Land. Therefore, he has a special responsibility to uphold the Truth, for it is through him that the Divine Feminine assures prosperity, justice, peace, children, even appropriate weather for each season. Just as the king is responsible for the well-being of the realm, so are we responsible for the well-being of our own lives.

In another Irish myth, Cormac, King of Tara, is lured into a realm of the Otherworld known as the Land of Truth, where he discovers the Pool of Wisdom and is given the Cup of Truth. Now, the Cup of Truth has supernatural qualities. It breaks apart when lies are spoken over it, and reassembles itself when the truth is spoken across it. Cormac brings the Cup back with him into this world where he can render wise judgements in disputes and arguments among his people. And yet, we might suspect that the Truth that the Cup responds to is also that deeper cosmic truth for which the king is held accountable, on which his entire realm depends, not solely the passing truths and falsehoods spoken by individual men and women of a given age.

The Cup of Truth shattering in the presence of a lie has a direct parallel to the disruption in nature caused by the triple death: the sky falls, the sea rises up, and the earth cracks open. Although each occurs in nature, none are considered the normal course of natural events. They are disruptions, moments of chaos, in what we perceive as the orderly sequence of nature.

The Celtic love of the dramatic and the desire to view one's life in heroic and cosmic terms lies within this concept of the triple death. The sky falling refers to the sun, moon, stars, lightning, or meteors hitting someone on earth. The sea rising up suggests a tidal wave or a great flood that washes ashore taking human life. The earth cracking open mercifully occurs only when massive tectonic plates shift enough to cause an earthquake. While totally in the realm of the natural, each is an aberration from the usual rhythms of the natural world.

Calling upon the elements of God to allow the triple death acknowledges that a person's broken promise has serious cosmic ramifications, analogous to severe disruptions in the natural world. Is it possible that the universe, like the Cup of Truth, would shatter completely if everyone lied, broke promises, and went back on their word? Is it possible that those honest individuals who keep their promises, speak the truth, and live up to their word are in fact holding the universe together?

The Pledge to the Elements can be a profound spiritual practice to deepen a sense of personal responsibility for one's life, as well as developing a sense of place in the greater cosmos, or what we might call Life Itself. While we do not live in a heroic world where we would pledge our lives on our spoken promises — and few of us would want to suffer the fate of King Lóegaire if we swore oaths to the elements and then broke them — there is a way to incorporate the core features of this practice into our spiritual lives.

For people with an animistic perspective on reality, the elements of nature are conscious beings, able to respond to human supplication. For theists, the God of the elements is the ultimate intelligent being behind the many faces of nature, which we might think of as 'the masks of God'. The Irish language contains a suggestion that both of these theologies might in fact be one and the same. The Irish word for elements is dúile and for nature is dúlra. An Irish term used for God or the Creator is Dúileamh, a word rooted in the idea of nature and the elements, and almost untranslatable into English except by phrases such as the 'Being of the Elements', the 'One Who Is the Elements', or the 'Spirit of Nature'. Perhaps it does not matter, therefore, whether we make our pledge to the elements themselves (the dúile) or the Divine

Being behind them (the Dúileamh). Either way we are sworn, witnessed, and held accountable.

So how can we do this?

Here is a formula I use in my training programmes in Celtic mysticism for restoring the Pledge to the Elements to the central place it once held in the old Celtic moral code. When you need to make an important decision in life involving a change in behaviour or a departure from your habitual ways of living, pray over it to learn whether it is appropriate to make the Pledge to the Elements concerning it. Examples might be eating healthier foods, getting more sleep or exercise, spending more time with loved ones, being more patient or tolerant with someone at home or at work, giving up some harmful activity, volunteering more time to community events, donating more money to worthy causes, taking steps to change your job.

If it seems appropriate to make a Pledge to the Elements, plan to make the pledge over four days. One day is set aside for each of the four elements. Each day will require prayer, ritual, and dedication. Spread out the four pledges over at least four days so that you are involved with your commitment for a length of time, to impress the seriousness of your intention upon your deepest mind and heart. In most circumstances we should not call upon the elements to witness important decisions on the spur of the moment.

Let's say you are pledging to be more tolerant and patient with someone at work. Decide where and when you will make your pledge to each of the four elements. For example, go down to a river for the pledge to water or stand outside on a rainy day to let the rain wash over you. Climb to the top of a hill or hike to the base of a mountain to make your pledge to the earth. Go to a hilltop on a windy or foggy day to make the vow to the air. Build a fire, get up at sunrise, or stand outside on a clear starry night to make your promise to fire. These are just a few suggestions from many possibilities. The point here is to place yourself directly in the presence of the physical elements.

Stand before each element, face it head on, and say a simple prayer, something like the following: I promise you, O River of Water (or Rising

Sun, or Southerly Wind, or Beauty of this Mountain), that I will try sincerely and to the best of my ability to be more patient and tolerant with So-and-So at work, and to be more patient and tolerant with Life Itself.

After each prayer, close your eyes and ask that element to give you a sign or omen that it will support you in this promise. With your eyes closed, rotate clockwise in the spot where you are standing until you feel an urge to open your eyes. As you open them, the first thing that catches your attention is the sign, whether it be visual, audible, or sensory. Accept it as an omen that the element has heard you. Treasure it, be grateful for it, think on it when you feel tempted to break your pledge. Over the four days or so, you will have completed the pledges, and you will be witnessed.

Now what is the judgement they will pass on you should you not live up to your promise? The spirit in which to make these pledges is that of appropriate accountability. Ask the elements to hold you accountable in ways commensurate with the seriousness of your vow and the violation of it. Obviously you are not asking for death, physical injury, or severe disruptions in your life if you lose patience with So-and-So at work. But serious or repeated failures should elicit some kind of reprimand, hardship, or sacrifice that you will recognise as just retribution for not living up to your pledge to the best of your ability. Examples might be: an event you were looking forward to is cancelled, your television breaks down the night of a special programme, your outdoor event is rained out, you come down with a cold and have to miss going somewhere, you have a flat tyre. These are all in the nature of dis-appointments, setbacks, and episodes of bad luck that will not disrupt your life out of proportion to your pledge and your failure to fulfil it. The important point is that you recognise these mishaps as the judgement of the elements that you have in some way failed to keep your promise.

When this happens, renew your vows in a spirit of humility. You can do this either by repeating the steps you took originally, or in an abbreviated form, speaking the words of the pledge to each element and asking for additional strength and help in the future. In fact, you do not have to wait until you break your promise to repeat the pledges. Make them every day if necessary to remind yourself of them and to strengthen your commitment.

The elements are not simply adversaries or stern judges waiting to catch you in a weak or compromising moment. They are participants in your moral life who bring Otherworldly focus to your resolve to live more consciously. Realise equally how your own commitment to the truth of your life, like the Celtic king's commitment to truth itself, contributes to the order and the beauty of the universe. Have faith that your efforts to be true to your word become woven through the greater fabric of nature, reinforcing the orderly rhythms that make our lives possible.

The elements, and the God of the elements, will treat us fairly. Honoured to be invited once again into our moral universe, they will respond to us both in support and in judgements that will keep us true to our decisions. We might recall that these are the same elements found in the Irish blessing that asks that the road rise to meet you, the wind be ever at your back, the sun shine warmly on your face, and the rain fall gently on your fields. These are the same elements invoked in an old Scottish blessing that says, 'The love and affection of the sun be yours, the love and affection of the moon be yours, the love and affection of the stars be yours, the love and affection of the dew and wind and rain be yours — the love and affection of every living creature be yours.'

If this is the universe we live in, how can we fear calling upon the elements of God to bear witness to our lives?

Soldier's Heart

✼

Patricia McDowell

Pat McDowell Aakhus (paakhus@usi.edu) is an American of Irish and Scottish descent. Wolfhound Press has published three of her novels: The Voyage of Mael Duin *(1990),* Daughter of the Boyne *(1992) and* The Sorrows of Tara *(1994). She teaches creative writing and literature at the University of Southern Indiana. Raised Anglican, she is a converted Catholic with a growing faith in analeptic thought, as Robert Graves put it, or time travelling, or genetic memory.*

On Samhain Eve some years ago, the late historian and archae-ologist Elizabeth Hickey of Tara led me over stone walls and through fields, chasing away herds of cattle with her cane, all the while keeping track of her seven cairn terriers, looking for the Ford of Slaughter. We found it, a narrow crossing of the Boyne River, near the ruins of an old abbey. She knew where it was, though it had been many years since she had been there. It was at that very site, in the year 528 CE, according to the *Annals of Ulster*, that Muirchertach mac Erca, Rí Éireann, King of Ireland, subdued the old tribes of Tara. There were no survivors. It was there, years later at Samhain, that the king had terrible flashbacks — the ford rose up, filling with blood and corpses. As he climbed the hill towards the 'blue stones of the Brug' to escape his hallucinations, long-dead blue-skinned warriors rose up from the mound to be killed again. On the night when the dead cross over, Muirchertach was haunted by images of war. Soon they would destroy him.

Mrs Hickey had prepared a picnic lunch, and we sat among the ruins of the abbey; she made sure I got the piece of Samhain barmbrack with the gold ring hidden in it. It was a beautiful autumn day. We talked of Muirchertach, of the novel I was writing, of the violent memories that drove him mad. 'You know,' she whispered to me, as though it were a secret, 'I have always believed that Shakespeare witnessed a murder. You see it in *Macbeth*, of course.' She shuddered. 'He couldn't forget it.'

Muirchertach and Macbeth have a common malady, one represented in much of ancient Irish literature. During the American Civil War, it was termed 'soldier's heart'; in the First World War, shell shock. At one time during the Second World War more men were being discharged for combat fatigue than were being drafted into the war. Today the same malady is called PTSD, or post-traumatic stress disorder; it is believed that of the million Americans who experienced combat in Vietnam, half suffer from this most common malady of war.

It is a malady found in many epics of antiquity: *Gilgamesh, The Odyssey*, the Breton tales of Chrétien de Troyes. Early Irish literature too focuses on soldier's heart — *Aided Muirchertach mac Erca* (The Death of Muirchertach), *Buile Shuibhne* (Sweeney Astray), *Imram Curaig Máel Dúin* (The Voyage of Máel Dúin), each tells the story of a hero's madness brought on by battle and of his quest for healing. Hardly an Irish narrative does not include it; battle madness is found in the *Táin Bó Cuailgne* and the Fianna cycle. Frequently, the hero's primary objective of vengeance is abandoned, and the adventure turns into a spiritual quest. In the end, as the hero is healed, reconciliation delivers a pacifist theme rather than a simple evocation of the glory of war.

Sweeney's madness descends during the Battle of Magh Rath (Battle of Moira), a historical seventh-century Irish event. During the conflict, Sweeney continually violates peace by breaking truces. As a result he is cursed with 'mad spasms' by the cleric Rónán. When he hears the howls of the armies engaged and looks up into the sky, he is possessed with a dark, inhuman energy that drives him mad. Vertigo, revulsion, spasms and paranoia grip him. He drops his weapons and is transformed into a bird, exiled from his own kind.

Vivid descriptions of battle frenzy can be found in many Icelandic and Norse narratives. A Viking berserker may be struck with fury in the midst of battle and transformed into his totem animal, usually a wolf or bear. Nowhere is the warrior's transformation into a state of battle frenzy more explicit than in the *Táin Bó Cuailgne*, describing Cúchulainn. When the 'warp spasm' comes upon him, each hair stands up straight as spikes made of iron tipped with fire; one eye is small as a needle, the other large as the mouth of a cup; his mouth gapes to his ears, and a halo of fire rises from the top of his head.

A goddess is often responsible for the frenzy. In *The Iliad*, Athena ignites Achilles' battle fury — crowning his head with a golden cloud and from it lighting a fire to blaze across the field of battle. Irish warriors are inspired by no less than five battlefield goddesses: Fea (the Hateful), Badb (Fury), Nemain (Venomous), Macha (Battle herself, who sent labour pangs on the men of Ulster for their lack of compassion), and the Mórrígan, queen of war. Most appear shrieking over the heads of warriors during battle and descend as ravens or crows when it is over. Medb of Connacht, as Sovereignty, warrior and primary instigator of the bloody *Táin*, joins their ranks.

On the surface, *The Voyage of Máel Dúin* seems to be a travelogue of supernatural adventures, similar to *The Voyage of Saint Brendan*, but with more Celtic elements. However, despite similar details of landfalls and fantastically viewed natural phenomena, Máel Dúin does not seek the white martyrdom, the hermit's exile of peace. Like Odysseus, he travels from wonder to wonder, trying to get home. Emotionally damaged by war — his father's brutal killing and his own subsequent rejection by the community for having failed to avenge him — he seeks peace. How familiar might that rejection seem to the many hundreds of thousands of Vietnam veterans in their own homecoming to America?

Máel Dúin's illness drives him towards revenge but prevents him from achieving it. As a result of divine will, chance or serendipity, he is lost at sea and gradually encounters spiritual healing. It is not an easy road; the way is filled with nightmares, hallucinations of giant ants and other icons of death, horrid battles in which two creatures flay each other perpetually. Gradually, the images of horror are replaced with splendid images of rebirth and resurrection. One of the last is the aged dying eagle who renews himself by diving into a lake. When Máel Dúin finally does reach home, he discovers that his enemies are no longer his enemies; there is no need for vengeance.

It was this unusual non-violent resolution to a heroic epic that initially drew me to Irish literature, to translate the *Voyage*, and write a novel based on the fragments. I found the pacifist themes again in *Tochmarc Étaíne*, the Wooing of Étaín (which became my novel *Daughter of the Boyne*). Further research led me to the Ford of Slaughter and a Samhain picnic with Mrs Hickey, as my work on the *Death of Muirchertach mac Erca* became *Sorrows of Tara*. The argument is the same: war is terrible and its effects on individuals devastating. The action of each epic is the working out of madness caused by violence — a condition, PTSD therapists say, that is 'a normal reaction to an abnormal situation'.

The flashback hallucinations that Muirchertach experiences are some of the most horrific in literature: decapitated warriors with hacked-off limbs who rise up to fight again, the blue warrior-corpses reanimated, the Ford of Slaughter rising up full of blood. Though he has lost his ambition for conquest and desires only peace of mind and domestic happiness, Muirchertach's past keeps coming back; inevitably, it destroys him. The sorceress Sin (winter storm) seduces him in order to murder him, driving him first more deeply into madness so that he will know his crime — the murder of her family and annihilation of the tribe of Tara. *The Annals of Ulster* were wrong; there was one survivor. Sin was a little girl and saw the horrors. There is no reconciliation, only recognition of wrong.

That Samhain afternoon, Mrs Hickey climbed down into the souterrain where the child Sin had hidden to escape death. There was no telling how old the chambered tunnel was. Iron Age? Early Christian? Since Mrs Hickey had last climbed down, thirty or forty years earlier, it had further deteriorated. She dropped down into the dark, her lantern shattering; it was difficult for her to climb out. Being less brave and only thirty-eight, I decided to forgo the adventure.

Soldier's Heart

We went instead for a whiskey by the fire at the Conyngham Arms in Slane.

Those suffering from PTSD recognise the range of side effects — explosive anger, depression, desires to court danger in order to feel alive, alienation. Like many returning veterans, Muirchertach, Máel Dúin, Sweeney and Odysseus try to get home. Home is not just a place, but a return to civilian life, the normal life, work, family, memories without pain, sleep without nightmares. Like Muirchertach and Sweeney, Odysseus has bad dreams.

When we first encounter Odysseus he sits sobbing on a rocky shore, his wet eyes scanning the bare horizon of the sea. When Kalypso offers to help him go home, he doesn't trust her. He will 'take no raft she grudges him out to sea'. As far as his wife and son know, he is dead; after all, he has been missing in action for ten years. Stripped of fame, fortune, crew, even of his name, he is swept naked onto an island where, out of hospitality, he is entertained with songs of the Trojan War. He cannot stop weeping.

Before taking his place in his home as husband and father, Odysseus takes on the role of the beggar and is received into a shepherd's house in the forest. Part of his healing is to experience the despair and isolation of others. Stripped down, he finds kinship with the poor and with animals; he is first recognised by his loyal dog. This simplicity and identification with animals is a motif throughout all the early stories about battle madness. When healed, Odysseus's instincts work perfectly. Spectacular physical feats, such as shooting an arrow through a row of spaced hatchet loops, would be impossible without grace. Healed, he sees clearly and dispenses justice. Men show their true natures in his presence. He puts an end to violence.

In the most ancient story of all, Gilgamesh, the king of Uruk, suffers greatly from the death of his beloved comrade in arms, Enkidu. Gilgamesh believes that he himself should have taken the blow and died. His guilt is enormous. He abandons his city and reaches the shore of the Sea of Death, where a maiden serves him the drink that refreshes and heals the wounded king — another Celtic motif. 'I can not stop crying,' he says to her. When he grows calm he places butter and honey in the water for Enkidu.

Chrétien de Troyes's *The Knight and the Lion*, likely based on an old Breton tale with similarities to *Buile Shuibhne* (Sweeney Astray),centres on the lucrative medieval war game — the tournament. Despite being outlawed by the Church (those killed in them were denied Christian burial), tournaments drew the avid participation of most of the aristocracy, including Chrétien's patrons. Chrétien's hero Yvain, recognising that he has lost everything because of his obsession with the games, goes mad. Everything he sees adds to his paranoia and claustrophobia. In an attempt to escape from his own grief and guilt, he runs from his friends and family, entering the magical wilderness forest of Paimpont in Brittany.

He remembers nothing, not even who he is. He steals a bow and arrows from a young boy, lives naked in the forest, stalks animals and eats them raw. Having lost all sense of proportion in battle, he must be restored to the natural order. What is it to be a beast? He is like Sweeney astray, an animal in the wilderness. He must return to his origins to find the way back; it is through nature that sanity can be restored. What is community? A hermit in the forest sets out mouldy bread and water on a window ledge to feed the wild man. Yvain brings the hermit meat. This simple reciprocity, a gesture of hospitality, is the first step to healing.

A maiden finds Yvain asleep in the forest, naked like an infant, and recognises him by a scar on his face, the mark of warfare. He is so weak he cannot stand. The maiden covers him with her cloak, healing him with a magic ointment given to her by Morgan the Wise, King Arthur's sister (not evil in this story, but a woman with gifts of healing). She rubs the ointment on his temples and forehead, then all over him, down to his toes. His madness leaves him. Joined by a companion, a lion, he uses his martial gifts to protect others, not for the glory of war. In a long series of adventures, in which he is obliged to save damsels — sometimes two at once, in different places, at the same time — he at last joins his lady, who loves him, 'and he forgets his hardships'.

At the time this was written, Henry II of England, driven by guilt for the assassination of Thomas Beckett, went to the stream in Glen na Gealt in Dingle to be cured of his madness. I looked for this place in 1990; it wasn't in any of the guidebooks. An elderly man at the post office in the village of Camp gave me directions, assuring me that though the place wasn't signposted, it was easy to find. 'Sure,' he said, 'I've seen them, naked, drinking out of the stream, like animals.' To get the cure one must strip naked, drink water from the stream and eat the cress that grows from the riverbank. It is a lovely site. My husband, children and I put our feet and hands in the water for good measure, but our courage stopped there. One hopes the midges weren't so bad when Henry visited.

Perceval, another Breton tale retold by Chrétien de Troyes, rich with Celtic myth, also depicts the effects of a life of combat. A flesh and blood evocation of the Sheela-na-gig — 'ugly as the pit of hell, her eyes two little holes tiny as rats, a cat's nose and the lips of a donkey. Teeth yellow as egg yolk flecked with blood. Humpbacked she was, and her legs twisted like two willow branches' — tells Perceval that because of his actions, ladies will lose their husbands, lands will be laid waste, maidens will be raped, and knights will die. He ignores her and continues to seek out the most dangerous adventures. At last, deranged and amnesiac, he comes upon a hermit on Good Friday, recognises that his desire to pursue violence is a sin, and begins to heal. Perceval is unfinished; it breaks off mid-sentence. Perhaps Chrétien de Troyes died, or he went on crusade with his patron Philip, Count of Flanders, host of tournaments. But one can sense the direction the story is taking. Like Yvain, Máel Dúin and mad Sweeney, Perceval will find his way; nature will heal him.

What drew me to Irish literature initially was its pacifist themes. Among the magical, violent and heroic acts, the greatest were acts of compassion — forgiveness of self and others. These are not political stories, meant to draw lines or to assign blame. All victims of violence deserve compassion. These same notions are reflected in the poetry and prose of some of my most gifted writing students, themselves

Vietnam veterans suffering from PTSD. Their lives are different from mine; I experience war through literature or film, while for them the suffering is real. Telling stories is part of healing, as the Irish have always known. The stories come out of Ireland's gentle landscape, grass and stone, from the ruined forts now ringed with hawthorn and furze. Those hurting from the effects of soldier's heart are wise to seek wild places and the comfort that nature brings.

Before World War II, my father was a musician and a composer. Afterwards, he gave up music and became an Episcopal priest. Twenty years later, suffering from alcoholism, depression, explosive anger and paranoia, he was forced to leave the priesthood. He told me that he was composing music in his head all the time; sometimes it gave him a headache. I heard him speak only once about war, a brief answer to my young brother's direct question: Did you kill anybody in the war? He said he had killed many civilians, but he had not seen them. When my brother was older, Father told him that as they marched, they buried multitudes of dead, dragged them from the Rhine, its water poisoned by corpses. But he was lucky; he was not wounded; he didn't see the faces of the ones he killed. He never took a day off, but once a year he went up into the Sierra Mountains by himself.

Men with soldier's heart have a hard time coming home. Many who have seen violence, or lived with violence — those for whom dreams are no refuge — are drawn to wild places. Nature gives no sympathy and no judgement, only the certainty of instinct. In the lee of a mountain or a stream, we may find what we had lost — instinct, purpose and peace.

A Celtic Mary Magdalen?

✤

Elizabeth Cunningham

Except for a grandmother of unknown but possibly Irish origins, Elizabeth Cunningham (www.magdalentrilogy.com) is not Irish. Probably a Celt of some sort and definitely one in spirit, she is the author of four novels and a collection of poetry, all published by Station Hill Press. The most recent, Daughter of the Shining Isles, *Volume One of* The Magdalen Trilogy, *introduces Maeve, the Celtic Mary Magdalen. It was named one of the best fantasy titles by the American Library Association in 2000. She is an ordained interfaith minister, priestess and counsellor who celebrates the Celtic Wheel of the Year.*

I am not Irish. That is why I am writing this essay — to explain how someone who is not Irish can be captivated by the Irish spirit. But of course it is possible that I may be Irish, at least an eighth or so. My grandmother, born in the United States in 1888, was adopted as a newborn from an orphanage by two women, one of whom had been disinherited by her family for studying medicine with the Blackwell sisters. In that gilded age, many Irish women were in domestic service to families of steel, rail, or coal magnates and may have been pressed into other services by sons or masters of the house. At least that is how my grandmother suspected that she came into existence. (And the curse of Macha, who afflicted the Ulstermen with labour pains for five nights and four days, be upon the memory of any man who molested my great-grandmother, be he or be he not my great-grandfather.)

You might reasonably suppose that Mary Magdalen was less Irish than I am and that Jesus was not Irish at all. But as Maeve remarks (here I mean Maeve, the Celtic Magdalen and the narrator of my trilogy-in-progress), 'Everyone is a little bit Irish.'

Despite her name — more on that later — it is not clear that my Maeve is Irish either. She is born on Tír na mBan, the Land of Women, an island in the Celtic Otherworld. *In Daughter of the Shining Isles*, Maeve and her pal Jesus meet on Anglesey (Mona), the site of the Druid college that was sacked in 61 CE by the Romans. Mona was only a short journey from Ireland, making it a strategic stop for traders in the gold that was mined from the Wicklow Hills. Those Druids were no fools.

I have been in Ireland only once, when I was seventeen years old, footloose and otherwise loose, living on a diet of whiskey, chocolate, and bar peanuts, which I sang for, literally. I'd spent most of the summer in Scotland, first at a youth camp, then hitchhiking in the Highlands. I decided I ought to see Ireland, too. Despite having read W.B. Yeats, J.M. Synge, Lady Gregory and James Stephens, I did not know what to do with myself or where to go. After pub-crawling in Dublin, I hitchhiked to Galway. I remember very little of the trip except a ride with a sinister man who wore one black velvet glove and lectured me unceasingly on the dangers of hitchhiking, detailing the horrors of what could happen to rash young girls like myself. I was terrified that he might demonstrate, but, thank whatever spirit was looking out for me, he forebore. In Galway I fell ill with stomach flu and was turned away from one B&B because of my unhygienic appearance. Apart from being greeted in Irish by an old man on a country road, I remember little else about my time in Ireland.

So why a Celtic Mary Magdalen? The character who evolved into Maeve first arrived in my life as a line drawing of an ample woman sitting naked in a kitchen. Mouthy from the beginning, she told me her name was Madge. She soon took on colour — Madge-ick marker being my artistic medium — demanding a shade called 'neon fiery orange' for her hair and using up marker after marker labelled 'peach' or 'flesh' because she did not like to wear clothes very much. (Does she begin to sound like some primeval Irish goddess?) I continued to engage with this engaging personality by drawing pictures of her. With each portrait she revealed more of herself, literally and figuratively. She liked to eat chocolate naked. She engaged in theological debate while in the bathtub. She was involved in the visual arts as a painter, founder of the whole-body-no-holds-barred school of art. She supported herself as a prostitute. She was not interested in being in any of the too-conventional novels I proposed.

'Look,' she said, 'first I want my own book of cartoons, then we'll talk.' Not that she ever stopped talking. And so the Book of Madge came into being, chronicling her adventures as a peace prostitute in the Gulf War, founder of such subversive organisations as TWAT (Tarts with Attitude Triumph) and WITCH (Women Inclined To Create Havoc). This book was later displayed in an art show called *War and Peace*. Thus I fulfilled her first requirement.

It was under a full moon in February that it happened. It was a mild, even balmy night, so warm I could lie on the bare ground, always a risky thing to do under a full moon. It was not long after Brigid's day, and perhaps she was having some influence on the weather. In her native land she inaugurates spring in February, something difficult for a North-eastern North American to grasp. I was thinking idly of how I'd often toyed with the idea of writing a novel about Mary Magdalen. But I had always dismissed it as too hokey, too like bad Hollywood. Then suddenly I made the connection. Madge Magdalen! Holy shite! Is that who...?

Yep, she said. I thought about her, her fiery hair, her irreverence, her inability to shut up or stay out of trouble. Why, you're a Celt! I said. You're the Celtic Mary Magdalen! 'You finally figured it out,' she said. You want to be in a novel about the Celtic Mary Magdalen? 'That's the one.' Big smile. Thumbs up.

So thinking Yeats, thinking The Chieftains, thinking lovely swirling Celtic knotwork, I set out to do research. I was soon appalled. The Celts, I discovered, had a reverence for severed heads. Warrior hordes of them had rampaged across Europe sacking cities and occasionally depositing the odd sacrificial body in the bog. Are you sure you want to be a Celt, I asked her. She was. So I persevered.

There were things I couldn't help liking about the Celts. They relished words and believed in the power of words to cure or kill. In single combat, the verbal challenge — a lengthy affair — was as important as any other martial art. Celtic warriors often rode naked into battle terrorising their enemies with hair and body art and the wonderful, terrible sounds they made. The unifying force among the frequently skirmishing tribes was the Druids, men and perhaps women for whom extensive training in the art of poetry was a requirement.

It seems possible that the Celts, who ended up in the far Western reaches of Europe (Ireland, Western Britain, Brittany) encountered an older indigenous, possibly more matriarchal, culture and instead of conquering and trampling, they fell into a kind of fearful love with it, incorporating the older deities like the Cailleach into their pantheon. It may be the persistence of that older culture that gave rise to the Celtic Otherworld, where a wanderer may lose herself today. When I read the stories about an Otherworldly Isle of Women, home to warrior witches who trained the best of the Celtic heroes, I knew my Celtic Magdalen had found her place of origin.

Thus our Maeve, as she comes to be called, has eight mothers — one womb mother and seven foster mothers who 'all succeed in their determination to lactate', all eager to teach her everything a hero ought to know. When she is born, they give her a childhood name, to protect her from being stolen by the bean sídhe, although, as one of them remarks, 'for all intents and purposes, we are the bean sidhe'. When their darling reaches menarche, they begin her sex education with tales of the infamous Queen Maeve of Connacht who, they tell her, delighted in offering the men of her choice 'the friendship of her upper thighs' and had never been 'without one man in the shadow of another'.

One moonlit night our hero (she doesn't like the word heroine) goes wandering. She seeks a vision of the Appended One, her name for the strange being she glimpsed across the worlds in a magic well (another standard feature of Celtic landscape). That's right: Jesus of Nazareth taking a leak. Remember, she has never seen a male human being before, so she could not help but be struck by his apparatus. On the night in question, perhaps influenced by her mothers' stories, she encounters instead none other than Queen Maeve of Connacht, who has just relieved herself before going into battle. (Yes, there is a lot of pissing in this book.)

'There,' said Herself, giving her bush — as orange as mine! — a shake and stepping aside to survey her puddle with pride. 'That's better. Fergus is impatient, but I always say: Never go into battle with a full bladder. It's so distracting, not to mention you might piss yourself in front of the enemy. And this will be a famous place of a famous battle, because I'm going to whip that Little Hound Dog son-of-a-bitch Cúchulainn's ass once and for all, so I am. And to mark this place, my stream, noble and mighty, will become a great lake with many channels. And from this time forward in all the worlds this place will be called Queen Maeve takes a leak.'

'Queen Maeve of Connacht!' I gasped, recognising one of Boann's stories come to life.

'The same,' she said, obviously pleased with her identity.

The two converse about battle and prophecy and of course the Brown Bull of Cuailgne.

'Hear me now and understand. The White Horned bull was mine, born into my own herds. And when it left my herds to join Ailill's, people said it was because the White Horned did not want to be ruled by a woman. Now do you think I can let a slur like that stand? My sovereignty is at stake.' Queen Maeve stepped closer to me. 'Your sovereignty is at stake and the sovereignty of every woman. There's only one way to restore the balance between Ailill and me, between all women and men. There's only one bull of worth equal to the White Horned Bull of Connacht.'

'The Brown Bull of Cuailgne!' I cried, stirred by her speech.

'Exactly!' She beamed at me.

Before too long, it dawns on our young woman that if she wants to know about beings with appendages, she has come to a veritable fount of information.

'What is it like to go with a man?'

'Colleen,' she said, 'I don't need prophecy to know that you're not long for Tír na mBan. What's it like? Think of having a flame-tipped spear rushing inside you. No, no, dear, it doesn't hurt. I don't mean that. It's flash after flash of lightning and the dark, weighty roll of thunder. Sparks fly upward. Stars burst in your breasts. The darkness blazes. And if it's really good, the fire comes right up out through the top of your head. It beats a cattle war all hollow. I'd rather fuck than fight any day. But you can't have great sex without sovereignty. Never forget that!'

Before they part, Queen Maeve asks for our hero's name and enjoins her:

'Keep fighting for our sovereignty. Without it, there can be no balance between men and women. No blessing, only battles.'

So if I had ever wondered — and I tend not to question the Muse; the more bizarre her instructions, the more likely I am to follow them — here is an answer to the question: Why a Celtic Mary Magdalen? Like her namesake, Maeve embodies sovereignty, being not the disciple or follower but the companion and partner of her cosmic counterpart. In the spirit of Celtic hero-women, she even gets to be his saviour literally. Could she have been who she was without this — let's call it Irish spirit? Surely there are stories of hero women all over the world, in every culture, in the Bible, too. But for whatever reason (and maybe it's the spirit of my unknown Irish great-grandmother reclaiming her own sovereignty), in seeking her true name, Maeve and I turned towards Ireland.

Out to Another Side

✣

Bob Curran

Bob Curran is Irish-born, from County Down on the edge of the Mourne Mountains. After living in North Antrim, he recently moved to Derry. Among his many books are Field Guide to Irish Fairies *(Appletree Press),* Creatures of Celtic Mythology *(Cassell, London),* Complete Guide to Celtic Mythology *(Appletree Press), and three books from Wolfhound Press:* The Wolfhound Guide to the Shamrock, The Truth about the Leprechaun *and* Bloody Irish. *He is Northern Co-ordinator for the De Cuellar Trail, which follows the traces of the Spanish Armada in Ireland, North and South.*

'Look there,' said my grandfather, pointing upwards towards the sky, 'and tell me what you see.' And I, no bigger than my own son today, turned my five-year-old eyes heavenward.

'Clouds, Grandda!' I answered with some confidence. And so they were — awkward-shaped, irregular bundles of wool, drifting lazily far overhead and away across the County Down mountains. He shook his head.

'Look again. Don't you see castles, ships and men on horses? Don't you see women standing at the doorway of their houses, watching for their men to come home from the fields? Don't you see birds flying and darting, and trees and rivers and meadows?' I looked again.

'They're clouds, Grandda,' I repeated. He shook his head, and we turned for home.

So I failed my first exam.

He was right of course. Many years afterwards, long after he was dead, I would stand on that same spot and look at the sky, watching the drifting battlements of some mighty fortress or the sails of some unknown ship swell in the freshening wind or a man on a horse chasing a hare across a field of intense and endless blue. It was another world. I could well believe that centuries before, some ancient warrior had stood on that same hillside and witnessed that same alternate reality, looking into what came to be known as the Otherworld.

Although the Otherworld appears to have played a central role in much of Celtic mythology and folk-tales — it was the land to which the hero Oisín was spirited away and from which he was allowed to return for a day after one hundred years had passed; it was the land about which the poet Angus dreamed and from which the sidhe brought him inspiration — it was never clearly defined. It was a vague other country that impinged upon our world but was never really part of it, although sometimes it crossed over into ours. The folklore of the Hebrides records that the island of Eilean Mor in the Flannan Isles was often referred to as 'that other country' and was regarded as a fragment of another world, trapped and held within our own. Stories grew around the place, the stuff of local folklore — how strange lights and even stranger figures were often seen there, always at a distance and always at twilight. What better time, as dark took over the world and the barrier dividing one world from the other grew thin?

Where had the notion of the Otherworld come from? A number of sources have been given, the first a fusion of landscape and memory. The Celts were settlers in Ireland, but before that they had been travellers. Many historians, such as Peter Berresford Ellis, suggest that they came from beyond the Alps to settle in the valley of the River Po. Wherever they came from, they were first mentioned in recorded history about the third or second millennium BCE. The word 'keltos', from which the word 'Celt' was derived, was not their formal name, but rather meant 'secretive' or 'hidden'. It was first applied as a nickname by the Greek Hectaeus, who mentions 'a hidden people' who shunned formal records of their civilisation and wrote nothing down. Their records must have existed in memory, association and symbolism —

those things that trigger the senses and stimulate the imagination. Which brings us back to the Otherworld.

In their travels, the Celts must have moved across many different landscapes and witnessed many strange things — towering mountains, boggy lowlands, endless plains. Not having written language as such, they may have committed such places to memory and folk tale. And so these places took on a colour and dimension of their own, becoming something fantastic. Moulded by memory and imagination, these lands became regions of mystery and awe, slowly metamorphosing into another world that lay just beyond reality.

As my grandfather was to teach me, such a mysterious land could sometimes be glimpsed by ordinary mortals, though not through the physical eye. A world forged from imagination could only be seen by those who were willing to see it and then only with the heart. This world, no less real than our own, existed amongst the towering cloud formations in the skies overhead or amid the distortions of the evening shadows as the day began to fail and fade. It was best to look for the Otherworld at dusk — 'between the lights', as the country people said. Along some lonely road, the comfortable, familiar world of the everyday began to slip away, to be replaced by an alien realm that remained until the light was finally gone. Those things we recognised and knew so well took on stranger aspects — sometimes more menacing, always more eerie. Things at a distance, distorted by the change of light, assumed mysterious shapes and took on new guises. This is how it must have seemed for the early Celts settling in new places and into new situations.

Who lived in such a country? Legend and folklore populates the Otherworld with all manner of beings — ancient gods, fairies, diverse supernatural creatures. In the Celtic imagination, it became a place of great beauty ruled over by an immortal and beautiful fairy queen whose name is sometimes given as Niamh of the Golden Hair. In the Fenian or Fionn Cycle, it is Niamh who lured the great Celtic poet Oisín, son of the hero Fionn mac Cumhaill, into her realm, from which he could not escape without her permission. After many months of pleading from Oisín to return to his own land, Niamh grudgingly granted his wish. He was to be allowed to return for one day and then only on condition that his feet never touched the earth. Mounted on an enchanted horse, he crossed the barrier between the Otherworld and our own realm. Although he had seemingly spent only a few months in the Otherworld, a hundred years had passed in this one. Oisín found everything changed. Places he knew were no longer there; he found the people more self-centred and brutish in their ways. He now longed to return to the tranquil and beautiful realm of poets and scholars that he'd left behind. Nevertheless, he reached down from his saddle to help some men move a roadside rock. His saddle strap broke and he fell to the ground, becoming an old man the instant he touched the earth. Before the astonished eyes of the workmen, Oisín turned to dust and blew away in the wind.

There are some lessons to be learned from this ancient Celtic tale concerning perceptions of the Otherworld. The first is that it is a world apart. Even time passes differently there; an evening spent on Otherworld soil might be a thousand years in our own. And secondly, those who returned from it — and some never do — never view their own world in the same way. Because they had absorbed the values of the Otherworld, the mortal world now appeared coarse and brutal, almost alien to them. Having lived amongst the fairy-kind, those who returned were changed, no longer a part of their former world. Both their manners and their ways of interacting with others were noticeably different. Accounts concerning those who had returned describe them as 'vague and dreamy', with their eyes fixed on 'other things' not visible to ordinary mortals. Some accounts further describe them as 'filled with a great longing'. They had taken on the qualities of thinkers, visionaries and poets. They had become one with the spiritual world forged in the Celtic imagination. They could no longer fully interact with our own world — as when Oisín touched the ground — since that would destroy them, cause them to lose their new-found innocence and imagination. The Otherworld, then, served as a metaphor for the poetic, bardic and creative elements of Celtic culture.

But let us not get too comfortable with one theory and neglect others. With the advance of Christianity across the Celtic world, the idea of the Otherworld gradually changed, becoming strongly associated with the Christian Paradise or Afterlife, which may have had its roots partly in the Jewish idea of Sheol. The Otherworld became the place to which mortals went after death, a limbo world from which the dead watched, and sometimes influenced, events in the mortal sphere. Folklore rose to this belief, weaving a veil between our own world and the Otherworld through which the inhabitants of one realm could peer into the other.

The Celts viewed death differently than we do today. For them, death was not a finality but a progression from one state to another. The idea of rebirth and reincarnation was very prominent in Celtic religion — all those who died would return in some other guise in the fullness of time; death was but a transition between one life and another. 'The Druids,' wrote Julius Caesar, 'attach particular importance to the belief that the soul does not perish but passes after death from one body to another.' Within the context of this belief, the Otherworld assumed the status of a halfway house between one incarnation and the next, a place where the dead awaited their rebirth in some other body or form. It was a place where the prayers and pleadings of those whom they had left behind could still reach them — a prayer for favours or for protection that they could supernaturally grant.

The medieval Church was not slow to realise the financial advantages of fostering that idea. The Otherworld became a place where the dead waited before passing on to their eventual reward, perhaps a forerunner of the Christian Purgatory. And it was here that they remained until the requisite Masses were said for them by those whom they left behind. Of course, individual priests who began to make a tidy sum out of this belief — no soul could pass on from the Otherworld until Masses were said — fervently encouraged it.

To reinforce such a notion, the Church also taught that the dead, like Oisín, could sometimes come back from the realm beyond. This brought a subtle shift in perceptions of the Otherworld. At first such returns were non-threatening. Under a general dispensation from God Himself, the dead could come back from the Otherworld at certain times of the year — usually 30 April or May Eve, and 31 October or Hallowe'en — to see their descendants, sit at their own firesides and enjoy those things that they had enjoyed in life, a pipe of tobacco or a glass of whiskey. These were not insubstantial ghosts or vague phantoms but solid, tangible beings who could experience the mortal world once more in real and concrete ways.

Sometimes such a return was accomplished when the family was still awake; at other times it was done in secret when they were asleep. In 1993, my wife Mary and I spoke to a grand old gentleman in Wheathill, County Fermanagh, who told us that as a young boy, he remembered his grandfather, recently dead, returning from the 'Other place' to sit briefly with the family just before they went to bed. The corpse never spoke, nor was he spoken to, but simply sat down in his usual chair — which had been left for him — and smoked his pipe just as he had when alive. Our informant recalled climbing upon the corpse's knee and finding the touch of his skin very cold.

I have no reason to doubt the old gentleman's story. Every Hallowe'en night Annie Kennedy, an old lady who lived quite close to the area where I was born, would sweep her hearthstone and then sprinkle it with the gleeshins or remnants of the fire. If in the morning the ash was disturbed, she knew that her long-dead relations had been in her house and had been sitting around the fireplace. It was a comfortable belief — the dead came from the Otherworld to enjoy what life still had to offer them and to be welcomed by their family. They could see and be seen, and sometimes touched, by those whom they still loved and who still loved them. They could protect and reassure those who came after them. A comfortable belief indeed!

However, the Church was soon to change all that. If the Otherworld was a place of waiting, like Purgatory, then souls could only be released from it and allowed to pass onto their eternal rest through the actions of their descendants. If, say, Masses were not said — and if the Church was not paid for saying them — then the dead would remain in the

Otherworld indefinitely and might even return from it to take awful supernatural revenge upon the negligent. Thus, the Otherworld became a place from which the dead often watched and judged the living. It became a place of fear into which mortals could be carried by the hostile dead as punishment and from which they could not return. There were stories from all over Ireland of dead mothers who returned from 'the Beyond' or from 'the clay' to take away the young children whom they had left behind and of lovers who came back to take former partners 'away' into the Otherworld. That other realm slowly began to take on a sinister aspect, the clouds overhead assuming more menacing forms. Rather than a longed-for world of poetry and beauty, it became a threatening world inhabited by dark fairies, the dead and other supernatural creatures.

'Be careful,' Annie Kennedy used to tell me. 'For one bad thought is enough to have you carried away.' Annie knew all about fairies and dark spirits. At least so I thought as a child.

With the growing notion of menace came a whole assortment of beliefs about the Otherworld. It was Tír na nÓg — literally 'The Land of Youth' — the land where the fairies dwelt and to which they would carry irresponsible or irreligious mortals away. No one grew old there but neither could they come back to their own world. They were held as ever-youthful and immortal prisoners amongst the fairy kind. Or it was Annwfn, the Welsh Underworld, ruled over by a ferocious sorcerer king, Arawn, who hunted across the nightbound countryside for souls to take back to his mysterious kingdom. Always, there was an air of menace and dread.

The notion of 'carrying away' began to loom large in the lore of the Otherworld. Many characters from Irish legends — the majority with their roots in actual Irish history — reappeared in these stories and attempted to lure mortals away into that other realm. Donn Bin Maguire, an ancient king of Fermanagh, emerged from the haunted realm that lay somewhere under Binaughlin Mountain near the village of Florencecourt every seven years to carry away the best-looking girl, the strongest man, or the greatest scholar in the county. Similarly, Earl

Gerald Fitzgerald, the sixteenth Earl of Desmond, rose from a hidden kingdom far beneath the waters of Lough Gur, Limerick, every now and again, to draw away local men and women to act as his servants. The story of the immortal 'Wizard Earl' is recounted by the noted Irish writer Sheridan Le Fanu, who heard it from Miss Anne Baily, whose family owned the lands around Lough Gur. In all these stories, the imminence and threat of the Otherworld is heavily stressed. It is no more than a few steps away, below neighbouring mountains, below local loughs and trees, its inhabitants ready to tempt or snatch away the first mortal who passes by. The mystical realm is not only different and exotic in the Christian world, it exudes a palpable air of danger and of supernatural dread. Now it truly is a place apart — a place of unquiet spirits.

The idea of the Otherworld has undergone subtle changes across the years. Under the influence of the Christian church, it has changed from an ethereal fairy place — a refuge for poets and dreamers — into a haunted realm, the abode of vengeful ghosts and phantoms, a kind of demonic Purgatory. From being a place longed for, it became a kingdom to be feared and to which men and women could be carried away against their will. And yet, there is still something mystical and poetic about it, a hint of the fairy world. It is still to be seen in the shapes of clouds, the movement of the wind on the water, the stirrings of the mist on the mountains. Despite the best efforts of civilisation and of formal Christianity, the Otherworld can lure the imagination into it and carry away the senses even yet.

And, as I stand on that same hill as I did all those years ago and look skyward once more, I can just about glimpse vestiges of that other realm amongst the trailing clouds. Here are battlements, there a ship, there too the edges of an unknown and fabulous forest. After all these years, the Otherworld is suddenly very close. And I think of my grandfather. I wish that I could tell him that I can see now.

A Primer of Irish Numbers

James MacKillop

James MacKillop is an American-born Scottish Gael, descended from Jacobite soldiers who stood at Culloden Moor. Former President of the American Conference for Irish Studies, he is the author of six books, including The Dictionary of Celtic Mythology *(Oxford).*

In modern English, we use the word 'digit' to mean both 'finger' and 'number', and we are never confused about which is which. The word derives from the Latin *digitus*, which could mean either 'finger' or 'toe'. The digit as number is one of the ten symbols or logograms that we use to count from 0 to 9 — Arabic numerals that entered Western culture after ancient times. But *digitus* could hardly have meant logogram, which did not yet exist in the West. Latin and earlier English usage reflected the Indo-European pattern of employing numbers from one to nineteen as adjectives rather than as nouns: one finger, one person, one clan. It is as if all counting under twenty existed in algebra story problems: two men fighting, three horses racing, four princes contending. In such a context, a number not only enumerated, it defined.

In early Europe, people could touch the numbers they used. Huge numbers that we can write effortlessly — the amount of a lottery prize, the national debt or the light years to a distant star — were unknown. To signal that they were dealing with an extraordinarily large number, people favoured multiples of the known and palpable, as we find in the Bible: twelve times twelve, or forty times forty. Common speech did not employ a numerical count for what could not be experienced.

The identification of counting and fingers is what gives us the decimal system. Early societies where many people went barefoot or wore open sandals favoured the vigesimal system, counting by twenties; thus 'twenty' means 'two tens,' 'thirty' means 'three tens'. Old Irish, unique in the Indo-European family, shows vestiges of a quinary system, counting by fives or by one hand. The Old Irish déec, or déac, means literally 'two fives'. The Irish would eventually adapt to the decimal system, but in their earliest calculations the people of Hibernia did not mimic their fellow Europeans. Some of their native initiative can be seen in the powers attributed to three, and also three times three or nine, and three times nine or twenty-seven. The significance accorded such numbers resonates throughout many early narratives.

No tract on early Irish numerology survives. Neither do we hear of a tradition of esoteric or occult knowledge attributed to certain numbers. What we find instead are patterns of attributions. People, animals or objects are often cited in groups of three, nine or twenty-seven. The reader senses that this is more than a coincidence or a convenience of logistics. We sell eggs by the dozen because they stack conveniently or neatly that way, not because of an ancient mystique for the number twelve. Twenty-seven, however, is not especially handy, nor is nine. But they relate to one another.

Competing systems of numerology in the West ultimately fall into two tracks, one originating in Greek tradition, the other in Hebrew. Irish calculations tend to favour the Greek or Pythagorean (sixth century BCE), which sees numbers as clues to an underlying structure of the universe. The repetition of numbers in different circumstances enhances their value as indicators of an order beyond the visible. The other, most associated with the Jewish Cabbala, asserts that the number of letters in a person's name contains an essential truth about him or her. Such a belief also assumes that nothing pertaining to the person is random or indifferent. While a quasi-cabbalistic belief in numerology retains a substantial following today, there is no trace of it in early Ireland, perhaps because so many Irish names lacked standardised forms and spellings. But repeated citations of the numbers three, nine and twenty-seven, as well as the numbers five, twelve and seventeen, imply the shadowy outline of a vocabulary with connotations that a number might carry. Irish numbers may lack the assurance of the cabbalistic numerology, but there are intimations of a discernible order.

The value placed upon numbers may vary widely — nine elevated above eight or seven, for example — but nothing suggests a break in inexorable numerical succession, never three before two, nor four before three. The solitary number one having no associations, it is with two that we begin to count.

Two: Not an often-cited number, two carries implications of service or servitude. The sídh of Angus Óg has two pigs: one living, the other cooked and ready to be eaten. In the twelfth-century Vision of Angus, the hero encounters scores of young girls, chained together two-by-two. The hated Bres in The Battle of Mag Tuired carries two silvery pointed spears. Cúchulainn is often accompanied by two ravens, skilled in Druidical secrets, who announce his presence to the warring hosts. The hero Fionn mac Cumhaill is usually trailed by his two hunting dogs, Bran and Sceolang, who are by descent his own nephews; the third dog, Lomair, is sometimes added, but storytellers preferred that there be two. In Christian times Saint Brigid and Saint Patrick were known as the 'Two Pillars of the World'. No other saint — Colum Cille, for example — was ever designated a third pillar.

Three: The favourite number of early Ireland, whose full citations could probably fill an entire volume. The prestige given to the number three is hardly unique to the Irish. Pythagoras cites three as the perfect number, signalling beginning, middle and end. A tripod or three-legged stool, as for the Pythia at Delphi, is stable and will not rock. Three can represent life (male, female and progeny) and time (past, present and future). Three evokes both the physical world (sky, earth and underground) and space (before, behind and right here). Myth theorist Georges Dumézil argued that the symbolism of three reflected the tripartite division of early European society: farmers, warriors and clergy. Triple-deities are found widely in pre-Celtic Ireland, as suggested by the three-faced stone head found at Corleck, County Cavan. Earlier still, the great passage-grave at Newgrange features interlocking spirals whose number is three.

The Gauls and Celtic Britons in pre-Roman and Roman times worshipped deities whose tripling anticipates those of the Irish. They may be three-faced, like Gaulish Mercury, who was also triple-phallused. Sometimes they are tightly linked to one another, forming a triad, like the mysterious hooded Genii Cucullati of Roman Britain. The names of three important Gaulish gods, Esus, Taranis and Teutatis, are mentioned together so often that the Roman poet Lucan asserted that they must be a triad.

Early Ireland was represented by three female deities, Ériu, Banba and Fódla, who appear together in the pages of the great legendary history of the island, the *Labor Gabála* (Book of Invasions). There are three gods of craft, Credne, Goibniu and Luchta. Tlachtga, patroness of a great medieval assembly held in County Meath, was raped by the three sons of Simon Magus and gave birth to triplets. Linked to the great County Armagh hill fort Emain Macha are three possibly divine heroes named Finn, known collectively as Finn Emna. The ferocious British pirate Ingcél Cáech who sacks Da Derga's Hostel has three pupils in one terrible black eye.

Joseph Vendryes asserted in 1952 that triune figures — trinities or three figures seen as one — often have a single dominant personality and two ciphers. He alludes to early Irish dynastic records that cite triplets all with the same name. This argument may well pertain to several triads in mythic literature, such as the three goddesses named Macha who all have separate stories and distinctly different husbands. So it is with the three figures known collectively as the Mórrígna: Badb, the supernatural, crow-like woman who visits places of battle before and after conflict; Macha, herself a triune figure; and the Mórrígan, the great goddess of war fury. Despite their seemingly discrete identities, they are always associated with one another and are easily confused. Cipher-like too are the two brothers of Noíse, lover of Deirdre. Those two brothers, Ardan and Ainnle, stumble awkwardly in modern, romantic adaptations, where it makes little sense that the tragic queen should run off with three men. Taken to its origins, the story may not tell of three men at all but rather one seen three times.

Triplism also shaped learning in early Ireland. The fascination with groupings of three unites with the need for mnemonic devices to produce a pattern of versification known as the triads in both early Ireland and Wales. The monumental Welsh *Triodd Ynys Prydad*, the Triads of the Isle of Britain, deals with weighty questions of native learning, poetry, law and medicine. In contrast, the ninth-century Irish *Trecheng Breth Féne*, or Triad of Judgements of the Irish, numbers only 214 examples, some of them dealing with geographical information or with homey but witty paradoxes in the observation of natural phenomena.

Further evidence emerges in visual expression pre-dating the beginning of writing. The style called La Tène flourished in Europe from at least 600 to 200 BCE. Its influence spread to the British Isles and continued until after the advent of Christianity. While characterised by swirling complex forms, as well as an obsession with an S-shaped figure, La Tène also demonstrates a fascination with triplism. Three-tined decorative figures adorn jewellery and metal-ware. In some instances the figures may be elongated, with one tine stretching off in the distance, disguising the distinctive triplism. In La Tène style we also find the original for that intricate, woven-together figure that appears in much later Celtic art, including early Irish illuminated manuscripts — the 'Celtic knot'. It flourishes today in popular culture from earrings to skateboards. And it has three tines.

Three-tined figures provide national symbols for two other members of the Celtic family, Brittany and the Isle of Man. Brittany, an independent Grand Duchy until 1532, has several such symbols, the best-known of which are the sign for the ermine, a black stroke the shape of an evergreen tree with three narrower black strokes emanating from the tip, and the trefoil, more pertinent in this context. In the Breton instance, the discrete spirals of this trefoil join at a central point in what appears to be a design taken from an ancient megalith. The Manx triskelion probably derives from non-Celtic sources, as the concept and the very word for it are Greek. The version found on this island in the Irish Sea is homelier than its classical antecedents, with a slightly bended knee and a shod foot. But it is the triplism of the figure that attaches it to the Isle of Man.

For instant recognition, of course, the trefoil and triskelion falter when compared with the shamrock. Its use is wider than that of the harp, as seen on the coinage, or the green/white/orange tricolour, itself modelled on the *tricoleur* of Republican France. Strangely, there is no hint of triplism in the word's etymology. The modern Irish 'seamróg', the diminutive of seamar, clover, was the same in Old Irish: semar, clover, and semrach, little clover or shamrock. The Irish seamróg and the English 'shamrock' are both generic terms for similar-appearing trifoliate plants. On St Patrick's Day the Irish ambassador gives the president of the United States a bowl of what we would elsewhere call wood sorrel (*Oxalis acetosella*, of the family *Oxalidaceae*), which means that this is the official shamrock. But 'shamrock' can as readily apply, both in Ireland and elsewhere in the English-speaking world, to any of various plants in the pea family (*Trifolium dubium*), such as white clover (*T. repens*) and suckling clover (*T. dubium*).

A similar ambiguity dogs the shamrock's status as an analogue for theological instruction. Every schoolchild knows the pious legend of Saint Patrick explaining the divine mystery of the Trinity to the native Irish, who already had their own associations with triplism. It is also true that the shamrock, in whatever form, is part of the regreening of the island taking place in mid- to late March, a cycle that pre-dates the advent of Christianity. In its modern usage, the shamrock seems shorn of its aetiology. There are no implications of faith when it appears on tourist gimcrack, on upmarket Beleek ware, or on the tails of aircraft flying for the national airline, Aer Lingus. Like the trefoil and triskelion, it is more national than Christian.

Four: In Tommy Makem's song 'Four Green Fields', the four provinces of Ireland that we have known since the Renaissance are implied: Munster, Connacht, Ulster and Leinster. There are four provincial halls at Tara. Emblems for the four are commonly placed in quadrants of the same frame. Earliest Irish records count the numbers differently. The Old Irish word for province, céiced, actually means 'fifth,' as in one-fifth of a whole. And so it is with the modern Irish cúige. Sometimes the additional province may come from counting Munster twice, one for East Munster, a second for West Munster, or more commonly the area along the Boyne, Old Irish *Mide*, coextensive with the modern Counties Meath and Westmeath, can be considered a province by itself.

One explanation for this juxtaposition of four with five is found in the *Lebor Gabála*, in which early invaders divide the island among four sons, followed by later invaders who divide it among five. The divine Tuatha Dé Danann have five leaders when they confer before the Second Battle of Mag Tuired. Alwyn and Brinley Rees, heavily influenced by Georges Dumézil, write in their study *Celtic Heritage* that four represents the farthest corners and five the centre of the whole. Yet four is juxtaposed with five even when there are not specific references to the map. Niall Noígiallach is called Niall of the Nine Hostages because five are from Ireland and four are from foreign lands.

In other instances four can have currency when not juxtaposed with five. It takes four men to lift the eyelid of Balor of the Evil Eye. Angus Óg, the god of love and poetry, has four kisses that are changed into as many birds. Fiachna mac Báetáin, the Ulster king, asks for security of four cows when dealing with the king of Lochlainn. In the *Táin Bó Cuailgne*, after the hero Cúchulainn finishes his tryst with Fedelm, he leaves four heads of slain enemy by a ford of the river as a warning to invaders.

Five: Although it lacks the glamour and power of the number three, the number five can imply certainty and strength, perhaps a vestige of early Ireland's quinary system. The classical commentator Diodorus Siculus observed that the ancient continental Celts held sacrifices every five years. As Peter Berresford Ellis notes in his *Dictionary of Celtic Mythology,* Fionn Mac Cumhail counts in five, as do the people of the sídhe. There are five masters to each art, Cúchulainn has five wheels painted on his shield.' The mysterious Fiachna at the Second Battle of Mag Tuired sports a five-pointed spear, as does Ailill in the eighth-century *Táin Bó Fraich*, an antecedent of the epic *Táin Bó Cuailgne*. Tara has five different names.

As mentioned above, five often seems to vie with four in calculation, as if it were a correction or improvement of four. The tightest unit of the family is the geilfine, comprising an innermost circle of five persons. Cormac mac Airt encounters a fountain with five salmon, and Connla's well has a fountain with five flowing streams. As Ellis also notes, 'There are five great roads in Ireland, five provinces, five celebrated hostels, five paths of law, five prohibitions for provincial kings.'

Six: As the double of the magnificent three, six has a surprising lack of utility in early Irish narrative. Emer, a wife of Cúchulainn, possesses the six gifts of womanhood.

Seven: The potent magic accorded to seven in the Middle East and the eastern Mediterranean preceded Irish tradition and inevitably influenced it, although the lines of communication may be hard to trace. The powers attributed to the seventh son of a seventh son, still a lively belief in Irish folk life, to take a prominent example, derive from beliefs originating farther east. Perhaps inspired by the seven-day week, Irish narrators often measure time in sevens. The Tuatha Dé Danann do not tire if they fight for seven years. For seven years weapons are prepared under the charge of Lug Lámfhota, Mac Datho's pig is nurtured for seven years on the flesh of fifty cows. The first fire at Tara lasts seven years. When Fuamnach transforms Étaín into an insect, she is blown about for seven years. Among the Children of Tuireann, when the brothers kill Cian, in the form of a pig, they bury his body for seven years. At Lough Riach white sheep are cast into the water every seventh year at the proper hour. In early modern tradition, a mysterious tree is seen at Lough Gur every seven years when the lake dries. Flidais had several cows that fed Ailill's army every seventh day.

Alwyn and Brinley Rees argue that the hero Fergus seems to have symbolised the week, as all measurements of his huge body are given in sevens — the so-called 'heptads of Fergus'. But seven is also associated with king Conchobar mac Nessa, as seven prophets foretold his advent seven years before his birth. He attained the kingship at the end of his seventh year, and the feast he gave at Samhain lasted for seven days. Seven attaches itself to other Ulster heroes in measures other than time: Cúchulainn has seven fingers, seven toes and seven pupils in his eye.

Remembering that the Thebes of Boeotia has seven gates, as does the city on the Nile named for it, we should not be surprised that many Irish spaces are also defined by sevens. The Dún of Cúchulainn's amazonian teacher Scáthach on the Isle of Skye has seven walls. Seven Ulster champions carry the lath to build Briccriu's hall. And there are seven doors in Da Derga's Hostel.

Other numbers used extensively in discernible patterns are nine, twelve, seventeen, twenty-seven and thirty-three. Curious associations accrue to almost every number under fifty, such as the thirty-one islands visited by the voyager Máel Dúin, but the patterns appear so infrequently as to limit our ability to assign a meaning to them. Above fifty, prominent citations of specific numbers are not common and may not draw upon widespread shared assumptions about unspoken powers. The early Christian Church in Ireland, for example, sometimes measured time in an 84-year cycle, a choice more likely explained in ancient learning, much of it originating far from Ireland's shores.

A fuller dictionary of Irish numbers has yet to be written, but the reader here will have already discerned the directions such a study would take. Ireland, while an island, never ceases to be a part of Europe. While we cannot ignore antecedents of Irish cultural expressions found elsewhere on the Continent or in western Asia, the defining elements of that culture are found in the island itself. When the Irish were themselves alone they could name the world through their own words, and they could count it in their own numbers. Holding up three fingers to signify three items or three divinities is something any human could do, but in Ireland the three alone, or represented in a commonplace trifoliated clover, could also signal the anticipations of nationhood.

Soulsmith for the
New Millennium

Mary Condren

*Founder of the Institute for Feminism and Religion in Dublin, Mary Condren is the
author of* The Serpent and the Goddess *(Harper San Francisco).*

This article first appeared in Concilium, *Vol 5, 2000, edited by María Pilar
Aquino and Elisabeth Schüssler Fioriorenza.*

Some went to Mass. The circle-dancers danced. A yoga group was in
full session in the corner. A tree-hugging group swayed in the distance.
Chanters wafted Indian music. Some just went to breakfast.

The amorphous group and the texture of that morning in the west of
Ireland testified to the far-reaching changes in the landscape of Irish
religion and spirituality. These women — Catholic, post-Catholic,
Protestant, pagan — met to celebrate, excavate, and liberate the
traditions and legends surrounding the spirit of Brigid.

For the past 150 years, clerical and religious abuse, the betrayal of
innocence, a dead hand of colonising clericalism, and wars fought
ostensibly over religion, have paralysed the Irish religious imagination.
But against this backdrop, the figure of Brigid — metaphor, muse,
goddess, saint and keeper of the flame — emerges today to rekindle
Irishwomen's spirit.

For the past seven years, we in the Institute for Feminism and
Religion have taken various aspects of the traditions surrounding Brigid

and woven them into a festival celebrating her feastday: 1 February, the first day of spring in the Celtic calendar. The journey has just begun; our questions have barely been asked.

In the year 2000, the quest took us to Belfast. One hundred and thirty women from all traditions and none gathered to explore the spirit of Brigid through music, crafts, poetry, artwork, dance, and reflection — peace workers, community activists, artists, poets, psychotherapists, teachers, full-time parents, musicians, and theologians. All returned at the end of the weekend to their homes in Ireland and abroad — renewed, refreshed, energised.

The darkness of winter was over: a new spring had arrived. Hope had triumphed over despair; life over death. Brigid's daughters, Keepers of the Flame, committed themselves to nurturing the seeds of her fire for the coming year.

But one might be entitled to ask: Why Brigid? What is she? Goddess, saint, or myth? Why does her spirit still inspire today's Irish poets, artists, musicians, and soul seekers? What might the traditions of Brigid have to offer to contemporary women's search? In this article I will attempt to sketch out some of the possibilities and point toward some of the implications.

Although in the Roman tradition Brigid is known primarily as a fifth-century saint, and foundress of a monastery at Kildare, the spirit of Brigid reaches back much further than that. By taking over shrines, churches, and mythological sites, the figure of Brigid has effectively incorporated many aspects of the wisdom literature of ancient Ireland.

Today, we draw on her pre-Christian roots, the archaeo-mythology of her sites, her *Christian Lives*, and the rites to be found even in contemporary folklore, to bring women together in search of new cauldrons to hold, ferment, and nourish our hungry spirits. Against the backdrop of marching bands, violent oppositions, and the patriarchal mythologies crucifying Irish cultural and political life for the past thirty years, Brigid's spirit is fresh, untainted, and multivalent.

Lighting candles, we explain — tongue-in-cheek — that these are pre-Reformation candles. The old dichotomies collapse under the weight of laughter; the old orthodoxies strain to the sounds of music; the old dogmas sway in the dancing of freed spirits.

But this is not to say that the spirit of Brigid is ungrounded. The female spirit of Old Europe personified, her healing shrines are found in the most remote places. In European history, her sons, warriors of the ancient Celtic tribe Brigantiae, fought off the colonising efforts of the Romans — the last defenders of old Europe.

Given her European background, the newly emerging Christian Church needed to negotiate with her. Brigid is said to have acted as Mary's midwife in giving birth to Jesus. Moreover, according to popular culture, she saved their lives. When Herod's men sought to slaughter the Innocents, Brigid (drawing on ancient Lupercalia imagery) ran through the streets to distract them, allowing Mary to escape.

In Irish folklore, when Mary was too embarrassed to submit to the rite of churching, Brigid again came to her rescue. She took a rake, inverted its prongs, stuck candles in each one and placed it on her head. Preceding Mary into the church, she drew the congregation's attention away from her friend, allowing Mary to enter without shame or embarrassment.

In return for such great friendship, Mary is said to have granted Brigid a feastday ahead of her own Feast of the Purification, 2 February. In reality, 1 February was too deeply rooted in popular rite and tradition to be amenable to the Gelasian policy of converting ancient pagan festivals to those of the Church.

Brigid's ambivalent status, her rootedness in the rites, artefacts, and rituals of the Celtic soil ensured that her stories and legends have been passed down from generation to generation; her relegation to folk-culture ensured that her rites have remained relatively free of clerical intervention; her female gender (she can't be taken seriously) ensured that she escaped the efforts to colonise the female spirit. Her multivalency now ensures that meditating, reflecting and theorising on her images, symbols, stories, and rites can once again inspire, encourage, and nurture the emerging struggle towards integrity of women today.

In the *Lives of Brigit*, mythological and saga themes constantly emerge and are indistinguishable from her legends. At her birth, her mother had one foot inside the door and the other outside, bridging the world of pagan and Christian. Her mother was a slave; her father, a free and rich man. She forms a perfect bridge or threshold between the worlds of pagan and Christian, rich and poor, women and men. Brigid in her saintly aspect constantly eludes the attempts of hagiographers to tame, colonise, or neutralise her.

Among her many characteristics, Brigid was patroness of healing, poetry and smithwork. For the millennium year in Belfast, our theme was Brigid as Soulsmith. In the words of poet Anne Kelly, we invoked her:

> You who turned back the streams of war
> whose name invoked stilled monsters in the seas
> whose cross remains a resplendent, golden sparking flame
> come again from the dark bog
> and forge us anew.

In previous years we had celebrated various aspects of Brigid, among them, midwife, warrior, outlaw, healer, wounder, and crone. Each year we carefully discerned the aspect of Brigid that appeared most appropriate to our historical situation. In the millennium year, as our planning committee met in Belfast, we yearned for change, for hope, for anything that would combat the great Either/Or of Irish politics. We knew that Brigid was patroness of healing, arts, and smithwork. What kind of resources for healing or change might her energies bring this year? Soulsmith captured perfectly the image we sought, and so in the planning months we reflected on what this could mean, starting with the most obvious character in Brigid sources — the blacksmith.

The blacksmith, the traditional figure of alchemy, magic, and culture, was a feared and revered figure in most traditional societies and Indo-European mythology. He transformed nature to culture, forged the instruments of agriculture, shod the animals and often maintained the village fire. When we turned to the sources, however, we found there was much more to Brigid and the blacksmith than originally met the eye: Brigid's smithwork proved to be quite unique.

In old Irish mythology, in The Book of Invasions, we find evidence that the figure of the blacksmith was distinctly problematic. The king of the Tuatha Dé Danann (People of the Goddess Danu), King Nuadu, lost his arm in battle. Because he was now physically blemished, Nuadu had to resign from the kingship.

His resignation made way for Bres, of the Fomorian race, (one of the invaders) who was granted the kingship provided he treated the people well. However, Bres began to levy heavy taxes on the people and they groaned under the weight of the oppression.

In the meantime, Dian Cécht, blacksmith of the Tuatha Dé Danann, had made Nuadu an arm of silver, but he was still technically blemished and the arm had begun to fester. But Dian Cécht had a son, Miach, and a daughter, Airmid, both doctors. Going to Nuadu, they actually grew another arm for Nuadu, using the words: sinew to sinew, and nerve to nerve be joined. Nuadu was able to resume the kingship and dethrone the oppressive powers.

But they had reckoned without Dian Cécht. Profoundly jealousy of his son's achievement, Dian Cécht attempted to kill Miach. Three times he wounded him seriously, but on each occasion, Miach was able to heal himself. On the fourth and final attempt, Dian Cécht succeeded.

Airmid was grievously distressed at what had happened and went to her brother's grave. On Miach's grave, 365 types of herb were growing: one for every day of the year, for every nerve in the body, and every human ailment. She began to gather the herbs, arranging them carefully on her cloak, systemising their properties. Dian Cécht, incensed at the powers of his son and daughter, irretrievably scattered the herbs. The legend ends that had it not been for the jealousy of Dian Cécht, the blacksmith, we might have lived forever with medicines to cure all ills.

The story clearly reverses some mythological themes. Death enters the world, not through Eve's sin or Pandora's chaos, but through the jealousy of the blacksmith father. Like Antigone, Airmid attempted to honour her brother's memory, but was caught up in patriarchal jealousy and rivalry.

Already, therefore, the figure of the blacksmith is problematic. Miach and his sister, Airmid, drew not on the transformative power of metal, but the transformative powers of life to bring about their healing. The culturally constructed silver arm cannot compete with the power of life itself. The rejection of their arts would have far-reaching consequences.

The ambivalence of the blacksmith recurs in another tale, The Battle of Moytura. Irish legend tells of many invasions, but the invaders were always made welcome, provided they respected the ways of the Irish and honoured their goddesses. For instance, they were allowed to come to Ireland provided they honoured the ways of the goddess by giving the goddesses' names to the land. Marriage and syncretism traditionally enabled the Irish to tolerate diversity, to welcome the stranger.

In The Battle of Moytura things began to take an ominous turn. Goibniu was the smith of the Tuatha Dé Danann, but the weapons he made were magical. Brigit was also a member of the Tuatha Dé Danann and in order to cement relations between two distinct peoples, she married one of the invaders, Bres of the Fomorians.

Goibniu made a weapon for Rúadán, son of Brigit and Bres, who thanked Goibniu by turning the weapon on him, attempting to kill him. Goibniu survived the triple attack but then turned the weapon on Rúadán, killing him. The story reverses some traditional mythological themes. In many world cultures patriarchy is established when sons kill their mother, or split her in two creating heaven and earth. Men live above the earth, often in the heavens, while women are relegated below ground. The stories signal the rise of patriarchal culture, a theme of which the storytellers were aware and sometimes foretold.

On hearing of the death of her son, Brigit shrieked and wailed. According to the text, this was the first time shrieking and wailing was heard in Ireland. The Battle of Moytura ends with an ominous intonation from the Goddess, Mórrígan, signalling the end of matri-centred Ireland:

Mary Condren

Peace up to heaven,
Heaven down to earth,
Earth under heaven,
Strength in every one,

I shall not see a world that will be dear to me
Summer without flowers,
Kine will be without milk,
Women without modesty,
Men without valour,
Captures without a king ...
Woods without mast,
Sea without produce ...
Wrong judgements of old men,
False precedents of lawyers,
Every man a betrayer,
Every boy a reaver.
Son will enter his father's bed,
Father will enter his son's bed,
Every one will be his brother's brother-in-law ...
An evil time!
Son will deceive his father,
Daughter will deceive her mother.

Clearly the culture of weapons, made possible by the new metal skills rather than magical arts of the blacksmith, is distinctly problematic: the spirituality of the old pre-Celtic matri-centred Ireland was antithetical to the new spirit now being introduced. In the Christian *Lives of Brigit*, this theme continues.

In one version of her Life, Brigid had a bishop, Conlaed, who was particularly fond of fine vestments. Brigid gave these vestments away to lepers, beggars, or to whomsoever she felt needed them more. Several times she had to make the clothing reappear to appease Conlaed's wrath. A crisis arose when he appeared one day in search of them, and all she had to offer was a garment like the skin of a seal's head. Exasperated, Conlaed set out for Rome for the third time, presumably to get more vestments, but Brigid said to him: You will not get there and you will not come back. And so it was fulfilled, for wolves devoured him. Possibly it was in relation to this and other incidents that a famous refrain of the early Celtic Church was composed:

> To go to Rome, much labour, little profit
> The King whom thou seekest here,
> unless thou bring him with thee, thou findest him not.
> Much folly, much frenzy, much loss of sense, much madness (is it), since
> going to death is certain, to be under the displeasure of Mary's Son.

In another version of this story, however, Conlaed is not a bishop, but a smith. The garments of the religious officiaries of old Europe, the garment like a sealskin, referred to the power to be found by returning to the womb, symbol of the source of life itself. We know that in the old Indo-European tradition officiating priests curled up in such garments during their rites. The seal was a symbol of immortality, but equally, the sealskin garment simulated the womb. In other rituals (possibly later) kings bathed in the blood of the slain mare, or entered menstrual huts at specific boundaried times to immerse themselves in female entropy.

The old European priests entering the sealskin garment, the cave of Newgrange, or Loch Derg were returning to the womb of the earth for re-birth and regeneration. Even the early Christian Churches remembered this: figures known as Sheela-na-gigs were often placed on the door lintels. Foetal-like in appearance, they held their genitals apart signifying to the person coming in that they were re-entering the womb/church, a place where our origins were honoured and remembered. The church was a place of peace: weapons must be left aside; the power of life and death remained the prerogative of divinity.

This anecdote by the early Church historian, Bede, is telling in this respect:

When the Chief Priest of the British, Coifi, had heard the message of Christianity (CE 627), he, together with the king, renounced his faith and set about destroying the temples and altars that he himself had previously dedicated. And so Bede relates, 'He formally renounced his empty superstitions and asked the king to give him arms and a stallion — for hitherto it had not been lawful for the Chief Priest to carry arms or to ride anything but a mare — and thus equipped, he set out to destroy the idols.'

In the culture of the blacksmith, social prestige has resided not in the ability to enhance and co-operate with the life-force and the earth, but in the military ability to effect victory, develop weapons, and dominate through various forms of grandiosity.

Whether smith or bishop, Conlaed represented the emerging culture where nature was not enhanced but superseded. The fine vestments were outer garments of grandiosity, pretension, and power. Holiness and awe were not naturally encountered in the artefacts of nature, but socially, culturally, and artificially induced by the ostentatious garments of religious culture.

It goes without saying that only privileged members of the privileged sex could wear such garments. Moreover, such new religious officiaries would have to free themselves of all the symbols of abjection, that is to say all reminders of origins — menstrual blood, milk, contact with women. Not accidentally, the twelfth-century Synod of Cashel forbade the Irish to baptise their children in milk — one of the last symbolic remnants of matrilinearity.

A clear set of oppositions appears to be emerging. The first is the cultural transformation represented by the blacksmith — the culture of rivalry, ostentation, war, destruction and death. The other is the transformation found when entering the womb/earth/cave or other representation of birth and re-birth, the transformation made possible by contact with the sources of life itself. The fires of the blacksmith apparently turn nature into culture, but what kind of culture and at what cost?

The problem may well be related to the profound cultural changes induced by the manufacture and culture of weaponry that the blacksmith made possible. Scholars as diverse as Marija Gimbutas, René Girard, and Riane Eisler have argued that profound cultural changes were brought about with the introduction of weaponry.

Girard points out that while animals fight, they seldom fight to the death. However, the human development of projectiles and missiles short-circuits the instinctual brakes to mimetic crisis found in animals. Therefore, he argues, the rise of weapons and the ability of humans to use projectiles in their battles is what finally distinguishes humans from animals.

Patriarchy has thrived on developing and maintaining various dualisms — heaven/earth, sacred/profane, male/female, culture/nature, pure/impure. Such dualisms and logical oppositions are now clearly exposed as predicates of power relations. Nevertheless, they continue to grip unsuspecting imaginations in their power. This culture was sacrificially achieved by the profound cultural splitting at the heart of the last two thousand years of patriarchal development. Such sacrificial practices and theologies are lethal in their consequences.

At the turn of this century, against the sacrificial fires of the First World War then burning throughout Europe, a young Irishman, James Joyce, set out, self-consciously in his own words: 'to encounter for the millionth time the reality of experience and to forge in the smithy of my soul the uncreated conscience of my race'.

At a time when the boundaries of Europe were being re-drawn, Joyce's definitive gesture embodied Nietzsche's critique:

> But blood is the worst witness of truth; blood poisons and transforms the purest teaching to delusion and hatred of the heart. And if someone goes through fire for his teaching — what does that prove? Truly, it is more when one's own teaching comes out of one's own burning!

Joyce's craft was exile; his anvil, loneliness, and his gesture broke definitively with the security of his upbringing. One of the first modernists, his intellectual and moral courage inspired a whole new generation of intellectuals to break with the sacrificial oppositions and their political and religious counterparts.

Today, Irishwomen are perhaps being asked to go further: to encounter again the transforming powers of Brigid, our Soulsmith for the new millennium.

What were these transforming powers? Brigid as patroness of smithcraft had transformative powers that lay in a very different kind of fire than that used by the blacksmith. At times of battle, like the Mórrígan, she used magic mojo, psychic warfare, rather than weapons, to confuse the opposing sides. She put them to sleep and gave them sweet dreams of victory without harming anyone; she placed clouds between opposing sides in battle so they could not see one another. At one of her major sites, the Curragh in Kildare (the Church of the Oak), no weapons were allowed to touch her sacred oak tree. Not only did Brigid give vestments away, but she also gave her father's sword away to a passing beggar.

The smith fires of Brigid are also quite different. In her church at Kildare in the fire-temple (the remains can be seen to this day), her nuns tended the fire for twenty days. On the twenty first, they left it to Brigid to tend it herself. Like the Vestal Virgins of ancient Rome, whose dedication and purity of intention safeguarded the integrity of the political order, Brigid's nuns were charged symbolically and actually with maintaining the fires, the symbolic heart (hearth?) of the state.

Fire was also the means through which Brigid knew if her nuns had been faithful. Every morning, one of her nuns, Darlughdacha (the Daughter of Lugh), went to collect the seed of the fire. On one unfortunate morning, when she returned, the fire had burned through her apron, symbolising that her purity had been compromised. Shamefully, she confessed to Brigid that indeed a blacksmith had admired her ankles Brigid told her to put coals in her shoes to purify herself once again, and Darlughdacha eventually became her successor at Kildare.

The stories bear evidence of an old purification fire ritual, but the importance for us is that Brigid's followers were charged with holding the seed of the fire on behalf of the community. The fire would not burn them provided they remained focused and undistracted by flattery.

Like her counterpart, Sul/Minerva, in her fires at Bath, the fires of Brigid did not burn. This theme emerges clearly in her Lives. When she was born, the surrounding people saw pillars of fire shoot from her house, but were amazed that the house was intact. At her ordination as bishop (another story!) a fiery column shot from her head and was seen for miles around. Brigid was known as the Fiery Arrow.

In an old Genealogy of Brigid, those who invoke her protection chant the following words:

I shall not be slain
I shall not be wounded
I shall not be prisoned
I shall not be gashed
I shall not be torn asunder
I shall not be plundered,
I shall not be downtrodden,
I shall not be stripped,
I shall not be rent in two,
Nor will Christ let me be forgotten.

Nor sun shall burn me,
Nor fire shall burn me,
Nor beam shall burn me,
Nor moon shall burn me.

For Irishwomen today our questions are these: What kind of fire does not burn? How do we keep Brigid's flame alive? How can we guard and protect the seed of the fire? These were the questions we wrestled with in Belfast at Brigid's festival. In the space here, I can only make hints and suggestions for our future journeys.

As a nun in the prophetic tradition Brigid took mercy as her distinct virtue. Her transforming powers, her smithwork, are allied to those of healing and poetry. Her fire is the fire that burns within, the life-force infused at birth into each one of us.

Her festival traditions recognised as much. On the morning of Brigid's day, traditionally women took a seed of the fire, put it in a sock, and went out to pound the earth. They were waking the *gneart* (life-force), reminding the cold winter earth that spring had come. Their song was significant:

> Today is the Day of Bríde
> The serpent shall come from the hole
> I will not molest the serpent,
> Nor will the serpent molest me.

On 1 February the serpent, the symbol of regeneration, was said to come out of the depths and was referred to as the noble queen. As part of the festival, an effigy of the serpent was pounded.

On Brigid's Eve, women placed her cloak outside the house. Through the night, the spirit of Brigid was said to pass over, blessing the cloak with her spirit. In the morning, the women took the dew-soaked cloak back in, cut it up into little pieces and used the pieces to cure the sick — animals, pregnant women, and even delicate birds.

At one of our festivals, a woman told how her grandmother used the brat (the cloak) to wrap sick birds, which she then placed in the ample folds of her breast for warmth. Her chirping granny came alive again through her memories.

Brigid may be patroness of smithcraft, but her anvil was that of the soul; her alchemy, that of the spirit; her fire that does not burn, the life-force within. Attentive to our soul-work, we keep the life-force ablaze and focused on the work of justice and mercy.

This exploration has barely scraped the surface of the rich traditions surrounding Brigid, or even her patronage of smithwork. Many other aspects can be explored, and in our future festivals we will continue to gather together under her cloak diverse groups of women committed to soul-work.

At the festival in Belfast, in our final gathering, we forged our spiritual weapons for the year ahead, drawing on her symbols. We invoked the protection of her dew-soaked cloak; we cleansed ourselves with water from her wells; we drank milk from the pure white cow; we dipped her bread in the honey of her bees to nourish us for the journey ahead.

In a nuclear world, the old images no longer serve us. Our attitude toward the earth, our bodies and our souls must change. Our repudiation must give way to a profound sense of gratitude and responsibility. From the sacrificial fires of patriarchy, we must shift toward the burning fires within. From the burning fires of the Inquisitions, we must now turn towards authentic sources of empowerment by committing ourselves once again to becoming, daughters of Brigid: Keepers of the Flame.

In Search of Crios Bríde

Barbara Callan

Musician and songwriter Barbara Callan was a mighty woman, a moving force in the folkloric and spiritual revival in Connemara until her death in early 2001 from cancer, at the age of fifty-two. Her songs exploring and describing women's spiritual journeys have been sung across Ireland. She was the wife of ecologist, Dave Hogan, and the mother of two boys, Kevin and Brian. An earlier version of this memoir appeared in The Beltane Papers, *an American journal of women's spirituality.*

Significant moments in our lives are sometimes planned, like the longed-for birth of a child. More often they are unexpected — the first meeting with a lover, the death of a parent, the dawning flash of an insight, moments that come like the touch of a butterfly's wing. So it was for me that my first sight of the Crios Bríde ritual by a Renvyle hearth was an unexpected, heart-stopping moment; and in stepping through that circle of straw I began a journey to my spiritual homeland.

The year was 1990. The time was Brigid's Eve, the time to mark the passing from winter into spring, celebrated by the Celts as the festival of Imbolc at the beginning of February, and from early Christian times as Lá Fhéile Bríde or Saint Brigid's Day. It happened that my husband Dave was involved in a heritage project in the Letterfrack/Renvyle area, led by archaeologist Erin Gibbons, and the group had decided to revive the custom of the Crios Bríde that had survived in the Renvyle area until well within living memory. I was lucky to be invited along to the re-enactment.

We set out on a night of some starlight and some rain, carrying the crios Bríde kindly provided by Paddy Fitzpatrick of Eagle's Nest and his mother Molly. (Molly Fitzpatrick, a native Gaelic speaker and, as they say in these parts, 'a mighty woman', died in January 1997, aged ninety-three.) The crios turned out to be a *súgán* rope (a rope plaited from twisted strands of straw) joined to make a huge circle — big enough, as Paddy said, for a tall man to walk through. Indeed, one woman told us that her neighbour used to put her cows through it. 'But she,' she added, 'was very religious!' Around the circumference were four small Brigid's crosses. Well-instructed by Paddy and Molly, our plan was to bring the crios from house to house as had always been done, though in this case we would especially target the houses where the old people lived.

At the first door we boldly knocked, our cry 'Ligigí isteach Brighid agus a crios!' (Let in Brigid and her girdle!) hanging on the night air. Sure enough, the door was opened with the answer 'Céad míle fáilte romhat, a Bhrighid, is roimh do chrios!' In house after house we were welcomed in with a mixture of surprise, shock, wonder and joy: Brigid was returning home.

The ritual involved each member of the household stepping through the crios three times clockwise, then gathering it up in their hands and passing it three times round their waists, while we chanted prayers in Irish all the while. Some of the old people had tears in their eyes. For us, there was overwhelming surprise at the ritual's stunning power. To watch a family, from old grandmother to youngest child, go through the crios was moving beyond words. We were all spellbound, and before the night was out almost all of us would go through the crios ourselves.

Incoherent as I was about the experience, I remember on my way home coming to the awesome realisation: 'This is the Goddess!' I was convinced that what I had taken part in was an ancient rite of spring, a fertility rite. This intuition was confirmed for me five years later as I pored over Professor Séamas Ó Catháin's book, *Festival of St Brigid*, and found its first chapter brimful of lore on the fertility aspects of Brigid customs. In my understanding, fertility includes all aspects of creativity, but at that particular time literal fertility had a special relevance for me: nine months later, just before the festival of Samhain, I gave birth to a much-wanted second child.

I was later to learn that the Crios Bríde custom was once widely practised in Galway. As far as I am aware, in the manuscripts of the Irish Folklore Commission there is no reference to the crios outside Galway and Mayo. However, in 1996 a Louth friend found a man in the Omeath district who knew how to make a different kind of crios and, intriguingly, it appears in Derry poet Seamus Heaney's collection *Seeing Things*, in the poem 'Crossings'. So perhaps the use of the crios was more widespread than is recorded.

Soon after the event of the Crios Bríde, I went to quiz my good friend Mary Coyne who grew up on Inishbofin. Had the Crios Bríde been made on Inishbofin? No, it hadn't, but she remembered well the custom of the Brídeóg (young Brigid) from her childhood. All the young girls from the village would go from house to house on Brigid's Eve carrying the Brídeóg, a doll representing Brigid as a child. At each house they would be given some eggs, flour, sugar or raisins. These offerings they brought back to one of their mothers, who would help them make cakes for a party held a few days later. Only the girls were allowed at this party, which of course led to attempted cake raids by the boys. The Brídeóg was also the custom on Inishturk South, and indeed was widespread throughout the country — often, though not always, confined to girls. Overall my feeling was and still is that these traditions of Brigid are of tremendous significance for women, a living link with a hidden spiritual heritage that celebrates the sacred feminine.

Who was Brigid? The rather pious images of the saint I remembered from childhood were much broadened by reading Mary Condren's book *The Serpent and the Goddess*. The image of Brigid giving away her father's sword, for example, gains immeasurably in power in light of a succeeding Abbess of Kildare being known as a woman 'who turned back the streams of war'. And for those women trying to deal with the gender imbalance in the Churches, encouragement leaps across the centuries in one early biographer's tale of the bishop 'intoxicated by the grace of God', who read the wrong words at Brigid's profession and made her a bishop!

To the early Celts, Brigit was a triple goddess of poetry (and prophecy), healing and smithcraft, as well as being concerned with childbirth and the abundance of crops. She was also, it would seem, strongly linked with the sun. In many many ways, the lives and the folklore of Saint Brigid resonate with the symbols of the goddess: for example, Saint Brigid is associated with cows, and indeed with a white cow — the sacred cow of the goddess remembered in Galway in the name 'Inis Bó Finne' (Inishbofin — Island of the White Cow). The goddess Brigit is everywhere connected with fire (fire of inspiration, fire of healing and fire of transformation), and Saint Brigid's nuns at her convent in Kildare kept a sacred fire alight for many centuries. That fire was re-kindled in 1993 by the Brigidine Sisters; perhaps part of what it stands for is a re-awakening of women.

In 1994 when I began to write songs, one of the first I wrote was 'Amhrán do Bhrighid' (Song for Brigid), in which I tried to fuse together what Brigid had meant in the past and now what she meant to me. I was invited to bring this song to a women's gathering, 'Celebrating the Festival of Brigid', at the end of the following January in Termonfeckin, County Louth. Not too far from Termonfeckin is Faughart, reputed birthplace of Saint Brigid, which has several holy wells and a series of stones for healing different parts of the body. One of the wells is in a graveyard where, my father told me, many of my ancestors are buried. I readily agreed to come and offered to bring the crios Bríde.

I went to Paddy Fitzpatrick to ask if he would lend me the crios he had previously lent to the heritage group. He no longer had it. 'But,' he said, 'I'll make you a new one, if we can get the straw.' He needed oat straw for strength, he told me, and it had to be full sheaves, which meant it had to be hand-reaped. The problem was that very few people locally bother growing oats any more, though formerly it was an integral part of farming practice. However, he would visit that evening the one man on the Renvyle Peninsula who might have it, and, if he got it, he'd make the crios and bring it over to me in Cleggan.

Several days went by and no crios. I asked all over Cleggan for oat straw. Might there be some at Cleggan Farm for the horses? Yes, there was indeed, but it turned out to be baled straw, chopped too small to be of any use. With only a few days to go, in desperation I headed down the pier to my friend Paddy Halloran, famous skipper of the Inishbofin ferry. By any chance would there be some oat straw on Inishbofin? 'Oh I doubt it very much,' Paddy said slowly, 'the old ways are gone on the island. But I'll certainly make enquiries for you.' I could see Paddy warming to the challenge. An hour later, as I was collecting my son from the pierside playgroup, Paddy came running up, waving a piece of paper. 'I have it for you! It's on Inishturk!'

That morning had seen the first break in weeks of bad weather, and, of course, there was a boat in from Turk for supplies. Paddy had accosted young Augustine O'Toole, who said his father had some oat straw. My hopes rose — his father, Paddy O'Toole, is a friend and takes a great interest in folklore. I phoned him. Of course I could have some.

But what about the chances of another boat being in in the next few days? 'Even if you can't get it to me in time, I'd still like to have it for the future, Paddy,' I pleaded.

'Oh, don't worry, I'll do the best I can for you.'

Next morning he phoned. 'It's on the post-boat to Renvyle,' he said. 'I've asked him to deliver it to Paddy Fitz but I think it would be better if you could meet the boat.'

I chased over to Renvyle by car.

The problem was to establish where the boat would come in. People had differing opinions — Gurteen pier, or back at Dooneen harbour — but luckily I spotted the Renvyle postman: he'd surely know. He directed me to a stony beach beyond Renvyle House. I ended up in Roz Coyne's house, overlooking the beach, chatting and drinking tea for an hour as we scanned the sea from Inishturk for signs of a post-boat. There were none. We mused about what the post-boat would look like — surely quite big. Just as I was phoning Dave in Letterfrack, to see if he could wait any longer, a currach appeared from nowhere. But that couldn't be the post-boat, could it? 'It could, it could,' urged Dave.

And so it was that I went running down the beach at Renvyle, to meet a currach bearing the precious load of oat straw. As the boatman threw it across to me, I had the sense of plucking the last strands of a nearly-forgotten tradition, from one of our westernmost islands, to carry them back to the centre. My running steps were in many senses a race against time. Almost without stopping, I sped back to the car, then it was up to Paddy Fitz's house, nestled under the mountain. His son, Johnny, met me.

'You got the straw.'

'I did. Is Paddy in?'

'He is, but he's in bed with the flu.'

'Johnny, could you ever make it for me?'

'Oh, don't worry, I'll get him up this evening and we'll do it together.'

And they did. It was a most beautiful crios Bríde, of gleaming yellow straw, interwoven with rushes 'for the green of the spring', as Paddy explained. It turned out that he himself, on a visit to Turk, had helped to reap the straw. I brought the crios to Termonfeckin, where it was the focal point of our opening ritual for women from all over Ireland. It stayed in our sacred space for the weekend for people to go through, and, when we were leaving, it went to Northern Ireland, to some of the women who help to 'turn back the streams of war'. It seemed the right thing to do.

Later, Paddy graciously agreed to make me another crios, this time with Dave as apprentice. This one, fittingly, was for a Brigid workshop in Letterfrack, where women from this area could explore some of the rich heritage kept alive in one of its last outposts, this corner of Connemara.

My story of the crios Bríde is one small link in the reappearance of Brigid as a source of inspiration in Ireland. This phenomenon has seemed to sweep the country in the past ten years, touching people from all walks of life. One could say it signalled that it was time to develop a spirituality that is female-inclusive. And, indeed, not all those re-attuned to Brigid have been women. In the folk tradition, the indications are that the Brídeóg was originally a ritual involving young girls, and the crios Bríde was originally carried by young boys. Can we see our way to a spirituality that honours both the feminine and the masculine? That is one of the challenges for the new millennium.

Meanwhile, a beautiful crios Bríde, made from Inishturk oat straw by a prayerful group of women led by Mary Scanlan of Carraroe, found its way back to Inishturk for Lá Fhéile Bríde 2000. And in the Renvyle peninsula, the Crios Bríde tradition has spontaneously re-emerged.

Part Three

The Coming of the Cross

*T*hese days, a posting flies around the Internet every 16 March urging readers to wear a colour other than green on the feast of Saint Patrick as a protest against the destruction of Ireland's ancient ways by the coming of Christianity. Allusion is made to inquisitions and massacres of the pagan faithful, and the text concludes with a suggestion that the image of a snake would be an appropriate anti-Patrician emblem for the feastday.

Inquisitions? Massacres? Destruction of pagan ways? Not in Ireland. (We'll get back to the snakes in a moment.)

According to legend, Patrick brought Christianity to Ireland. In fact, it is likely that bearers of the good news had been there before him, for the Christian world had already witnessed the war of ideas that Augustine of Africa waged against Celtic theologian Pelagius. The latter contended that all creation is good — including such matters as sex and death, both of which made Augustine sufficiently uncomfortable that he made a special effort to exterminate the 'happy heresy' for too closely resembling paganism, ignoring the likelihood that his own spiritual vision harkened back to his days as a follower of the dualistic Persian sage Mani. Augustine got canonised, while Pelagius was doomed to the hell of heretics.

From whence Pelagius hailed is unknown, but that the Celtic world could, by the late fourth century CE, produce a theologian of his renown suggests that the Christian message was heard and embraced by more Celts than Rome acknowledged. Thus, Patrick's mission to Celtic Ireland, however significant, was probably not the first. Rather, he stands as a personification of an unknown number of early missionaries who endured privation and danger to spread the word of their Lord.

Because the lives of Patrick and other early Christian figures were embellished into *Lives* by the addition of mythic motifs, truth is hard to tease out of the tangle. Patrick was said to have been brought as a slave from Britain to Ireland in the fifth century CE. He escaped but, after ordination, felt the draw of the green island of his captivity. Returning there, he converted many — from high estate to the meanest — and brought Ireland into the first European Union. Probably the most famous Patrician story is that of his sermon on the shamrock. On the night that the annual spring fires — marking Bealtaine, not Easter, for pre-Christian Ireland did not celebrate the resurrection of anything but vegetation — were to be lit on royal Tara, Patrick jumped the gun by igniting a blaze on nearby Slane Hill. Druids, no doubt scandalised by his political and spiritual one-upmanship, raced over. Thereupon Patrick preached the gospel to them, offering as a symbol of the tripartite God the three-leafed clover. Celts were familiar with triplicity, as Patrick surely knew from his own upbringing and from his years of servitude in Ireland. So his selection of that commonplace plant both showed the cosmic similarity of the Christian vision to that of the Celts and pointed out a radical difference in its focus on the lowly and overlooked of the earth. The Druids, it was said, were quickly converted.

Thus, no colosseums nor lions, no inverted crosses, no roasting over hot coals, no gouging out of eyes, none of that lurid stuff of Italian martyrology. Christianity arrived, abbeys and convents were set up, literacy spread, but otherwise things went on rather as they had before, at least for several centuries. Bishops (including that female bishop, Brigid of Kildare) were charged like Celtic kings with providing for the needs of their tuath or tribe. In fact, many bishops were drawn from the ancient nobility, although those of lesser status could rise in the ranks as well.

Monastic life in ancient Ireland took two forms. There were the highly organised monasteries like Kells and Lindisfarne, still renowned a millennium after they closed. Such centres were part university, part think-tank, part commune; administration of such a complex beehive of activity must have taken impressive skill. Equally significant were those tiny isolated communities — a few ragged monks out on the Skellig rocks — where constant prayer was the point, not church politics or training of scribes. Both monastic forms left their mark on Ireland, as well as the rest of the Christian world.

There is some contention over how independent the early Irish Church was from Roman influence. Some contend that celibacy was not the rule and that married clergy were acceptable; some find hints of alternative sexual preference in Saint Brigid's choice of female room-mates. No reformist or revolutionary religious movement, sociologists contend, ever claims to be inventing a new way; they always harken back to a forgotten golden age of ideal harmony. Thus, both those who claim that Celtic Christianity offered great latitude for currently unorthodox practices, and those who disdain such claims, see themselves as following the old straight path. Only history will tell which will become tomorrow's accepted orthodoxy.

Oh, yes, about the snakes. Snakes were not indigenous to Ireland in historical times, so Patrick could not have evicted them. The early *Lives* speak of Patrick waging war with demons, who may or may not have had serpentine form. A ram-headed snake is found among continental Celtic gods, so it is possible to read the story of Patrick driving snakes from Ireland as an emblem of his extirpation of paganism. But paganism didn't stay extirpated for longer than it takes to say 'out with the snakes!' Worship at holy wells, which goes back to Celtic times if not before, continued under the patronage and matronage of various saints; festivals were converted, with Imbolc becoming Lá Fhéile Bríde, while Lughnasa turned into Reek Sunday; and monks set to work transcribing the great myths of their ancestors. Astonishing what a lack of lions will do for religious tolerance.

Old Ireland's Pugnacious Saints

❋

Richard Woods, OP

A dual national since 1988, Fr Richard Woods splits his time between Chicago and the family cottage in Wicklow. His maternal grandmother hailed from Tyrellspass, Westmeath, and various other forebears were from Cork and Tyrone. Now visiting professor at Dominican University, he has taught at Blackfriars Hall, Oxford; Loyola University, Chicago; and Emory University, Atlanta. A Dominican friar with an interest in spirituality and the medieval mystics, he has published ten non-fiction books, three novellas and one novel; he has also co-authored a novel with Anne McCaffrey, edited four anthologies, and authored articles on spirituality and Celtic studies. His most recent works are The Spirituality of the Celtic Saints *(Orbis Books) and the novel,* Epiphanius Tighe and the Dragon of East South Water Street *(Authors' Choice, from iUniverse.com). His web site, Dragonthorn, can be found at www.op.org/rwoods.*

S aints are dangerous. They bring on trouble — mostly for themselves but also for other people, even long after they have gone to their well-deserved and eternal rest. Perhaps especially in that respect. A few years ago, the canonisation of Edith Stein, a seemingly innocuous Carmelite nun killed by Nazis at Auschwitz, seriously strained Vatican–Jewish relations. More recently, the Masters of Beijing waxed apoplectic when the Pope enrolled a number of Christian Chinese executed during the Boxer Rebellion in the ranks of the holy martyrs. Stein, many Jews claim, went to her death because she was of Jewish origin, not because she was Christian. And the Chinese bosses huff:

'Western imperialist agents! They got what they deserved.' 'Not so,' retort incensed Catholics: 'The Nazis herded Stein, her sister Rosa, and many other Catholics of Jewish origin into the death camps to warn the Dutch bishops in particular not to continue denouncing Nazi anti-Jewish policies. And Chinese Christians died for their faith in Christ, not in street cars, cheap beer or Coney Island.'

And so it goes. But if saint-sharing across party lines remains difficult for religious rivals, it is not an entirely new phenomenon. Nor are troublesome saints, of which Ireland — one of the earliest Christian nations of the world — provided several hundred named individuals. Some of the most notable fought even each other as well as against kings, bishops, tribal chieftains, bandits, and anyone else within cursing distance. Others proved posthumously contentious, visiting doom on the heads of those who vexed their spiritual progeny. Contentiousness did not prevent rival churches and monasteries from laying claim to the corpses of holy men and women after their funerals, a dilemma the Irish typically resolved by a miraculous multiplication of bodies, so everyone went home happy.

Like most Catholics over the age of fifty, I grew up under the impression that saints are larger-than-life examples of Christian holiness, granting the existence of non-Christian saints who somehow managed to achieve spiritual pre-eminence 'without benefit of clergy', as the saying goes. They are lifted up so that we can imitate them while disclaiming any intention of doing so lest our humility fall under a cloud of unsaintly suspicion. (Excepting Mother Teresa of Calcutta or Padre Pio, to call someone a living saint has been code for considering them physically, morally, intellectually, and psychologically inept. This is especially true of clergy, about whom litanies of incompetence typically conclude with the disclaimer 'but he was a very holy man'. Or they used to, anyway.)

Yet the very intensity of their holiness, like the spotless purity of the Virgin Mary and the sublime patience of Job, digs chasms of inimitability between saints and ordinary sin-prone mortals, despite legions of martyrs and countless hosts of virgins and confessors urging us on to ever greater virtue. The more awful their holiness, the more difficult to emulate. But it is still possible to revere what one cannot successfully imitate, or even want to, and there has always been a place for the saints as Christian culture heroes — miracle workers, defenders of the oppressed, heavenly champions to whom one could appeal for help in battling illness, injury, war, famine, earthquake, unhappy death, recalcitrant bus tokens, and, on occasion, other Christians.

Early Irish saints leaped effortlessly into the ranks of heroes. In their time, they were, no doubt, men and women of prayer, simplicity of life, generosity, perseverance, and patience. But they were remembered by later generations as giants of the faith, formidable contenders against wickedness in high and low places, prophets brimming with divine chutzpah, larger-than-life figures embodying the righteousness of God and the ideals of tribes and peoples, ultimately becoming their guardians and celestial patrons. And as such they would surely have healed and blighted, raised the dead or killed by a word, uncovered or dried up wells, made peace and war, slain dragons, and disputed mightily, incessantly, and successfully with just about everyone, including, on occasion, the Almighty God.

Not surprisingly, like Holy Writ itself, the records of the saints of Old Ireland require some judicious exegesis to liberate small but precious nuggets of fact from mountains of later embellishment. Although trekking the mountains of fiction is entertaining, fact is truly there, preserved between glowing lines on translucent vellum as well as in the names of crumbled churches and monastic cells, holy wells, caves, and time-worn paths athwart mountain ridges. Prone to limp from prodigious senescence and the encroachment of human forgetfulness, collective memory may require crutches. But it still moves even when it wanders a bit, and the ancient tales can still prove dangerous. Be warned.

Stories of heroic sanctity provide the scaffolding for other kinds of memories as well — the boundaries of church property etched by a saint's spade are likely to be recalled and made memorable by association, particularly if a thumping good yarn is involved. Similarly, disputes over ownership, precedence, and jurisdiction are likely to be remembered as contests resolved between saintly champions, as in the story of the debate between Saint Ciarán of Clonmacnois and his friend, Saint Columba. Arguing like fishwives over who was the poorer and therefore closer to Christ, the saints' verbal duel is finally cut short by an angel bearing an axe, an adze, and an auger. The angel upbraids impulsive Ciarán, the son of a carpenter, for daring to compare himself to Columba, for while he had abandoned only his father's tools to follow Christ, Columba, who was of royal blood, had renounced the very kingship of Ireland.

But Ciarán, who died relatively young from the plague that ravaged Ireland beginning in 545 CE, figures in a number of other stories containing at least the nub of historical reminiscence. *The Annals of the Four Masters* notes that in 847 CE the bishop-king of Munster, Fedlimid mac Crimthainn, succumbed to what was described as a wound inflicted by the long-dead abbot of Clonmacnois, whose ghost stabbed him in the belly with his bachall, or pastoral staff, in punishment for his crimes. Infidels might scoff that the violent-tempered old cleric died of stomach cancer, but at the end of the day a kind of rough justice was done, and who better to take credit than the volatile founder of Ireland's greatest monastic city, raided once too often by the rapacious Bishop Fedlimid? So far as I know, history failed to record the fate of the Elizabethan soldiers who finally burned the roofless walls of Clonmacnois, but I'm sure there's a story or two to tell.

Such medieval accounts reflect spiritual truth on a deeper level than mere historical fact, although fact may sometimes lie at the bottom of a ripping tale, like that of the expulsion of Saint Mochuda from Rahen around the year 635 CE. Remembered especially for the establishment of the great monastery of Lismore in Waterford, Mochuda had the temerity — being a Kerryman — first to found a monastery in the northern half of Ireland, thus transgressing ancient territorial boundaries. Although Rahen in Offaly flourished and came to house over seven hundred monks, the jealous harangues of the abbots of Clonmacnois, Clonard and Durrow led to a prolonged confrontation between Mochuda and the kings of Tara and Meath. After attempts to expel the old abbot and his monks failed, largely because of the defensive exploits of a Herculean, if dim, monk named Constantine, the royal troops eventually scourged Mochuda and his followers out of Rahen and sent them packing south. But not until the saint had roundly and effectively cursed every man-jack of them with a host of ills. Although Rahen survived for centuries, Lismore became one of the greatest monasteries of Ireland, known especially for its kindness to lepers, until it was razed to the ground by Anglo-Normans in the twelfth century.

Most of the accounts of saints in Old Ireland are stories about men, as was the case elsewhere in Christian Europe, probably because the compilers were monks. But many holy women were remembered and revered. And pugnacity was not absent from the record of their *Lives*. Even the holy Saint Brigid exacted divine vengeance on the thieves who rustled the monastery's cow; and they were borne away by a sudden torrent. Saint Gobnait, abbess of Ballyvourney, released her bees against a troop of marauders, successfully ending the attack. *The Annals of Ulster* record that in the year 552 CE the prayers of the formidable Saint Íte, patroness of Limerick and anamchara of Saint Brendan, worked defeat on the Corcu Oche of Munster at the battle of Cuilen.

With a few exceptions, the *Lives* of the Irish saints were put in final form centuries after their demise. As a form of heroic literature, they tended to follow a set pattern, much as did the *Lives* of illustrious figures from the classical past on which they were modelled. To begin with, the saint should have noble, preferably royal, forebears. Miraculous signs herald his or her birth, typically a vision granted to the saint's mother. Saints' fathers might be insignificant thugs, but their mothers are important and, not surprisingly, often become saints themselves.

Following a childhood memorable for small miracles forestalling embarrassment to the saint or sainted mother, such as multiplying butter or sheep, the holy adolescent is sent to a revered and saintly teacher to be schooled in the finer arts of divinity. Angels are likely to appear at crucial moments to supply needed advice and protection. Eventually, the fully fledged saint performs miracles astonishing enough to convince detractors of their authenticity, such as raising the deceased or, conversely, striking malefactors blind, dumb, ill, dead, and so on. In the case of a male saint, he eventually visits the Pope, an archbishop, or a church council, and is consequently ordained a bishop or archbishop. Female saints are usually made abbesses; only Brigid was ordained a bishop and that was by oversight on the part of Saint Mel, who, some sources suggest, had been over-tippling the altar wine. After a remarkable career, usually involving at least one major altercation with a saint of equal or greater prowess, she or he is alerted to an impending demise, including in the best instances exact date, time, and circumstances. Excepting later posthumous interventions, the story ends with a vision granted to another saint some distance away of the hero's entry into glory.

One of the more ripping yarns about bellicose saints touches on the literary tradition of ancient Ireland — the feud between Saint Rónán Finn, the abbot of Druim-iskin, and Mad Suibne, king of the Dál-nAraide. Suibne was a man of explosive temperament, as might befit a king, but when he seized from Rónán a tunic that had been intended as a gift, he initiated an escalation of retribution and revenge that led to his destruction.

The story has the ironic inexorability of Greek tragedy seen through the eyes of a midwife. Rónán and the other saints of Ireland ritually curse Suibne for his rapacity. Then, before the Battle of Magh Rath (Battle of Moira) in 637 CE, Suibne encounters Rónán in the woods, reading from his psalter. The king hurls the valuable book into a nearby lake and would have throttled Rónán on the spot had he not been deterred by battle preparations. This earns him a second curse. Just before the battle itself, while Rónán and his monks are blessing the soldiers with holy water in a last effort to prevent inevitable carnage, Suibne loses patience and spears one of the monks. Another monk pronounces the third and decisive curse — that Suibne himself would one day fly off the handle in similar fashion and meet his doom at the point of a spear.

Suibne's forces are overwhelmed in the fight, and the king is duly stricken mad. He takes refuge among the animals and birds of the forest, unable any longer to bear the company of humankind. His only friend is the gentle Saint Moling, himself a poet, who protects the mad king and to whom Suibne dictates each evening what he has witnessed in the forest by day. (A number of 'Sweeney' poems are extant from the twelfth century, and Moling's poems are themselves still remembered.) The final curse takes its toll when Moling's swineherd discovers Suibne talking innocently with his wife but, assuming the worst, he spears the hapless madman.

Unlike the narrow-souled missionaries of later centuries, the early Irish evangelists did not suppress the pre-Christian myths and sagas of the Celts, but copied them down, if sometimes with suitably monkish disclaimers when matters grew a bit too ribald or violent, thus preserving for posterity the oldest European literary heritage. They also sometimes incorporated them into the *Lives of the Saints*, most likely as a form of coded information, metaphorical clues as to the significance of later Christian heroes. For the most part, ancient sites were also left relatively unmolested. Despite medieval morality tales such as 'The Cursing of Tara' — which describes how Saint Rúadán, in a fit of holy pique, invoked heavenly vengeance on the seat of the High Kings, leading to its demise — the saints generally left such places alone. Some years ago, I asked an eminent Irish historian what happened to the Irish Druids, who gradually disappeared from the scene without great rancour, much less persecution. He glanced about cautiously to see if anyone in the department might overhear, then whispered conspiratorially, 'I think most of them became monks.' That would explain a lot.

Despite the surprisingly benevolent gaze turned on Ireland's pagan antecedents by Christian scribes — former Druids or not — recent writers, still smarting from the sting of post-reestablishment clericalism, have fantasised about a struggle between 'Roman' and Celtic Christianity in early Christian Ireland. But it just won't wash for a number of reasons. For one thing, the whole Western Church was

Roman, in that the language of the liturgy, law, and ordinary communication was Latin. Irish did not come into vogue in Church circles until the Middle Ages. And when disputes arose over differing liturgical practices in the aftermath of the English Church's rout at Streanaeshalch on the Northumbrian coast (misnamed the Synod of Whitby) of Colman and the Irish monks of Lindisfarne, the Irish Church simply sent a delegation to Rome to find out what was what. And that was that, although there were always hold-outs. Stubbornness is not a recently acquired Irish trait.

The real conflict was with the English Church, not because it was Roman, but because it was English. Even before the Anglo-Norman invasion, acute and sainted Church leaders like Laurence O'Toole (Lorcan Úa Tuathail) and Malachy O'More (Máel-Maedíc Úa Morgair — he of the spurious and much later 'prophecies' fame), realised that the glory was departing from native Church institutions, monasticism in particular. A new era was dawning and, like their contemporary political counterparts, Irish Church reformers recognised that the future of the Church lay in closer ties with the emerging European union, optimistically not to say presumptuously called Christendom. Not by chance, the fifteenth or sixteenth-century forgery attributed to Saint Malachy elaborates the history of the popes, not Irish abbots or bishops.

Soon, however, the Irish Church was claimed to have been deeded to the English crown for purposes of reform by the only Englishman ever to mount the papal throne — Nicholas Breakspear, a no-nonsense pope who took the name Hadrian IV. The papal bull was most likely a later forgery, but it worked. Someone in the English hierarchy seemed to think that Henry II might improve the quality of the Irish Church by repeating the wholesale replacement of native Irish bishops by imported Anglo-Normans in much the same way as Henry's great-grandfather, William of Normandy, had purged the Anglo-Saxon hierarchy after 1066. Although Henry preferred to meddle in his native France, his Plantagenet successors did precisely that, driving a wedge between the bishops and the lay members of the Irish Church as well as many priests and almost all the monks and friars, who tended to remain staunchly Irish.

Matters did not improve greatly during the Reformation. Beginning with Elizabeth's reign, most Irish saints for the next three hundred years got that way by being murdered on the grounds of religious affiliation or at least resistance to altering it. Some things don't change.

The worst of it fell during the Cromwellian period. Thousands perished anonymously in massacres at Drogheda, Limerick and elsewhere. Others were rounded up and executed for clinging obstinately to the old faith. Over 250 martyrs have been identified by name, seventeen of whom have been endorsed by the Vatican for eventual enrolment among the saints. The most illustrious of those who died rather than switch, Saint Oliver Plunkett, Archbishop of Armagh, was hanged, drawn, and quartered in London in 1681 during the infamous Popish Plot trials. The last official martyr, the Dominican friar Dominic Egan, died in prison in 1713. Since then, Catholics and Protestants have murdered each other chiefly as private citizens but no less abundantly.

More recent Irish saints resemble contemporary saints from other lands — religious founders like Nano Nagle and Mother McAuley, missionaries like Edel Quinn, holy abbots like Dom Marmion, even someone as unusual as the reformed alcoholic Matt Talbot. There may be something distinctively Irish about them, if only their self-deprecating humour and rock-like resistance to ecclesiastical intimidation. Given a few hundred years, however, they too will likely amount to something in the ranks of Old Ireland's pugnacious saints.

The Ashes of Memory

John Dominic Crossan

Born in Ireland, John Dominic Crossan was a member of the faculty of DePaul University in Chicago until his recent retirement; he now lives in Florida, devoting his life to lecturing and writing on the subject for which he is renowned, the historical Jesus. His books include Jesus: A Revolutionary Biography *and a memoir entitled* A Long Way from Tipperary.

I enter the fields and roomy chambers of memory, where are the treasures of countless images, imported into it from all manner of things by the senses. When I am in this storehouse, I demand that what I wish should be brought forth. For there are nigh me heaven, earth, sea, and whatever I can think upon in them, besides those which I have forgotten. Great is this power of memory, exceeding great, O my God, an inner chamber large and boundless! Who has plumbed the depths thereof? Yet it is a power of mine, and appertains unto my nature; nor do I myself grasp all that I am.

Saint Augustine, Confessions, *Book X, Chapter VIII*

*I*n western sensibility, the archetypal conjunction of spirituality and autobiography descends to us from the *Confessions* of Saint Augustine. And the integrity of that spirituality depends on the accuracy of that autobiography. One major index of that work's sincerity is its recognition of how a memoir must finally face memory and must ultimately meditate on the mysteries of remembering. Augustine remembers and remembers that he remembers. Augustine forgets and both remembers that he forgets as well as forgets that he forgets. All this he knows full well and dissects with a careful scalpel. But nowhere does he ever recognise memory's most fatal flaw, namely the terrible certainty with which it recalls incorrectly, the serene security with which it remembers wrongly. How does that rather important problem interact with spirituality and autobiography, memoir and memory?

What, if any, fiduciary bonds do we create with a reader when we place, in print however small, the simple assertion 'A Memoir' on the cover of a book? I do not suggest that, in absolute post-modern consciousness, writing a memoir should be only about writing a memoir. I simply ask whether stories should evince any awareness, within memoir, of the difference between fact and fiction, imagination and memory, and any awareness, within memory, of its uses and abuses, successes and failures, tricks and deceits. Or, more basically, are those naïve questions from another age, atavistic ethics in a world where fantasy and reality, documentary and drama merge smoothly together under the exculpatory rubric of entertainment?

I am quite ready to admit that somebody else's memory is much better than my own. I know that, while my memory for concepts and structures is excellent (I can give a weekend of lectures without notes), my recall for names and places is awful (I can forget who invited me and where it was a few months later). That is not my problem with memoir-memory. An author could be simply much better on details than I am. It is that some memoir-memories seem unlike any normal memory as that is understood in experimental psychology, cerebral neurobiology, or my own experience. It is not, of course, unlike the standard common-sense understanding that imagines data all stored away in memory as in a vault, available forever to some proper searching, available as more or less accurate recall rather than as constantly adapted creative reconstruction.

Objection. We all know that we never forget exactly where we were or how we learned about certain traumatic national events. Americans say it repeatedly, for example, about the assassination of President Kennedy. Maybe that is also true for events in an author's own life, for example, a traumatic childhood and adolescence. Maybe we never forget time and place, word and deed, speaker and spoken in such a situation. I have written extensively about the arrest, trials, execution, and burial of the historical Jesus and have called the hour-by-hour and word-for-word details of that story more parable than history. But many of my scholarly colleagues underline the trauma of that execution for Jesus' companions, and that shock, they assure my disbelief, is why the New Testament Gospels are so blow-by-blow and detail-by-detail accurate on the passion of Jesus. Traumatic shock, they say, be it over execution or assassination, must focus, improve, and guarantee our memory of its content.

So we Americans say this: I remember exactly where I was and how I first heard about Kennedy's assassination; I will never forget it until the day I die. But who is rude enough to contradict our account, crude enough to check it out, even where such is possible? And what would happen if somebody did?

The day after the *Challenger* explosion on 28 January 1986, 106 students in Psychology 101 at Emory University in Atlanta, Georgia, answered a questionnaire on when, where, and how they had first heard of the disaster. The accounts were then sealed until the autumn of 1988. The forty-four students still available were then asked to fill out a new questionnaire about that almost three-year-old moment of first information. Some did not even remember the earlier assignment. Most wrote divergent versions, some mildly but others wildly so. Confronted with those divergent versions, they did not back off, apologise, and assert that, of course, the former ones were more correct. No, it was the latter ones that were correct. How, indeed, could it be otherwise since those earlier ones were not enshrined somewhere in separate storage but had been completely erased and overwritten by the later ones? Finally, and most dismayingly, there was a strongly negative correlation between accuracy and certainty. The mean for accuracy was 2.95 out of a possible 7 but the mean for certainty was 4.17 out of a possible 5. Memory does exactly what it is supposed to do with the important details of our lives, namely, to be steadily reconstructive, to obliterate ruthlessly and forever the earlier versions it overlays, and to make us utterly confident about the final one to hand at the moment.

From the start of Frank McCourt's *Angela's Ashes*, for example, two divergent chords played incessantly in my reader's mind, and they continued their interaction to the very end. The major one was sheer enjoyment, a pleasure unalloyed then by any later authorial over-adulation. What I was reading was horrible but, as long as its author could describe it like this, he had clearly survived with mind and heart, humour and irony intact. The minor one was a nagging doubt about Frank McCourt's memory and about the genre of the book in my hands. Was this sheer, shining imagination, a fictive child-persona created, no doubt, out of actual events, but no more 'a memoir' than was James Joyce's *A Portrait of the Artist as a Young Man*? Maybe it was just a novel based on a life, a portrait of the artist as a young boy? I take that minor chord to major status here.

Everything in the first thirty-five pages of *Angela's Ashes* takes place before the family 'returned to Ireland when I was four'. Most of us get the significant details of our earliest years from the narration of our parents or the gossip of our extended families, that is, from the memories of others. Frank McCourt has a memory about sending his younger brother Malachy to the hospital when 'he's two, I'm three'. He drops him off the see-saw and sends him in for stitches on a teeth-clamped tongue. Maybe he remembers directly, maybe indirectly, so let that be. In any case, it's three years after birth, and direct memory is already possible (my own earliest one is at four). But what about three months after conception? How does memory operate then?

He tells us that he was conceived prior to his parents' marriage. It took his mother's married cousin-sisters to enforce the proprieties. His father attempted flight, first drank all his money 'to celebrate his decision and departure', did not get very far, and thereby ended up married about halfway between Frank's conception and birth. Any child could learn those general details from a documentary comparison of marriage and birth or baptismal certificates, from parental confession, familial lore, or tribal gossip. No problem there. But it is all told by a marvellous six-person, interwoven exchange between reluctant husband-to-be Malachy McCourt, Cousin Delia and husband Jimmy, Cousin Philomena and husband Tommy, and Joey the speakeasy's bartender. Frank-to-be is safely at home within his mother's womb. It is also a very funny multilogue, but who remembered it then and/or who recalled it for Frank McCourt later on? Maybe it was a case of oral tradition passed on within the family?

I have spent my professional life reconstructing the historical Jesus from and against the first written gospel records. Many of my biblical colleagues invoke oral tradition to claim continuity and accuracy from the Jesus of history in the late twenties to the Jesus of gospel in the seventies through nineties of that terrible first century. Maybe there was always and only oral tradition there, but maybe there was also and more often deliberate creation. In gospel then and in memoir now?

When Frank McCourt was four, those same redoubtable cousin-sisters decided that his family should return to Ireland. They wrote to his maternal grandmother requesting funds, and the letter is given in a full and verbatim version. Was a copy kept of the original and later recovered? Is this documentation or fiction? What protocols of factual reconstruction or fictional creation control such a transcript?

I go back to my own recent experience in writing *A Long Way from Tipperary*, a book claimed as 'A Memoir' on its cover. I too cite there a written text verbatim, but I was fourteen and still have that schoolboy diary (because my mother was a perfectionist and stored away anything that might ever again be needed). I also cite the Latin letter that dispensed me from my vows as a monk and from my vows as a priest. But that too is because I kept it. It was dated 'die 4 Julii 1969', and I thought it might be evidence that somebody at the Vatican had a sense of humour.

The protocols of ancient history and especially of ancient biography allowed the fictional creation of lengthy speech-in-character or even event-in-character. Classic examples are the troop-addresses that the historian Tacitus placed on the lips of the British general Calgacus and the Roman general Agricola as they faced off for the island's ultimate control near the Grampian mountains of Scotland in 83 CE. Calgacus says of the Romans that neither east nor west has glutted them, that they plunder, butcher, steal, and call it empire, that they make a desert and call it peace. Agricola says of the British that their best have long since fallen, that now only cowards and shirkers are left, and that they are not bravely making a final stand but are simply frozen to the ground in fear.

Those twin speeches were invented by Tacitus in a memoir about his own just-deceased father-in-law, Agricola. Classical scholars are used to such creations, although biblical scholars are much less willing to accept them on the lips of Jesus. Is 'Father, forgive them for they know not what they do' a Lukan creation giving Jesus speech-in-character or an actual saying on the cross heard by women disciples and preserved through orality or heard by soldier guards and transmitted through bribery? Since I myself find many such creations in ancient gospels, why should I be surprised to find them in modern memoirs? But, of course, those ancient writers said openly that they were writing gospels and not memoirs about Jesus. Gospels are good news. Good is from somebody's point of view, from a Christian-Jewish and not an imperial Roman one, for example. News is something to be updated regularly and deliberately, from the historical Jesus of the first-century twenties to the written gospels of the seventies, eighties, and nineties. The term 'gospel' admits creative reconstruction and gives you four examples in case you miss the point and would like to make comparisons. The term 'memoir' claims memory, does it not?

There is clearly a difference between autobiography and memoir. The former probably demands a degree of checking and researching, dating and placing, that memoir can validly avoid. Memoir can simply claim that this is how I remember it. But, once again, what minimal self-consciousness about memory should appear in a memoir?

Some time ago I appeared with many other scholars on a television special 'From Jesus to Christ: The First Christians'. A few days later a priest from California wrote to ask if 'you and I were in the sixth class with Brother Grennan in 1943/44 at Naas, County Kildare'. We had indeed been primary-school classmates but, as we talked by phone and corresponded by e-mail, it was clear that my memory of those distant days was woefully defective while his was still brilliantly clear. He recalled the names, pedagogical capacities, and caning proclivities of each year's teacher from among the Christian Brothers. But I had left Naas around June of 1945 and never returned, while my classmate had stayed continually in contact, even from America ('I will visit next year and advise with the latest'). Did that abrupt departure and continued absence affect my own memory?

Early in 2001 the BBC programme 'The Lives of Jesus' was shown on Irish television. I had appeared in it from Rome and Ravenna (catacombs and cathedrals are nicely cool in high July). The following Sunday I received a call from a secondary-school classmate and fellow-boarder at Saint Eunan's College, in Letterkenny, County Donegal, between 1945 and 1949. He sent me our official 1945–46 class photo and could tell me what had happened to all of our classmates. Once again, his memory reduced mine to stuttering silence. But, as he wrote: 'Having lived all my life on this island I have been able to keep in touch, directly or indirectly, with a substantial number of our Saint Eunan's contemporaries.' Same point as above. Just as I had left one month after primary school ended, so I had left one year after secondary school ended. Those ruptures at ages eleven (Kildare to Donegal) and seventeen (Ireland to America) profoundly damaged my memory's continuity, but similar ruptures at ages four (Brooklyn to Limerick) and eighteen (Ireland to America) do not seem to have harmed Frank McCourt's to any significant degree. Should I admire his better memory or envy his better fiction? And how much fiction is acceptable in memoir?

Is this just a tempest in an Irish teacup? For Erin boys, go brawl? Who cares where the lines between fantasy and reality merge in a memoir? Just enjoy it, whatever its genre! The title is *Angela's Ashes* not *I, Frank McCourt*. It is not a revolutionary accusation against 'the poverty; the shiftless loquacious alcoholic father; the pious defeated mother moaning by the fire; pompous priests; bullying schoolmasters;

the English and the terrible things they did to us for eight hundred long years.' Neither is the title *A Star Called Margaret*, or *Oliver*, or *Eugene*. It is not an exercise in magic realism where knowledge, voice and memory are available even in the womb. Maybe I should just think of it as Blarney Realism, as a new sub-genre of memoir that would negate my own carping questions about memory?

Memory, however, is a serious responsibility, and an awareness of its fragility and creativity, of its inaccuracy despite certainty, and of its subsequent erasure of earlier data by later strata, is a terribly important social necessity. Without it, we can never understand eyewitness identification that is securely given but completely wrong, or false memory syndrome that is absolutely sincere but totally false. Without it, we can have, and have had recently, families torn apart, reputations left in shreds, and lives ruined forever. And all that can happen from a memory totally secure and able, as it were, to close its eyes and see it all in sharp visual detail.

I remember in just such sharp visual detail our maroon Vauxhall car in the late 1930s and the black one that replaced it in the late 1940s. In both cars, my mother preferred to sit in the back seat in order to be farther from the flying glass when the inevitable crash occurred. It never did, but I got to sit up front with my father from as early as I can remember. Further, in 1949, the deal was that, if I learned how the engine worked, my father would teach me how to drive. I did, he did, and thereafter I got to drive the car for family outings. I even got an illegitimate driver's licence that same year by writing my birth-date as 1933 not 1934 in the mailed-in application (no documents, no tests, in those days).

If I close my eyes now, I can see all of that in sharp visual detail. I can see clearly, for example, the manually operated sun-roof (an oxymoron in Ireland?), the fixed bonnet with hinged lift-up flaps on either side, and that bonnet's dual chrome-coloured strips narrowing from front to back and thereby distinguishing a Vauxhall from other cars. But now comes a tiny terror. If I am driving, my father is always to my right. If he is driving, I am always to his right. The steering-wheel is always on the left side. Were I challenged today, under oath in a court of law, to describe exactly what I see in my mind's eye, I would have to claim that we had and had successively the only two left-hand-drive Vauxhalls in the Ireland and Great Britain of the 1930s and 1940s. I know that is wrong, and I can correct my memory conceptually but not visually. The wheel is still on the wrong side in my mind's eye. A half-century of American experience has overlaid completely and thereby destroyed forever what my mental knowledge knows but my visual memory denies.

How fantasy and reality, fiction and fact, interact in memory is a profoundly serious question. To write 'a memoir' is to raise that issue, or else let's just call memoir fiction and worry no more about memory. But we live in the land of memory, in the land of memory where the shadows lie.

Confessions of a Recycled Catholic

Janet F. Quinn

Janet Quinn is one of America's most highly regarded theorists and practitioners in the area of holistic nursing. She is the author of dozens of papers on the subject as well as a book on women's spiritual quest.

*I*t had been a long board meeting and I was looking forward to the six-hour drive home for a quiet time of debriefing. As we finished things up, one of the board members asked if I could give a ride to another one who was going to visit family. 'It's right on your way,' he explained. 'It really won't take you any extra time at all.' I agreed and, although ordinarily I wouldn't have minded, this change of plans did not thrill me.

My passenger would be Sister Charlotte Rose, a Religious Sister of Mercy, whose family lived just a few hours from where I was headed. I would be in the car for four hours, not steeped in solitude as I had imagined, but riding with a nun. Great. What on earth would I talk to her about? I thought that having completed twelve years of Catholic education a long time ago, I had had my last intimate conversation with a bride of Christ. I liked Charlotte well enough it seemed, but a nun? For four hours?

I did not do well. Some part of me seemed to have absconded with my usually respectful decorum and left Sister Charlotte to ride with a very angry, hostile, and unfortunately uncensored Recovering Catholic. For reasons I still don't understand, I felt compelled to tell her all the reasons why I hated the Catholic Church, as well as all the grounds on which I believed the Church would hate me. I reeled off a list of past digressions from Catholic goodness which surely would convince her that I was doomed — from the point of view of 'her' Church.

It hadn't been my Church for a long time. Having been raised in Brooklyn, New York, in a house between those of the McHenrys and the Fitzgeralds, I had never questioned that Catholic was the only way to be Irish. My father was the first of his line of Quinns to be born in America, a point simply understood, though much more clearly on Sundays. But the freedom of college and a recognition of deep wounding had changed all of that years ago. Now, at seventy-five miles an hour, this innocent nun was being pummelled by my rage.

To her credit, Sister Charlotte did not ask me to pull over at the next bus station but stayed put as the barrage continued. Finally, when I began to calm down and run out of horror stories, a gentle quiet descended over the car. Sister Charlotte looked at me with a tenderness I little deserved, and, without a hint of defensiveness or condescension, said two sentences that I have never forgotten: 'Janet, why don't you just drop it? Forget your fight with the Church; get to know Jesus.'

At the time I could not possibly know that she was right. She was well-intentioned, I would grant her that, but what she said had really nothing to do with me, it seemed. That was before the summer I spent on a small island off the coast of South Carolina doing immunological research — or at least that's what I thought I was doing there. Apparently there was another plan, which I shall share later, the result of which was my return to the Catholic Church as what I call a Recycled Catholic.

I, like other Recycled Catholics I have dialogued with, am not just a Returning Catholic, a person who has taken up where she left off with the Church because of one or another practical reasons. Returning Catholics often have not undergone any metanoia, or change of heart, from the time that they left. It is simply more convenient now to attend Mass on Sundays, or there is the need to raise the children with some form of religion. Of course, Returning Catholics may become Recycled through the grace available to them as they participate in the sacraments. Grace, it turns out, is relentless.

Recycled Catholics are also not Recovering Catholics, a euphemism for angry ex-Catholics. Recovering Catholics remain in a state of rejection of their Catholic heritage and typically have a good deal of disdain for the entire tradition and those who remain in it. One can often find large numbers of self-proclaimed Recovering Catholics in a wide variety of other religious or spiritually oriented groups. Years of facilitating workshops on topics related to healing and spirituality confirm this observation. Recycled Catholics may or may not go through this experience, but if they do, they don't stay there. It becomes a stage of the recycling process, not the end point.

I use the metaphor of recycling to describe the process that I, and many others, have been through. As Recycled Catholics we are different from when we left the Church. We are made of fundamentally the same stuff, but live it in a very new form. The conversion of physical form that takes place in recycling involves a transformative meeting between matter and energy. There is some stuff, some matter to begin with, and through the application of a force or an energy — chemical, mechanical or biological — the original stuff is broken down, and out of its essence something new is brought forth, some new form that may contain in it glimpses of the original but may also be quite distinct. In the case of Recycled Catholics, Catholic teaching about conversion would suggest that the energy being applied is not physical but spiritual, the force the power of the Holy Spirit, and the purpose nothing less than transformation of the entire person into a new creation.

Recycled Catholics talk about feeling compelled, pushed, drawn out, pulled under, attracted, out of control — all ways of describing a sense of having been acted upon. We often experience the initial disruption of our lives during the early stages of recycling as chaotic, random, out of the blue. Yet from the vantage point of hindsight,

Re-cycled Catholics share the understanding that this process was not random but the work of the spirit within the depths of our being. We also recognise that, despite our protests at the time, we could have said no. We could have stopped the process, and this, of course, is consistent with the Catholic teaching that we have free will.

The sense that one has been called by God to a process of conversion is completely consistent with basic Catholic teachings on the workings of grace. Saint Augustine writes about this as beautifully as anyone:

> Indeed we also work, but we are only collaborating with God who works, for his mercy has gone before us. It has gone before us so that we may be healed, and it follows us so that once healed, we may be given life; it goes before us so that we may be called, and follows us so that we may be glorified; it goes before us so that we may live devoutly, and follows us so that we may always live with God: for without him we can do nothing.

Thus, the transformative energy that powers the recycling process I am exploring here, that initiates it and supports it, guides it and directs it, can be understood to be the spiritual energy of grace acting within — grace unfolding. However, when one is going through this process of conversion, things don't seem graceful at all. It was only in the months following my return home from the South Carolina beach, when things started to settle down a bit, that I could articulate anything that even came close to the depth of the disruption I felt during my own conversion experience.

Conversion takes you, ready or not, to what feels like the edge of your sanity. You are drawn into the dark cloud of unknowing — irresistibly and inescapably drawn — beyond your fears, your defences, your protests; beyond your rationalist arrogance and superiority; beyond even the smallness of what you have allowed yourself to hope for all these years of longing and searching. You are dragged, kicking and screaming the death songs of the ego. Heart pounding, breathless, shaking uncontrollably, I found myself opening the door, scared to death, the creak of the hinge exploding in my head. Scared not of the place itself, but of the fact that I was there, doing this, and could find nothing in me that wanted to be doing it.

I acted because I was compelled by something I did not comprehend. Slowly, slowly, like walking through the mudfields of some faraway land, tiny, tentative, hesitant steps took me through the portal of a church in South Carolina, and the door closing behind me sounded like the lid of a tomb crashing shut on an unsuspecting tourist. I stood there, frozen, trying to be small, unseen, barely able to see myself, the light mercifully dim, eyes adjusting from the glare of sun on ocean and sand until finally, the images in the church came clearly into focus. On one side, a statue of the Virgin. On the other, Joseph and the Holy Child. The smell of incense pierced my memory and the flickering candles teased my still-blurred vision.

I was flooded with emotion by the sudden rush of intimacy I felt with these images, their welcome familiarity shocking and disorienting. In one timeless shattering moment I realised, in the place beyond all my carefully constructed resistances, and narrowly escaping the death-grip of my own controlling ego, that I was home. I turned and ran as fast as I could, onto my bike and down the beach, away, away, like I was being chased by a black bear through the mountains, until finally, behind the slammed, locked door of the tiny rented house, I collapsed, exhausted, weeping, terrified, ecstatic, and I prayed for my sanity.

Sanity, however, was not mine to have. God was after me the next day, and the next and the next. Riding on the beach, salty air filling lungs as the pace picks up, eyes squinting from the glare — free, free, it was good to be alive, good to move, good to be in control again, and yet the fear was right there, trailing me, breathing down my neck. I told myself that this time I could ride right by that church, without a glance, without so much as a thought. Even so, the bike leaned to the right and began its turn off the sand and onto the pavement. 'Stop this!' I screamed from some sane place inside. 'You are acting crazy.' But the words didn't even slow me down. I was once again standing outside the doors of the church, literally shaking and yet compelled to continue.

That time I took a few more steps until I was standing alongside the last pew. I thought that it might be good to rest my legs for a minute, so I sat. The cool wood, worn smooth over so many years, felt soothing against my hot skin; I could almost relax until, again, overtaken by emotion, tears streamed down my face and I leaped up and ran for my life — right into the priest who had come in to prepare for the morning service. I mumbled something about 'just passing through' and he said, 'Well, why not stay for Mass?' I politely declined and raced for the safety of the little beach house, where I continued to play hours of Jesus muzak in spite of my utter revulsion of it. I continued to be simultaneously ecstatic and terrified. Mostly I was afraid that I was really losing it — you know, 'it': sanity, my grip on reality, my common sense and critical intellect, rationality, and most of all, control. Well, that last was at least clear — fear or not, I was definitely not in control.

'Mass? Mass? Are you crazy? Have you lost your mind?' I resisted the voices clamouring in my head as I slipped on a skirt and prepared to go, this time in the car so I would not be damp and red-faced. I ignored the familiar shaking as I took a seat in the last row. There were only seven or eight other people there in the little island church dedicated to Stella Maris, Star of the Sea. They were all over the age of seventy, it seemed, and all seated a comfortable twenty or so rows ahead. I struggled to maintain composure and to remember the rituals.

Suddenly the priest was on the altar exclaiming, 'The Lord be with you'.

'And also with you', I replied instantly from someplace long ago. Oh yes, now we stand, now we sit, now we kneel, of course, of course, I remember, of course. The priest read the Gospel and I was transfixed. It was as if I was hearing the words being spoken from within my own heart instead of from outside me and through my ears. It was a feeling unlike anything I have ever experienced before. The shaking stopped and all fear was gone and I knew with every cell of my being that I was with the truth.

'A reading from the Holy Gospel according to Mark: "One of the scribes, when he came forward and heard them disputing and saw how well he had answered them, asked him, 'Which is the first of all the commandments?' Jesus replied, 'The first is this: You shall love the Lord your God with all your heart, with all your soul, with all your mind, and with all your strength. The second is this: You shall love your neighbour as yourself. There is no other commandment greater than these.'" The word of the Lord.'

Yes, I knew this as truth, as most certainly true. It was one thing that I knew. It's all, all, about love. In that little church at the tip of the island, Mary standing atop and looking out to sea, my recycling had begun.

To be a Catholic is about a particular kind of relationship with the Absolute, the Divine, the Ground of all Being, the Ultimate Mystery, God. I, like most Recycled Catholics I have spoken with, never stopped cultivating and being in relationship with God. But for a variety of complex reasons, we had to separate this relationship and its cultivation from Jesus Christ. Because Jesus Christ was the possession of an institutional Church that we could no longer abide, Jesus had to go, along with confession, Sunday Mass, and unquestioning obedience to the Pope. The mention of the name of Jesus, which in our youth might have been accompanied by a quick bow of the head or a swelling of the heart, now brought anxiety, squeamishness and even disdain. Sometimes the name of Christ could be tolerated, even revered, if it was preceded by the word 'the', making it clear that this Christ, 'the Christ', was not the man owned by orthodoxy, but the principle, the energy, available universally, the Cosmic Christ.

Over the years, education and experience seemed to confirm our estrangement. Ironically, it was often the rhetoric of the religious right that most served to deepen the commitment to remaining distant from Christ. Jesus loves some, but hates others; there are the saved and the condemned — the acceptable creatures of God and the abominations. Many Recycled Catholics went through a time when, if the only way to salvation was this Jesus, the Jesus of the institutional Church, we would just have to take our chances on hell. Jesus was thus further banished from our lives and our seeking, as we sought spiritual paths that felt less brutal, more inclusive, less about following rules and believing without thinking, accepting without asking.

So we read and studied and tried to practise other paths to God. After conversion, feeling no need to discard what we learned or experienced on the journey, we come back to our spiritual home with an expanded spiritual sense. In returning to our Catholic roots, our Catholic identity, all of these practices and experiences are enlarged and understood in new ways because they are experienced by and through a new self, a self grounded once again in Christ. The Catholic experience is most fundamentally about relationship to God through, with and in Christ. It is this mystery, this awesome experience that everything we are, all that we do, everything that we can become, is in, with, and through Christ, that draws Recycled Catholics back. With so many mixed emotions, with fear, resistance, guilt and the anger of years of hurt, and with love, tenderness, hope and ineffable gratitude, Christ is rediscovered as radical lover — as a doorway, a path, a guide on that path, and the destination of that path, all simultaneously. As conversion and recycling progress, the words 'it's a mystery' become the source of great awe, comfort and courage, rather than the grist for anti-Catholic jokes and the justification for ridicule and dismissal.

This mystery cannot be apprehended through the intellect or language, no matter how expertly crafted. Mystery can only be experienced and lived, opening itself one breath, one petal, one moment at a time within timelessness. Yet this is — has always been — the true spiritual call, regardless of the tradition one follows — to live the ultimate mystery more closely, more deeply, more trustingly day by day. The mystery of Christ is what Recycled Catholics were missing on our journeys away from home. Relationship with the mystery of Christ is what we come home to.

This relationship, this direct connection with mercy, with love itself, with the light of the world, with Jesus as the spirit who dwells in our hearts, transcends belief. It is the most compelling and the most defining experience of the Recycled Catholic. It is this relationship that drew us back to our Catholic identity. It is this relationship that teaches us, that comforts us, that keeps us Catholic, because it helps us to embrace the flawed and broken mystery that is Christ's Church here on earth, even as we may continue to wrestle with it. It is this relationship that grows Recycled Catholics more and more whole, that nourishes us with the gifts of the spirit, that sustains us in the dark times, and for which we give grateful praise and thanksgiving always. It is this relationship that attracts us to the Eucharistic celebration every Sunday; that so opens our hearts that the mystical understanding of the body of Christ becomes more and more real to us. It is this relationship that turns blind obedience to rules and laws and dogmas into devoted discipleship, making of us followers who would pay whatever price was asked for the greatest pearl. It is this relationship that is the most central joy in our lives and out of which we live the fullness of those lives, with all the unpredictability, struggle, pain and bliss that comes with incarnation.

We never do return to the Jesus we left, the Jesus who we learned to disdain — a Jesus who has more to do with the projections of human fear and brokenness than with ultimate reality. Rather, the Jesus of our liberation and our salvation calls us to freedom, open-heartedness and surrender, to a life lived in, with and through love, to the truth of who we are as Catholics — followers of Jesus Christ, disciples, students of his teachings and of his ways, believers of his promises — not because someone told us to believe, but because we have had the experience of redemption, of lives salvaged from meaninglessness and transformed, gratuitously and ultimately. We are called, as new selves, to be — as Jesus was — radical lovers, to live as if we really believed that the most important thing we can do, the greatest commandment, is to love. This, we find, is a fine path. More than adequate, this path, this journey to, with, in and through love is all we desire, all we need, all we hope for. It is enough. It is home.

Janet F. Quinn

Now, many years after our first uneasy sojourn together, Sister Charlotte is one of my most treasured friends. She is still a Mercy Sister, and I like that. I like the idea that at that time in my life when I was so angry and lost, it was mercy that spoke so directly to me, in words I couldn't hear at the time but couldn't forget later. It is mercy still that continues to speak to me. Sister Charlotte Rose was right after all.

Ðisillusion and Ðelight

✣

Anne Le Marquand Hartigan

*Anne Le Marquand Hartigan was born in England. Her mother was from Louth,
close to the prehistoric site of Newgrange. Anne and her husband returned there to
farm and raise a family of six children while she painted and wrote. Her award-
winning long poem,* Now is a Moveable Feast *(Salmon Poetry) arose from her life
on the farm. Hartigan has published four books of poetry as well as* Clearing the
Space, *a meditation on creativity (Salmon Poetry). Anne has won many awards for
her visual art, poetry and theatre, the latest — The Mobil Prize for playwriting
in 1995 — for her play* The Secret Game.

> nature is never spent;
> There lives a dearest freshness deep down things
>
> *Gerard Manley Hopkins*

I landed in this world with one leg on each of the islands of Ireland
and Britain. With an Irish Catholic mother and a Protestant father from
the Channel Islands, I was born and nurtured by them both in England.
From this confusion, I bit my way out. Our parents' approach to the
world of the spirit sets us on some path, which we take, reject or ignore
— or a mixture of these. This spiritual heritage is a given from which
we emerge like a bug from a chrysalis, hopefully with wings.

The spirit is what moves, propels, guides, prods, annoys, agitates. Is the
unknowable, the way ahead, the outside, the shadows, the breath, the invisible,
the vision, the connection, the disconnection, the halt, the gap, the space.
Emptiness. To be full. The uneasiness. The dark. The underneath. The
collapsed. Disconcertion. The volcanic. The eruption. Dis-ease.

At my Sacred Heart boarding school, Reverend Mother — the spiritual head of the community and a true Victorian — amused us when she delivered her rare exhortations. She loved to speak of 'School Spirit'. Unfortunately she lisped so it came out as 'Spivit'; we would wait for this with glee. The spirit was much in evidence in my school days. We were aware of souls. Our own immortal souls, others' souls, the holy souls, those dead, who waited in turmoil in purgatory while we, by 'offering up' — another frequent exhortation — could help them with 'self sacrifices', by prayers, by 'offering up Mass' to relieve their suffering and help them on their flight up to heavenly bliss.

On the Feast of the Holy Souls we could gain many indulgences by confession and communion. Then, with each visit to the chapel, we could gain a plenary indulgence that would completely wipe out the debt a soul was paying and give a swift and free access to eternity. We enjoyed doing this. Popping in and out to the chapel, wiping slates clean. How straightforward and practical was this spirituality!

> The spirit is design. Order. Form. Shape. Horizon. Imagination. Air, light. Hope and despair. The spirit moves us and moves on — moves us on?

We receive a spiritual heritage unconsciously from those who give us life. We do not choose this. It arrives with our mother's milk — and probably shapes us for life. My mother was a devoted Irish Catholic and a genuinely spiritual person, my father a nominal Protestant, but really a healthy pagan with a desire to serve humanity through his practice as a doctor. They met, fell in love, married. Both were separated from their own island's heritage, to live their married lives on the more prosperous island of Britain.

> The year and the hour that snatch our day warns us not to hope for eternal life.
> *Horace,* Odes, *Book IV*

Of that marriage union, the Catholic Church ruled okay. My father had to sign over, on the dotted line, the religious education of his children, so I, his only offspring, was brought up in the Catholic faith. I don't think this bothered him one way or the other, for he liked and admired nuns, but I think his family were none too pleased. The rules for a Catholic marrying a 'non-Catholic' then were less than warm: there could be no nuptial Mass; the couple could be married only at a side altar; there could be no flowers and no music. What a welcome my father received.

My parents had to face tragedy in the first year of their marriage.

My mother was in her mid-thirties when they married, seven years my father's senior. She feared that this — as well as being Irish and Catholic — was some sort of handicap to him, not socially acceptable, unhelpful to his career as a young doctor. My mother conceived twins on her honeymoon, but they died full-term babies at birth; she nearly lost her life as well. She was advised not to get pregnant again. How did they manage their married life? What happened to their lovemaking? Oh dear Mother Church, oh no, Father Church. No contraception. No no no. I know my devout mother could not have considered it. But my father was not a Catholic. What did he lose? What did they both lose?

> Where do my stillborn sisters lie?
> Orphaned in another's grave
> Did they lay you side by side
> Curved womb moulded naturally
>
> While my mother fought to live
> Tempest tossed upon her bed
> In another woman's arms
> Her sweet fruits were laid to rest

After five years my mother conceived again and gave birth. And then? I was reared most carefully and fully as a Catholic, Roman brand, in non-Catholic, now increasingly non-Christian, Britain. Almost every year we journeyed home to Ireland and home to Jersey. I was a good and well-informed Catholic girl. A sort of Irish Catholic girl, where

Catholics were looked down on, as were the Irish, who were dirty and drunk and had pigs in the kitchen.

I believed my faith entirely. There never appeared to be any arguments about religion between my parents. My mother, to her credit, never made any attempt to convert my father or suggest I should. I believe there were attempts by my father's family to have me educated at a Protestant school, but these were resisted by my mother, who paid my school fees.

And my soul where does it fly? How moves it? And where does it lie?

As a small child I wanted to be a saint. I thought the martyrs had it easy. Just get eaten by a lion and Bob's your uncle — there you are a saint with halo and everything, walking around on spongy clouds for all eternity. I thought I was somehow lacking because I could not feel like the small girl in a sentimental story the nuns told us, who wept when she dropped her prayer book, because of the hurt she caused Almighty God and his blessed mother.

Compared to the martyrs, we had it hard. We had to contend with sin. Confession and guilt, sins of disobedience, and the one considered worst by the nuns — impertinence. Then later, bad thoughts — what were they? — and purity and guilt. Go to Mass every Sunday, or else a mortler (mortal sin, danger of hell) hovered around and about, there to catch you.

The Catholic Church envelops you in ritual; the dates and days of each year are marked, in tune with the seasons, with the turning year and with the profound dance of the world. These rituals are human and faulty, but they are ancient, they are drama, they connect to human need and back to the pagan world. They can be sublime. This connection to the deep past is especially true in Ireland — here our knowledge and the function of such things as holy wells, patterns, Saint Brigid's Cross, and others are still practical symbols of devotion. However, many of the changes made since Vatican II, in an attempt to reach the people, have replaced plain chant with pallid music, traded

masterpieces for off-the-peg art, and weakened the word by removing
its poetry. The present Mass is a dull travesty. I am not saying the ritual of
the past is best — some of it was appalling — but that the best of the past
should be built on, with the best of the present and the future. The
mystery of fine architecture, music, painting, poetry, contains our spirit, is
born of it and allows it to move and fly and speak in singing tongues.

The Catholic Church, unlike its sister Protestant Churches, kept the
important profound connection with the female, through the place
given to the blessed virgin mother, Mary. This is a vital channel back to
pagan life, and more importantly, to woman. The Protestant Churches
are weakened by her loss. However, the Catholic Church has dimin-
ished its portrayal of Mary by removing her power, showing her as
docile, weak, obedient, oh so wishy-washy. Even in those days of my
devotion I rejected this model. I went through some kind of crisis when
becoming a Child of Mary. I felt a powerful rejection of the whole thing,
yet did not know where these feelings came from or what they meant.
Should I be taking vows at the altar about such things? A vow is a
deeply important commitment, not to be taken lightly. I came to terms
with the Virgin Mary when my imagination saw her as the moon
goddess, full of her own power. I could accept her as that.

At seventeen, I met a tall, dark and handsome man, also a Catholic.
We fell madly in love and, a few years later, married. I studied painting at University during those years. We moved to Ireland, then we
had six children, the first five in rapid succession. We lived happily
(and busily) for a pretty good, pretty long happy ever after. Father
Church's laws were against contraception. I truly believed then that to
break them would be an act against love itself, but this meant that we
had no time to ourselves as man and wife, to love truly and fight freely,
to forge our own life, no time to make a marriage, no time to have
important battles, no time to grow up before, helter-skelter, young and
unformed as we were, we were pitched into parenthood. The Church,
by becoming an institution, has learned to rule. When you rule you
exert power; in the hands of an institution, this can become a blunted
instrument.

I believed in love, in the body, in my love affair with the man I married — that this sexlovelife was our life. The Church's assertion that marriage was for the procreation of children? Not what I got married for. And hovering in the background at the time I married was an idea that if the mother's life and the life of her unborn child were threatened, the mother should give up her life for her child. I shut my mind to that. A great anger rumbled.

I read the mystics, the poetry of Saint John of the Cross, Saint Julian of Norwich, Teresa of Ávila. During our marriage we both read widely, including the Eastern religions, the Koran, Buddhist scriptures and poetry, Taoism, the Bible, anthropology, psychology. During our long years together we examined read, discussed, questioned, learned and lived.

Then came *Humanae Vitae* and nuns expelling our daughters from school because I didn't want them to attend weekly compulsory confession.

Earlier they had made First Communion, without confession, with a Dutch priest in a friend's kitchen. My daughters, quite rightly, have never forgiven me for causing them to miss the most fantastic day in the life of a small child in Ireland. First Holy Communion day, when the child is the revered centre of the family, when the child passes from babyhood into childhood proper. A brilliant day for every child. They were right and I was wrong. But I was not wrong about confession — I thought that in the form it was enacted at that time, it formed a false conscience.

The nuns, backed by the archdeacon, acted heavy-handedly, preventing our daughters' return to school unless they attended confession with the rest of the class. While we tackled this problem, I taught the children at home. Funnily, my daughters thought I'd just forgotten to send them to school, so they kept quiet, in case I remembered. We wrote to the Cardinal, and after a long wait we got an appointment and drove to Armagh to meet him. When he discovered we were not Reds Under the Beds but, strangely enough, sincere Catholics, he became quite human. Again, after a month or so of waiting, we received his permission for our children not to attend the compulsory confession at school. The nuns were all over us, the Cardinal had spoken.

Something had died. Gone. Life was different.

During this painful episode with the school and Church authorities, the deepest hurt to us was that no care had been shown for our daughters at all. Where was the Good Shepherd? 'Feed my lambs, feed my sheep'? This experience came quickly on top of the heavy blow of the publication of *Humanae Vitae*. This document showed a complete lack of understanding of the new aspirations among Catholics at that time. This was a time of great disillusionment to all who were part of the post-war idealism — the desire to make the world anew, to ban the bomb, that war should be no more, the importance of love and the family, to make good in all ways, such as developing organic farming, to bring about a just and equal society. Those who had thrown themselves whole-heartedly into these aspirations, this rejuvenation of spirituality, were the babies thrown out with the bathwater. We were not going to be permitted to be adults. To plan our families properly. To be full and vibrant members of the Church. How can a woman be part of a Church that does not acknowledge her equality? And does this not still go on?

At the same time I had come face to face with the fact that I did not see there was a God at all. This made an empty but an open space. All my horizons changed forever. I stepped into a new world. I looked God in the face but could not see his features. God's existence cannot be proven; maybe it should not be attempted. Immortality lies beyond us. Many, even those who still practise a faith, admit they do not think there is a life beyond this one. I simply do not know. These certainties are just not there for us. We live in a post-Christian world. I have moved into now and try to live there.

The spirit moves forward looking around and about.

Now, I jokingly say I am a pagan. That I gave my mother's religion a chance, so now I'm giving my father's a go. He would attend the Church of England occasionally, at Christmas perhaps. I remember an aunt of his asking him, 'Did you have a nice service, dear?' He could say yes or no, but could we? Goodness no. Mass could not be nice, Mass could not be questioned, it was the Holy Sacrifice of the Mass, where bread and wine became the body, blood, soul and divinity of Jesus Christ who was God. Nice? These are different planets.

The Western tradition of thought, through which our modes of looking are formed, trained us to see in pairs of opposites: black/white, body/soul, spirit/flesh, good/evil, light/dark, man/woman. This way of seeing lands us with continuing problems, insisting as it does on either/or rather than both-as-one-and-equal. On the conception of woman as flesh, with all the heavy baggage that that contains, rests the basis of the Catholic Church's denial of women of their full Christian rights.

Strangely, but almost obviously, this leads me to where I feel we are today in the year 2001, wallowing in the newness of wealth and freedom, celebrating continually the body brashly, foolishly, exploiting it maybe, but it is healthy to be back to a fundamental. We exist in body, our body brings us life and light, we are not a creature divided against itself, but a full one. Through our new attempts at equality between man and woman, we are struggling for harmony, mirrored and found in joyous sex. Sex is worshipped, sex has been released, sex is uncovered and seen, sex is everyday, sex is human and divine, sex is body and soul as one. What was hidden is revealed.

It is the new God. It is where we humans can move out, experience and attain ecstasy, and is that not a state the mystics strove to attain? We have come down to earth to find heaven.

Through and out and beyond we weave ourselves. I work and love through the work I do, the play I do, through painting, poetry, plays, loves, my children and children's children. It is my method of survival and attempt to understand this life. The artist (a word I do not like and use reluctantly) is on the side of anarchy. The artist has to risk.

Disillusion and Delight

Birth itself is a risk of death

Giacomo Leopardi

The artist cannot belong to caste or creed in any way that narrows the vision and excludes. It is the artist's job to step over boundaries, to risk death, to say the unsayable, to find new words and meanings. The artist can play jester too, speaking in riddles, saying what is not being said. To give a voice to those silenced. To celebrate life and death, in its most profound and most foolish. Playful and serious.

In Ireland, the Angelus is still sounded on the radio each day. To ring a bell is such a simple thing. Whatever the Angelus means or does not mean in itself, its ringing links us through the thousands of years that every civilisation in the world has rung bells, gongs, or resounding instruments. A calling out from one human to another. They are rung to celebrate joy, to mark marriage, birth, the end of war. To give respect to the dead, to warn, to keep in contact over large areas. Look how bells are hung from the necks of animals so the herdsman may know where they wander. Even the dreaded school bell.

A bell is a note we all recognise. It has its own universal language and voice. It is physically made, like ourselves, with a tongue. All can hear and know its meaning. So, like water, the bell has its own note. I am glad that here, in present-day, vigorous, growing Ireland, we have kept, almost by default, on our national radio, this strangely powerful connection between the past and future. The song of the bell is not in the possession of any religion. The ringing of the Angelus to call the faithful to prayer may be the origins. But the ringing of the bell is a universal symbol of our own spirit calling out on the wind. So we can remember to listen, inwardly and outwardly. The note for each of us will be different, but it is a connecting song.

Pilgrimage

Mary O'Malley

Hennessey Award-winning poet Mary O'Malley was born in Connemara and educated at University College, Galway. Her most recent collection, Asylum Road, *was published by Salmon Publishing in 2001. Previous collections, all with Salmon, are* A Consideration of Silk, Where the Rocks Float *and* The Knife in the Wave. *She has written for both radio and television and is a frequent broadcaster. She travels and lectures widely in Europe and the US. She lives in the Moycullen Gaeltacht in Galway.*

Let us begin in a stone city, low to the sea, centred on a fast-flowing river.

> So tender, I said. Remember this.
> It will be good for you to retrace this path
>
> When you have grown away and stand at last
> At the very centre of an empty city.
>
> *Seamus Heaney, 'Station Island'*

The city would not always be empty, but it would, at times, be cold, be metaphor, be itself. Begin this journey in a living city. Galway. As you drive from the courthouse, over the Salmon Weir bridge, towards the sinking hulk of the Catholic cathedral, built on the site of a jail and retaining something of its gloom, look to the right and you may see, some distance upriver, the rock where Galvia or Gailleamh, maiden or river-goddess, drowned. The rock marks the spot where she was waked and, according to oral history, that never-ending wake led to the founding of that Burghers' city.

In the words of Roderick O'Flaherty:

The occasion of the name

a very antient Irish distick expresses thus,

translated: *Ludit aquis mersam deluserat amnis*

Bresalii prolis, funere nomen habet.

In English this is given as:

Gailleamh, daughter of lasting Breasal,

Bathed in the full cool stream,

Where the bright branch was drowned:

From her the river is named.

Take the right-hand turn at the hospital, follow the road through Oughterard to Clifden, then to Ballyconneely, then right again to the village of Aillebrack. You will reach a monument to the flight of Alcock and Brown (who landed nine miles distant, in a soft bog, but we leave such quibbles to the cartographers) and a sign pointing to a golf course. There is nothing on either to indicate that this place has a culture of its own, that its people lived, emigrated, died, that their lives are important, worthy of note. Yet places such as this are the setting for local rows and epic events, as Patrick Kavanagh, uniquely among the English-language poets of his generation, understood.

The small grove of trees on the left is one of two small copses in the village. There is a ruined house, where there used to be a shop, up until about the 1940s. Every June there are beautiful scented red roses whose velvet petals drew a small girl scholar in to trespass on the way home from the two-roomed national school you have just passed on the right, and where I first heard the name Patrick Kavanagh spoken with affection and respect. Through the fields behind this ruined house there is a blessed well, The Seven Sisters Well. Why wasn't it called after the

Seven Daughters, like most wells of its type? The distinction seems relevant, although it is most likely a linguistic accident, a slight shift in translation. Nevertheless, I am one of seven sisters, and no doubt my sense of the name's significance is coloured by this biographical detail. An estate of holiday homes now stands close by, the proximity leading some to wonder whether the holy water is contaminated by their septic tanks.

Let us end this digression and follow the road past the golf course, which announces itself confidently. Follow the sign, pass the clubhouse, the greens, the nests of little dimpled balls. To your right is the village of Silverhill, where thirty-eight people lived in six houses in 1881. By 1891 there were only three houses, and fourteen fewer people. By 1901, the population had further decreased to seventeen, nine males and eight females. When I was a child, there was a handful left, one of whom rode out to do the shopping on a large white horse. The village, in common with small settlements world-wide, lives in the memory of its people, its stories are not, for the most part, recorded. Aspects of the people's lives are written in the landscape, and certain rituals such as this one, we know they observed.

Along the shoreline, great wire baskets of stones have been laid to prevent the future greens from eroding. They are intrusive in their ugliness, though some environmentalists favour them. The sand is perhaps expected to cover them, but now they are strung out along the beach like a mad detention camp, a sort of linear Long Kesh, designed for good, committed to holding back the Atlantic. What has this to do with Irish spirituality, I hear someone ask. More than we might think. A few hundred yards along a sandy track, you come to a barred gate. Stop, politely, as requested. You are on your own from here on.

This is where my pilgrimage begins, not in Galway, nor by a golf course, nor through a barred gate. 'The western coastline from the mouth of the Killary is thickly inhabited.' This was, according to James Berry's *Tales*, in 1798, when refugees found their way through and penetrated this labyrinth of nature. Berry also claims that the area was inhabited by a race of mortals the most heterogeneous in western

Europe, though later the Great Famine and emigration cleared them out. Be that as it may, by the 1950s, the villages were sparsely populated, the Famine was spoken of as a recent event and everybody had relations in America and England. This shore is inhabited now by a new race of mortals, the summer visitors, numerous enough though hardly heterogeneous holiday-home owners who migrate, commute, and seem scarcely touched by the fabric of the place. Now, houses are empty half the year, the price of building land too grossly inflated for a local to buy.

Fintan O'Toole asserts that, 'If you see a country in terms of its people rather than its territory, then, far from being small and well-defined, Ireland has been for at least a hundred and fifty years, scattered, splintered, atomised like the windscreen of a smashed car.' Hardly news here, nor does it present much difficulty, as the sentence might seem to imply, to people brought up to know that the world they could see was at best only half the story, people with a healthy scepti-cism for both maps and logic, living in the knowledge that what was important had not always been surveyed and that what was written down was seldom accurate.

To negotiate such perilous states between worlds, there were patterns, paths, pilgrimages to fixed places from where you could, having arrived and done the prescribed duties, set out again renewed.

And so a pilgrimage has to be made, a circling in the footsteps of people long gone, as much to say there is dangerous loss here, as well as gain, this land is more than a few fields, those fields are not merely sites. But that is not of course the real reason we go, which is both more complex and infinitely simpler. The real reason is this: every year, on 13 November, the people from the surrounding villages came, on foot, on horseback, in donkey and cart, then later on bicycles and in cars. They came during famine and during plenty, stepped down the stony path through the rocks in the bitter cold, took off their shoes, picked up their small stones, and began to circle the well seven times, each pilgrim's eyes on the whale shape of Dun Hill, or the grey sea, or, intent on keeping upright, his neighbour's cold blue feet ahead of him on the narrow muddy path. They came every year for centuries to make their station to Saint Cáillín, whose well this is. And as a child, every year, I came with them.

This is not only a personal journey, but a commemoration of the hope and desperation of a driven people who knew great hardship. Countless generations came here with their fears, their faith, the dangerous secrets of their watched lives. They came before, during and after the Famine; after childbirth, death and the immigration that was so close to death it was marked by a wake. Some of them must have come in joy because there was also dancing; they must have gone home and made love and been happy. Such activities were considered to belong in the realm of the intensely private, a view ingrained early and indelibly.

But why are people freed from the restraint of the Church, no longer bound by the old superstitions, still gathering for a ritual that is both private and communal, silent and whispered, and for which no priest is needed? And there are newcomers, people from outside the traditional catchment area of Errismore, Errisbeag and parts of Carna and South Connemara. What do they want from this station? What do they want it to represent? Do they think it picturesque, old-fashioned, significant? And if significant, in what way? Though I think it genuine, this attraction is a curiosity, and we suspect it, as if there were some kind of spiritual tourism at work, like that at Lourdes or Knock or Santiago de Compostela. Maybe we'll have bus tours soon, stalls, the religious supermarts of Christy Moore's song about Knock. After all, the great medieval pilgrimage ways were commercial routes, rife with robbery, chicanery and the sale of enough pieces of the true cross to deforest half of Sweden. But this was never the way here. Local saints were not commercialised in Connemara. Why are we so often fiercely protective of something sacred that is not ours to protect? If not ours, whose? That is a vexed question.

Let me stud the page with a few signposts, sketch a context: I was small in an era of banned books, tuberculosis, Noel Browne's campaign for decent healthcare for Ireland's women, before electricity, plumbing, television. Everyone waited for the Pope to reveal the third secret of Fatima, which was confidently expected to be apocalyptic and bad. The 1960s were causing havoc in America, but not in Ireland, certainly not in the west. Nothing much happened, no three-ring circus rolled into town. Big events were the tarring of the road, the arrival of electricity. There were giggling conversations about rock and roll music, even among the married people. That Elvis had young women thinking bad thoughts in the cinema in Galway, where they went in busloads to see *Rock Around the Clock* and shyly admitted they liked it. Then came the Beatles singing 'She loves you, yeah, yeah, yeah'. It was the beginning of the end of the world as our parents and their parents had always known it, or so we like to believe, wanting them to have been more innocent than ourselves.

Now it is necessary briefly to revisit childhood, that dangerous parish. What am I doing here? I never seek to go back. John Montague's assertion that one explores one's inheritance to free oneself and others is true of poetry, yet it could be that this journey is some atavistic, agnostic quest by yet another lapsed Catholic.

I am seven years old, they tell me I have reached 'the age of reason'. It is Saint Cáillín's Day, and this well, as much as the house I was raised in, is, in some indefinable way, home. The pilgrimage to Knock is for later, when I am older, to pray for success in the exams. The high point of the year, the annual bacchanal that is the visit to the Reek, the night climb in high summer — already there are whispers of goings-on with boys in the dark — is years away. How they managed in England and the North without the all-night vigil, the novenas, the scores of candles, it never occurred to us to wonder. Faith and desperation have no need of logic. Like poetry, they depend on more powerful connections. On what Raymond Carver called 'real influence' when he said, 'I am talking about real influence now, I am talking about the stars and the moon.'

This, then, is the annual big day out. I am with a few family members, a girl from the village. We walk up a steep hill, turn left over the stony path, down among the rocks until we see the well, with its circular mound, the pennies gleaming in cold winter light. There is a scatter of people there already, some circling, some putting on shoes and socks, others taking them off. A few more people are arriving, others leaving. All greet us and we respond, politely as we have been taught. A few ask who we are, meaning whose are we. Cé leis thú?

It is bitterly cold. It will rain. This will not stop us making the station in our bare feet, which will turn red, then blue, then several alarming shades of purple. None of us will die of either the cold or the drenching, because we are doing our duty to a saint. The well is always warm. The rocks hurt our feet. We offer it up. For a happy death. I don't know it yet, but the same happy death will be the cause of my falling out with the Church. This will cause me considerable anguish, the Church will remain unscathed when I leave because the Church is dedicated to death over life.

I begin, gathering the seven stones that will remind me I have finished my station when the last one has been thrown into the circle. My feet are not cold — they burn as I walk. We learned early about fire and ice. I leave a button or a penny behind as an offering and quietly step out of the line of pilgrims. I kneel at the well itself and say the statutory Hail Mary, Glory Be and Our Father, then bless myself and go and wash my feet in a mucky pool. I dry them as best I can with my socks, put those on, and finally my shoes. As I do, I watch the sea pounding the rocks below. I feel a strange elation, a powerful urge to run up the hill for no good reason. I'm holy, I think, holy. I can see my soul shining like a bright full moon. At Mass, I sometimes felt this way when the priest raised the host and rang the communion bell and we sang in Latin at Easter, but mostly in the church, I only felt good. Now I was holy, and holy was infinitely better.

It was many years before I understood that this euphoria, this altered state they call grace, was not what the priest meant by holy, not the same thing at all and it could be this distinction that brings me back here, to visit a childhood I cannot return to, an innocence I only partly want to retrieve. Whatever my personal objective, I have come to pay tribute to the people who invested this ground with the kinetic energy of their faith and passions, doing what we have always done, circling ourselves, walking our prayers and our verses and the runes of our despair into the cold November ground because, in the end, this is what we know, and all we will ever know.

While I am here, I watch this thin intense child, my young self, as she walks the two or three miles to my grandmother's house. There is seed cake and current cake and a party atmosphere. Old women kiss one another and the dúidíns are smoked in the bedroom, the women giggling like Arab girls. Sometimes they cry under pressure of joy or sorrow or some other great emotion. These exchanges are in a mixture of Irish and English, and we children are shown off, inspected and given money. Thus was our place secured, our sense of ourselves tied into the family and the tribe. This system worked well, for the most part.

There was one big woman 'from the hills' with a son, whom all were eager to marry off. She had a lisp and led him around like a young calf at a fair. The women laughed when she left, but they were fond of her. The children copied her lisp and laughed hysterically. After several years, a woman was got for the son, who turned out not to be a sissy at all, sired seven children, had a satisfied-looking wife. He left the women wondering and a few feeling cheated. An old man said the saint had great power. All this makes it seem that our lives conspired to be part of a bad Irish short story, but that would be a mistake. That would be to forget that in little over ten years the country changed from a peasant community to one with cars, televisions and washing machines and that the ageing daughters of those old women surf the net and fly to New York for weddings, funerals and the shopping.

I envy the visitors, those who are new to this, and 'find some comfort there'. I return a couple of times a year in full awareness of the treacherous tides around station island, the eddies in the philosophical whirlpool. It is the place I trust, the touching stone, the wild spot where the veil between the two worlds I was reared in is thinnest, and where it might, with faith or luck, occasionally open to reveal one through the other — especially in November, Samhain, the month when dead souls haunt the night and come crying for mercy and release, so that we who are left have to do penance and say Masses on their behalf, to release them from their torment. No one believes that story any more, but millions went to their graves certain of it. And what am I certain of? What will the veil open to reveal now? A void, blackness, the only light being the cold-boned face of the moon.

Two years ago I climbed the hill near the well at half past four in the evening. The sky held the last light over Slyne Head and dark clouds were piled up, threatening and stark. The skyline was brooding, the clouds backlit in places with red and purple light. As we arrived, a line of people struggled over the horizon against the wind. My friend mentioned Spain, drama, films, then commented that this was a very penitential time of year. Her local saint is Mac Dara, the patron of Carna, and his day is in July. 'But you have to go to the island for that, in a boat,' I pointed out. 'We'd all be drowned if we left the shore in this weather.' Saint Cáillín's island, half a mile off the coast, lies within sight of the well.

'Well, ye had an awkward bloody man for a saint,' she said.

Yet the people continue to make the station, imprinting their longing on the stones with their bare feet, then putting on their shoes and, because they are the lucky ones, going back to warm, lit homes to eat and dance and celebrate a life improved beyond the imaginings of our grandparents and great grandparents, improvements they would have approved. So why do we go? Does it matter?

Peregrination. Odyssey. Station.

I know only this — all journeys, no matter what the destination, are circular. They begin and end with yourself, alone, and the destination is not always what matters. But it matters enough.

I know that now, but I didn't always know it. I thought Heaven was the end, purgatory the coal-strewn ante-chamber, and pilgrimage the means of shortening the way. I thought all this because I was a devout child, desperate for miracles, wanting above all else to be good. What was I doing, at the age of seven, pale, thin, dragging an overdeveloped conscience around the miserable marshy fields, along the untarred road to school every day, where it was fed by a spinster teacher who press-ganged us all into the Legion of Mary and instructed us in the arcane detail of hell? And dragging it, like a sack of grain, home again in the afternoon. 'Déjà vu,' I thought, years later, when I first came across Sisyphus with his rock, warm with the comfort of fellow feeling. 'Been there, done that,' I said, superior because I thought I had left my rock behind in university.

That early pilgrimage is the map on which I occasionally negotiate that labyrinthine journey inside the self, tangled hopelessly and needing some outer shape to which, for the purpose of progress, I am pleased to conform. I go to circumambulate the well and because there I feel closer to my father's shade, to my grandmother's enduring presence and to the slow swing of some older dance, the equivalent of walking verses around an altar, of stepping out the rhythm of a line, as some believe was done by the poets before the time of Christ or Naomh Cáillín — at least Robert Graves would have it so.

I usually leave with a day defined in darkness, like the negative of an evening landscape outlined in the last watered light. There is less a sense of a prayer answered than of a god appeased, at least for a time. And there is a temporary slaking of that cursed desire that Máirtín Ó Direáin, in his wonderfully titled 'Malairt Duile' refers to as 'Duil i mbraon as tobar na ngrast'.

The rituals I grew up with were beautiful and gave me the basis of form, poetic and dramatic, and they brightened dull, hard lives. Of course, they also dulled and hardened bright lives. But they gave us the notion of sacrament, celebration, grace — and faith, which we might then, having gloried in, lose and always know what we had lost. That's the fall.

I am Created in God's Image, Therefore I Laugh

❈

Charlene Ann Baumbich

Charlene Ann Baumbich (www.dontmissyourlife.com) is a 56-year-old, mostly-Irish gal nationally-known in America for her lectures and books for both mainstream and Christian audiences. On her paternal grandmother's side she traces back to County Cork roots and while her father's father is described at family reunions as being 'mostly Scots-Irish', official tracing of the maternal line has not been confirmed, but everyone has been assured there's Irish blood racing through their veins, which continues to be evidenced today in Charlene's wickedly humorous take on just about everything she writes and speaks about.

*M*y father died in 1998. Just to help you hop aboard my sense of humour, I do not perceive that to be funny. Exactly.

My grown son Bret was blessed enough to get a chance to kiss his grandfather goodbye hours before Dad's death. Oh, he didn't kiss him goodbye because he knew my dad was dying. After all, Dad had just, within eight hours of The Kiss, had a pacemaker successfully installed in order to keep his merry heart beating. No, death was neither expected nor suspected; as usual, Dad had many plans under way. Although he was eighty-two, there were still bowling lanes to conquer for the Senior Olympics. There were still beautiful women — young, old and medium — with whom to flirt unabashedly. Three marriages behind him, a fourth always loomed just on the horizon, or perhaps next to him in a grocery-store line. Or at the golf course, on the dance floor, at a casino. Or in the doctor's office or driving next to him in a convertible — you get the picture.

No, my son didn't kiss his grandpa goodbye because any of us thought Dad was dying. In fact, I didn't even fly to Albuquerque to be with Dad for the procedure because everyone said it was so routine and, after all, my son was there to cheer him on and so was Dad's girlfriend. Bret kissed Dad goodbye because he was flying from his home in Albuquerque to meet me in New Orleans. When Bret asked my dad if he would be more comfortable if he postponed our trip and stayed with him for a while longer, Dad replied, 'Hell no! Don't worry about me! I've already been there and now it's your turn. I'll see you when you get back, and you can tell me all about it. I'm doing fine.' And he was doing fine, aside from the fact he would die within hours of Bret's departure. And so Bret kissed his grandpa goodbye and left to gather the stories with which he would return, something Dad taught us all to do very well.

When I'd booked the speaking engagement in Gulf Shores, a quick map gaze revealed I'd only be a smidgen away from New Orleans, and I knew the opportunity had arisen for a dream to come true. Finally Bret and I, mother and first-born son, were going to wallow in our long-awaited, much-discussed and highly anticipated adventure in New Orleans, land of ethnic diversity, jazz, blues, the Mississippi River, voodoo, sauces, gators, Mardi Gras, begnettes, Cajun everything. New Orleans: Land of all that overflows with earthiness and possibilities.

Within an hour after we'd each arrived in the Big Easy and ten minutes after we were sound asleep (long day and late travel for both of us and we wanted to be wide-eyed and fully alive for our great adventure), we were awakened by The Call: my father was dead. My laughing, ever hope-filled, moving-right-along, roughish, loving father was dead.

New Orleans: Land of all that overflowed with grief. Earthiness and possibilities, we assured ourselves, would still be there when we tried this trip again. Now, we were on our way to New Mexico, the Land of Enchantment (so the licence plates say) and an impending cremation.

Yes, Bret had kissed my father goodbye. I, as it turns out, had kissed him goodbye a month previously when I returned home after a happy visit with the father of my life here on earth. The one who taught me not only to say, but to believe, as we reached for our wallets with delight and abandon, 'I've got money I haven't even spent yet!' The one who taught me to live by the motto, 'It doesn't matter if you win or lose, but you're stupid if you don't want to win.' The one who asked me, when I was off and whining or angry or too sad about something, 'Why do you want to be that way?' and who always, by the simple asking of the question, helped me determine not to be. He would wrap his arm around me, pull me tight, then back off and grin at me with a generations-old, devilish twinkle in his eye undoubtedly inherited through his Cork genes. And so, too, I would grin the sight-yet-unseen, swaying grasses of Ireland back at him and we would both laugh and all would be well with my soul.

And now my father was dead and I was way too sad and I couldn't help being that way because my father was now dead and therefore wasn't there to help me not to be that way. Well, not exactly. Yet.

My mother died in 1975. Death wasn't funny then, either — although, like my father used to say when referring to life's ins and outs, 'As the worm turns', and sometimes the worm turns 'crazier than a fart in a whirlwind', as my mom's red-haired, mostly-Irish mom used to say. Colourful, huh? My mom's mother's mom was married five times and each husband died. Talk about a curious worm ...

But then the possibility of murder is not what I'm talking about. We are on the topic of death, remember? And how can I speak about death without first thinking about life, which systematically leads me to creation and the creator. And now I'm speaking about neither death nor life but God, who I cannot speak about without encompassing all of death and life and farts and swaying grasses of Ireland and worms and whirlwinds and all that is, seen and unseen. I am speaking about a God who I believe created a sense of humour, and I believe God did so after God first cracked himself up with feel-good, spontaneous laughter immediately after creating some of the ruddiest, rowdiest, red-haired-iest and roughish-est creations, namely us Irish and mostly-Irish folks who, in the darndest of times, explode and implode with laughter —

just like our creator. 'Twas we who first inspired the laughter of God (Which came first? The fairy or the belief in one?) and since we're created in God's image, we now all laugh. We hope. Sometimes even when it's not appropriate. And now I'm back to talking about death, which is getting funnier, all because of God.

My mom died when she was only fifty-six years old. A warm, laughing, gentle, brave, wide-eyed child of God, she blew a blood vessel in her brain. She lived two weeks to the day afterwards. No, none of this was funny. However, blessedly, both of my parents knew how to laugh at themselves and therefore modelled that it was perfectly normal to do the same. Once you can laugh at yourself, you can find humour in just about anything, whether you're trying to or not. This character trait is not only entertaining and in my opinion divine, but it is a pure and sparkly and much-valued inherited gift that I have been overjoyed to pass along to my children.

I spoke of this at my father's memorial service, which, of course, followed the actual cremation, my father's choice even though my mother had twenty-three years earlier been buried and the engraved headstone covered both their plots. Dad's wishes were to have his ashes sprinkled across them. Dad's cremation was, of course, preceded by the arrangements for same, following body identification, which also wasn't funny.

Brian, our younger son, flew in from Minnesota to help Bret and me with all that needed to be done, including dispersing my father's home and belongings. Together we very sad people sat in the funeral director's office discussing cremation and memorial service arrangements. During the course of this very sad conversation, I casually mentioned something about my father's pacemaker, and suddenly the funeral guy — who otherwise had been acting very limply funeral-ish — snapped into full posture. 'Your dad has a pacemaker?' he asked, voice elevating in pitch and urgency.

'Yes. He had it put in the same day he died.'

'This is very important information,' he said as he quickly shuffled through papers looking for the death certificate forms on his desk, scanning the details and then making hasty notations. I was wondering what could possibly be so important about a pacemaker, possibly now the only thing working about my dad.

'The cremationist must know this before a cremation! We were unaware your father has a pacemaker! It can be very dangerous to cremate someone wearing a pacemaker' — he used this active verb as though Dad was out on a date and sporting it like a corsage — 'since the pacemaker will explode in high heat. In fact, we recently had a cremationist injured over an incident like this!'

Suddenly, an explosion and implosion of laughter seized my entire otherwise very sad self. I involuntarily belted out so many continuous HAHAHAHAHAHAS that I could hardly breathe. I would almost collect myself, sigh loudly, then throw my head back and hurl into yet more fits of laughter. My sons and the funeral guy sat stone silent, staring at me in disbelief, undoubtedly fearing I had snapped from grief and stress and lack of sleep.

'Oh my GOSH!' I finally exclaimed between guffaws. 'Wouldn't it be just like Dad to go out with a BANG?!' I was nearly rolling out of my chair by this point and since I'm a mid-life female on hormone replacement therapy, the threat of wetting my pants loomed ever near — which suddenly made everything even funnier. My sons finally joined my laughter. They didn't laugh as heartily as me, but they laughed. They also settled their laughter long before I did; I needed to be handed tissues to wipe the tears from my face. I could think of no one other than my father who would think this explosion concept and entire, hysterical funeral home scene run amuck funnier.

Then as I blew my nose, suddenly, like a spiritual gust of inviting fresh air, I felt my dad's presence deep in my gut, his arm around my shoulder pulling me tight. It was as though I heard him say in fully animated and great story-telling detail, as I'd heard him say so many times in my life, 'Well, wait until you hear what I did today!' I could see his arms waving and his bushy eyebrows rising and falling as he milked the moment for all it was worth, describing bits and pieces of his body and that of a very surprised cremationist flying this way and that and the cloud of smoke and the ... I could hear Mom laughing in the background, covering her mouth out of habit the way she'd done for decades on this earth.

Should this have actually become Dad's story, the green Irish grasses in heaven would have rippled as his happy and exuberant and laughing, story-telling breath blew across the land, rising and falling, entertaining those seen and unseen. I can hear it with the same clarity I can imagine in my descendants as they repeat the ordeal in full details of what almost happened but didn't. Dancing eyes, pints raised, toasts made: 'May we all go out with a bang and enter the gates of God's heavenly laughter, ha-ha-ing in unison with all the universe!'

Of course grief is real. And painful. And long. But I cannot imagine getting through the process without the gift of laughter bestowed upon us by the Creator and passed along by my parents, nor could I even believe in a creator who didn't laugh. In Genesis I learn that I am created in God's image. And I laugh. And so, therefore, must God. And so, therefore, does the gift of laughter fluently minister to me in the hardest of times. I believe a sense of humour that rings with laughter bestows a velvet salve of healing powers. Oh yes, I believe laughter is divine.

There was divinity in the moment we *could* laugh when we began to go through my father's belongings and found the humour and 'good fortune' in the fact that his last two wives had uncluttered him of so many personal belongings that it had ultimately lightened our task. There was divinity in the moment we arrived at the cemetery and I realised Dad had put 'Together Forever' on their headstone and I began to laugh when I said aloud, 'with just a couple detours in between'.

There was nothing funny in actually sprinkling the ashes. No, there was nothing funny about losing the last physical pieces of my father to the earth. I cried profusely and, in fact, laid myself face down, prostrate, arms and legs spread across their graves as I wept for a long while, one son eventually nesting my head in his lap and the other stroking my legs as I wound myself down, saying a final goodbye ... imagined farewell kisses ... to the ones who raised me.

When I was finally emotionally spent, I sat up to a startling discovery: I was coated — absolutely coated — with my father's ashes. I held my arms before me as though a ghost had appeared, eyes wide opened with disbelief and mild shock. And once again, in the middle of my gut, my father's humour and laughter seized me. 'Well,' I said to my sons, 'let's go to the casino. Maybe Grandpa Dust is lucky!' (Fastest twenty bucks I ever lost, by the way; and then I remembered my dad saying how long it had been since he'd won. Not a winning roll for the Dadster.)

When my brother went to make arrangements at the cemetery to have Dad's death date etched in the headstone and the administrator couldn't find any records of the grave having been opened (and we learned what we'd done was illegal but obviously unre-doable — you know, rain and all that), there was divinity in the laughter that erupted from me when my brother told my son who told me that the guy looked up my dad's record, saw he hadn't been buried and asked my brother, 'So, just where IS your father?'

And so we laugh, and the laughter itself becomes a part of the healing.

It is the memories of the laughter of those gone before me that God uses to replenish my own giggling and singing heart. Like recalling the time when I was growing up and a fox fell through the window well into the basement of our farm house and went berserk. Mom, in a courageous and protective mother's fury, shot it. When I gaze upon the photo, I cannot help but laugh for joy. There stands Mom, fox dangling by its tail from one hand, rifle raised in the other, tears of terror — and laughter — flowing down her soft cheeks. I keep that cherished, photographic memory tucked away in the muff I had made out of its pelt after mom died. 'Thank you, Lord, not only for the memory, but for the mother who modelled joy and laughter and triumph in the midst of tribulation.'

Yes, I appreciate and love the God who fills my heart by lovingly and playfully guiding and healing me, always with a twinkle in her eye, ready to erupt into the laughter that rings out of my being and the being of my father and father's father and all the generations to come.

Soulfood and Lechery, Saint and Sinners

Michael Coady

Poet, author, musician and former teacher Michael Coady lives in his hometown, Carrick-on-Suir, County Tipperary, and is an elected member of Aosdána, the Irish academy of artists. The winner of a number of literary awards and author of three books from Gallery Press, he is also known as a broadcaster and a participant in arts events at home and abroad. He has a special interest in the Irish diaspora in America, about which he has written a family memoir, in his book, All Souls.

*I*n the millennium year, billboards all over Ireland carried a message from An Bord Bia, the State board that regulates food quality and promotion. A large full-colour photograph of a mouth-watering dish of strawberries was accompanied by the slogan: 'Purify yourself without going to Confession — Fresh fruit, for a naturally better life.'

As usual, the advertising industry reflects and surfs the Zeitgeist — in this instance playing on the increasing abandonment of institutional religious practice in Ireland, along with the prevailing conventional wisdom that holds that eating the right kind of food is the pathway to salvation. This is the overwhelming contemporary orthodoxy of the overfed and exploitative West, where the diet industry and its oppressive imperatives and compulsions constitute a kind of voodoo of our time, a quasi-religion, for the most part unexamined by its modern, educated hundreds of millions of subscribers to the sacred tenets of calorie count, lettuce leaf and low fat as ciphers for virtuous living.

Michael Coady

Where once we strove to save our in-dwelling souls through sancti-
fying grace, now we struggle to attain or at least aspire to a body shape
idealised and defined by movie stars or models. The sins of fornication
once thundered about from pulpits have been relaunched as
recreational pursuits, their erstwhile force and gravity replaced by a
secular consensus that decrees that sex is good but fat is sinful, with
obesity the mark of the damned — those unreconstructed sinners who
go through life not eating right, and not working out in the gym, the
pool, or on the exercise machine.

As an unrepentant and slothful diet and exercise sceptic, I occasionally find myself almost nostalgic for the medieval gravities and perverse
puritanism of the Irish Catholicism in which I grew up. It was a world in
which you carried an awesome personal responsibility for something
immortal and unique within you, called your soul. I hardly ever hear it
mentioned in church nowadays. The body, though theoretically the temple
of the Holy Ghost, was in ecclesiastical practice a damned nuisance that
wouldn't go away until safely cold and coffined. Up to that point the flesh
was hot stuff, occupying a central role in the great tussle between good
and evil. In those days sexual thrills came spiced with the flavour of the
forbidden and carrying the awesome price-tag of eternal retribution —
eternal, for God's sake — if not repented of and recounted in quantitative
and qualitative detail in the whispered dark of the confessional.

All of this has a funny side, a transcending element of the absurd.
The implacable fact of death is what makes religion relevant; the gift of
life is what makes sex important and love central; the saving mystery of
laughter is what makes the world supportable and humanity unique.
Religion in general is notoriously lacking in humour, its formal structures never allowing for the possibility that the supreme being may well
be the great arch-joker. If there's one thing that should convince us that
God has a subversive sense of humour, then surely it must be the
hilarious mechanics of sex — hilarious, that is, except for the panting
participants. But here's the kind of thing I was learning by rote by the
time I was eleven or so, and still not into puberty, much less in the way
of any opportunities for precocious promiscuity:

Q. Besides all wilful consent to immodest thoughts and desires, and all wilful pleasure in irregular motions of the flesh, what else is forbidden by the ninth commandment?

A. The ninth commandment also forbids all immediate occasions of immodest thoughts and desires.

I had no idea what irregular motions of the flesh might be, much less immodest thoughts and desires or immediate occasions, but the general message was clear: The body, and in particular the lower body, was very bad news indeed. Not only was unlicensed hanky panky itself illicit, but so was even thinking about it. The actual fantasising about carnal delights was not in itself a sin — the sin lay in taking deliberate pleasure in the thought. The Irish Catholic clergy, driven by a bleak post-Famine agenda of social engineering and population control restated as virtues of chastity and purity, had grown to regard the body, and especially the female body, as a most regrettable lapse on the part of the Creator. Eve and all her charms might never have been loosed upon the world if a brace of old-style Irish bishops had originally been to hand in an advisory capacity. But given that the Creator slipped up unaccountably in this regard, you needed to be eternally vigilant:

Q. What should you do in the morning after offering your heart and soul to God?

A. I should rise diligently, dress myself modestly, and entertain myself with uplifting thoughts, such as the goodness of God, who grants me this day to labour in it for the salvation of my soul, which day, perhaps, may be my last.

Life, perceived as a kind of pre-trial process played out in an ante-chamber inexorably leading to the hall of eternal judgement, was not meant for partying. But for all its joylessness and prescriptive legalism, the religion to which I was exposed came set within a deep cultural matrix of liturgy and language. It was anything but trivial in form or content. After all, by the time I was seven I was mouthing the awesome word 'eternity'. Along with the catechism that I learned by rote, as I grew up I was immersed in Latin chant. I haven't forgotten its cultural riches, and I am appalled by the banality of what has taken its place, much of it the musical equivalent of junk food.

For all of the pre-Vatican II religion that I would never wish upon my children, I'm conscious that I was exposed by default to a substantial cultural matrix ultimately rooted in the classical worlds of Greece and Rome as well as Judaism. At the same time, Hell, Heaven, Purgatory and Limbo were perceived realities that paralleled a worldly landscape fraught with unprotected mineshafts of sin down which you might plummet to damnation. Institutional religion was a grim business, regulated in infinite canonical detail, its governance entirely appropriated by a celibate caste of male clerics deep into social control. No wonder it has now run out of spiritual steam. If the nominal founder of Christianity could have slipped incognito into the average church on an average Sunday, he would surely have shaken the dust from his feet and headed for the hills, inviting the less respectable ones hanging about the door to join him in making a new start.

Now, says the millennium billboard, you may purify yourself through healthy eating, and without going to Confession. If dietary obsession and the idea that we are what we eat is the new religion, however, it remains in one sense still linked to an ancient and perhaps primal concept. Psalm 36 has these lovely words: 'O taste and see how gracious the Lord is' — the idea of tasting as perception and becoming, communion and transformation.

At the more carnal level, lovers in their passionate couplings hunger to taste and savour one another. What is kissing but symbolic feeding? Eros is never too far from the caring kitchen. I can think of one cookery programme on television revealingly called *Consuming Passions*. This features a male chef, but my personal weakness is for a couple of other television cookery productions starring women. Not blatant babes, mind you, but mature women who know what they're about ('really good pork begins with a really good, well-reared pig'). The one capable of inducing immodest thoughts and desires in me has an irresistibly white-starched-apron image and a slightly school-mistressy tone as she takes things in hand and expertly performs all the culinary foreplay. Then, when she has you weak with salivating anticipation, she's likely to smile straight at you and invite you to pop it in the oven. Shameless stuff, and guaranteed to make any flesh-and-blood man burn, or at least smoke.

The truth, as poets and impassioned cooks should know, is that all things connect, could we but perceive the links and correspondences. One evening I was ambushed by a connection between my dinner and a long-dead Italian saint. The revelation came as I struggled to remain open-eyed during a sermon. People have been dozing through sermons for centuries, but it takes a practised skill to succumb without your neighbours noticing.

There were some extenuating circumstances: a preceding late night and then the church packed for evening Mass at the local Franciscan Friary in Carrick Beg. Moreover, the weather was oppressively humid and, only an hour before, I'd had a fine dinner of corned ox tongue, new potatoes and dressed cabbage. It's a traditional dish of which I'm fond, and has some relevance here.

The guest preacher was talking about Saint Anthony of Padua. He's the lost-property specialist to whom in Ireland even dedicated atheists appeal after misplacing their car keys or credit cards. He lived from 1195 to 1231 and is not to be confused with Saint Anthony of Thebes, 251–350, the Egyptian hermit who gave a kick-start to monasticism.

Most of what the preacher was saying was coming at me dimly and distantly as I struggled to keep the eyelids raised and the head upright. Suddenly, however, I was jerked into a state of high alert. The man on the altar had just hit me with a piece of riveting information: Saint Anthony's tongue is still to the good over in Padua, though getting on in years.

Now, whether you yourself give this any credence or not is beside the point. You can be certain that the punters are constantly queuing up over in Padua for a glimpse of the holy man's tongue, said to be in remarkably good nick, all things considered. It was only an hour since I had been enthusiastically poking a knife and fork at my dinner-plate and through an unfortunate process of organic association the venerable relic over in Padua and the substance of my dinner became entangled together, in, well, a confusion of tongues.

I scarcely got a wink of sleep for the rest of the sermon, and the matter occupied my mind afterwards.

On the subject of relics I'm sceptical but intrigued. Holy Mother Church always maintained a cunningly fail-safe line on this: if relics assist some people in believing then they may be a good thing, even when their authenticity is suspect. For centuries, tons of shredded timber were circulating briskly and profitably around Christendom — each little fragment or splinter purporting to be a part of the True Cross.

Similarly, saints' bones and other reasonably respectable body parts or personal effects have also had a miraculous shelf life and popularity. To tell you the truth, only part of me finds this hilarious or repugnant. I don't quite know where I stand on the question of the saint's tongue over in Padua. A metaphor for eloquence? Maybe — but the literal thing itself, grisly in a glass case?

You could say that my head is Protestant and my gut Catholic, and the confused cohabitation of the two signifies an unresolved tug-of-war between magical fascination and rational scepticism. On the one hand, there is a kind of poetry of the people that must go back to the universal beginnings of religion and belief. And on the other hand, there is a highly developed intellectual tradition in all the great world religions. Reason without imagination is arid; imagination without reason can be dangerous.

If religion and local culture are intimately related, you might find yourself wondering what the tongue of Saint Anthony of Padua has to do with going to church in Carrick Beg. The Romanisation of Irish religious belief, organisation and practice was a kind of colonising mission that took a long, long time to accomplish. One of the most significant contentions in our literature is the argument in the Fiannaíocht between

Oisín and Saint Patrick. Oisín has returned from Tír na nÓg to revisit the heroic life he remembered; instead he is trapped in time and age and impending death. Patrick tries to persuade him to accept Christianity, but Oisín pines for the remembered Eden of the old pagan world and wants no dealings with new-fangled clerics or church bells or repentance.

What we really have here is the struggle in the Irish psyche between a native spirituality, based on wells and streams and woods and wonders, and the imperial Roman take-over through imported structure and dogma.

Patrick won out. Or did he? At the lovely holy well of Cuan and Brógán in the ancient parish of Mothel in the County Waterford hinterland of Carrick-on-Suir, on Pattern Day each July, I can recognise, played out before my eyes, the continuing tension between Oisín and Patrick. What the instinctive and ageless veneration of the well expresses is innately religious and also truly feminine — cyclical renewal, water and life.

Patrick's clerical emissaries have tried for centuries to reach an accommodation with the well and its unbridled custom. It's far older than their empire or its decrees, or even its own devotees in prehistory. In the case of the well of Cuan and Brógán, a permit in Latin from the Vatican formally allowed the local parish priest of the 1850s to link the annual Pattern in July with the special offer of a plenary indulgence on the day, simultaneously legitimising a financial levy at the site of the holy well in order to help build the lovely little church that stands in Clonea Power. Ten years after the Great Famine, the immensely influential and Romanising churchman, Paul Cullen, travelled to rural County Waterford from his archbishop's palace in Dublin to preach at the completed church's dedication.

Unlike most nineteenth-century Irish churches — heavily influenced in design and iconography by Italian vernacular models — that distinctive village church at Clonea Power has several stained-glass representations of traditional Irish saints, the putative pair associated with the holy well amongst them, and, in addition, some glowing twentieth-century work from the famed Harry Clarke studio.

What historical actuality, if any, may lie behind the saints of the well, Cuan and Brógán, and their likes? Our traditional Irish saints inhabit a kind of intriguing shadowland. I only recently discovered the speciality of Saint Dympna — who has, I'd guess, no official recognition. Come to think of it, the Vatican selectors have never been willing to draft our traditional saints into the Roman squad, notwithstanding how long most of us on this island have been supporting the Italian side. Anyway, I overheard one woman recommending Dympna to another. 'She's great,' she said, 'for the nerves.' I made a mental note.

The esoteric mythology of traditional saints may be encountered in Hubert Butler's extraordinary book, *Ten Thousand Saints: A Study in Irish and European Origins*. In it the author daringly sets out to prove that we inherited our saints from a pre-Celtic past in which they figured as ancestors of half-forgotten tribes. The forest of material examined includes some engrossing anecdotes and narratives. Let me, for instance, subvert received nineteenth-century pieties by spilling some little-known beans on Saint Patrick's kin and household.

What kin? Well, there was Saint Martin, Patrick's uncle, and Restitutus his nephew, while the household included Saint Erc his embroideress and Trenfer his strongman. Most interesting of all was Saint Lupita, his sister. Lupita, like Patrick, had been captured by pirates, along with her sister Tigris, and sold into slavery in Louth at the same time that Patrick was sold to Milchíu in Antrim.

Though she came to be called saint, Lupita had a colourful career path on her way to eventual last-minute canonisation. Mind you, it's said that she was also the victim of some malicious gossip. It was alleged that she was engaged in an unsavoury relationship with her nephew, Saint Mel, with whom she shared a religious house, but she managed to clear herself of that allegation through some miraculous intervention, and Patrick thereupon strongly advised her to get the hell out of that particular monastery and not be giving the family a bad name.

That should have been the end of it, but in no time the whole country was buzzing with the news that Lupita, fatally attracted to holy

men, had moved in with Saint MacNisse of Connor. As if he hadn't
enough on his plate, the long-suffering Patrick was forced to intervene again. What did he do but pray that the lecherous hand that
Saint MacNisse had laid upon his sister should fall off. It did, and Carn
Lámha or the Cairn of the Hand is where MacNisse's discredited hand
is buried.

It was becoming embarrassingly obvious by now that Lupita was
destined to strain the acceptable limits of even fifth-century mores and
would more than likely come to a sticky end that you wouldn't wish
on anyone's sister, let alone the national apostle's. And so, alas, it
transpired.

On the rebound from the handicapped MacNisse, Lupita fell straight
into the arms of Colmán of Clan Breasail. She was infatuated once
again, but it has to be said that she had also begun to be afflicted with
guilt and remorse, and about time for her.

One day she saw Patrick approaching and knew that this had to be
the final showdown. Out she went, deeply penitent, and flung herself in
front of his chariot to appeal for mercy. The brother might ordinarily
have been impressed, but on this particular day he was just too sick
and tired of the whole thing to stand for any more of it.

'The chariot over her!' Saint Patrick ordered his driver, and his
chariot was driven over her, not once, but three times. However,
the promiscuous Lupita's last-minute repentance ensured spiritual
salvation, and her penitential fortitude in the face of a vengeful
oncoming chariot was the very stuff of sainthood. She flew straight to
Heaven, and Patrick, fair play to him, even sang her requiem once he
had cooled down.

There was a slightly messy dénouement. One of Saint Lupita's
illegitimate children was Saint Áedán of Inis Lothair, and he begged
Patrick that the descendants of his illegitimate brothers and sisters —
who I have to reveal included the O'Faolain tribe — should have places
reserved for them in Heaven. Patrick agreed, but not without the
purgatorial injunction that they would always be sickly and prone to
ailments while in this world.

Whether members of the clan still enjoy that Patrician privilege entitling them to reserved celestial suites I'm not qualified to say, but the alleged O'Faolain sickliness is definitely a thing of the past. Perhaps they stumbled upon our contemporary path to redemption early on, and any ancestral taint of moral turpitude or proneness to ailments has long since been overcome by virtue of regular workouts and steadfast devotion to the right foods.

Part Four

The Troubles

*D*uring the very period when spirituality has become — along with cream liqueur and traditional music — one of its signature exports, Ireland has seen the orthodox practice of religion decline steeply. A mere three decades ago, Ireland was still the priest-ridden country that James Joyce had been so eager to escape fifty years earlier. And it wasn't just priests doing the riding; lay people lent a hand to keep the land safe for Catholicism. Censors cleaned the shelves of Edna O'Brien and the like, rural postmistresses had their own little unofficial censorship operation going, and that lascivious rock 'n' roll could be heard only from floating pirate radio stations. Ireland was the most Catholic of European nations, a land where men and women conceived children after marriage, bore them without interfering with the hand of God, and remained duly married until death did them part. Pubs closed down for the holy hour, everyone went off to Mass on Sunday, the Church set the curriculum in the schools, and all was well in the land.

We are speaking here, of course, about the Republic. In Northern Ireland, long-simmering economic warfare between descendants of mostly poor Scottish settlers and descendants of mostly poor Irish farmers finally broke out into literal war. The fact that the former Scots were Protestant while the not-so-welcoming Irish were Catholic made it seem, to the world and often to themselves, that the conflict was about religion. And indeed the language of religion was used then, as it is still used today, to cloak the roots of the conflict in land and resources.

The war in Northern Ireland was exacerbated by the Republic's Church-ridden state. Many in the North quailed at the thought of a United Ireland, if unity meant censorship, lack of access to birth control, and elimination of divorce. Sentimental images of carrot-haired lads and colleens skipping down the boreen to Mass while the kindly village priest administered sacraments to his devoutly murmuring flock brought shudders, not smiles, to those who feared Church-determined regulation of their lives.

But those sentimental images were, for many, just that: images. Reality was starkly different. There is a common joke in recovery circles that Denial is a river not in Egypt but in Ireland. Who guessed how many smiles were plastered over unspeakable pain? Lack of access to birth control drove some families into poverty, while those of means found other countries — including Northern Ireland — to provide what the Republic denied. Lack of divorce led to marital abandonment, a strategy practised disproportionately by men, while women were left without legal recourse, unable either to end the marriage or to force support payments. Some of the men who stayed did so at the expense of their children, who suffered beatings and, at worst, sexual assault — stories of which have filled the Irish newspapers for the past decade.

Religion once offered solace for such human misery. Such was the case with the two most significant blows to the Irish spirit, the Great Famine and emigration, which are impossible to divorce from each other. The indescribable conditions of the Famine forced millions into exile to escape the fate of the millions who died at home. Then, the

Church offered consolation to the bereaved at home and to those bereaved of their homeland.

Such consolation is not so easily accepted today. A 2000 study showed that half of Irish young people do not participate in religious services or do so rarely. The Church is no longer universally regarded as a safe harbour from the world's evils. For more than a decade, revelations about the unsaintly activities of the clergy have tested the faithful's commitment while driving away the doubtful. Young women, pregnant out of wedlock, were virtually enslaved in the notorious nun-run Magdalen laundries, forced to give up their children, sometimes worked to death. One of Ireland's most prominent bishops acknowledged not only a long-lasting affair but the offspring of that affair. Hollywood stars described their sexual abuse at the hands of priests, while villages learned of pastors responsible for the abuse of generations of boys. Early in 2001, the Vatican admitted the truth of a report listing Ireland as one of a handful of countries where nuns had been raped by priests and forced into abortions. The hypocrisy of an allegedly celibate clergy engaging in activities that they condemned the laypeople for has driven many sincere spiritual seekers away from the Church.

Those who did not personally suffer from these secret tragedies are sometimes heard expressing impatient nostalgia for that sweet sentimental image of Ireland past. But for those wounded or damaged by institutional or personal evil, the replacement of that image by the painful truth is part of the spiritual search, for forgiveness must begin with honest confession.

Spiritual Politics of Peace

Kelly Candaele

Kelly Candaele (Kcandaele@msn.com) is an Irish-American who was born in Canada and emigrated to the United States in 1958. His mother, Helen O'Callahan, was also from Canada and traced her roots back to County Cork. She played professional baseball in the 1940s for the Fort Wayne Daisies. Kelly has written extensively on Irish politics, history and culture for the Los Angeles Times, San Francisco Chronicle *and* Irish America Magazine. *He has produced several documentary films including* A League of Their Own, *the basis for the Columbia Pictures feature film, about his mother, and a film on Swedish Prime Minister Olof Palme. He says he is what Mike Harrington has called a 'pious apostate'.*

Travelling to Northern Ireland for the first time in 1989 was like entering Alice's rabbit hole. Crossing the border from the Republic, where daily life and human interaction seemed familiar, I entered a place that immediately struck me as darker, psychologically and socially more complicated — a society where the weight of history was reflected in people's names and faces, full of foreboding but also more intense. I felt like I was in a very strange world.

In Derry, a local guide, my own Virgil, interprets the political and social symbols of the native landscape. He tells me of the significance of an absent statue on the city walls, that of a Protestant hero blown off a pillar in 1973 by the IRA. He points out an unmarked armoured police car, which, he explains matter-of-factly, 'rides about ten inches lower than most cars and has a different licence'. Workers constructing a barrier near a police station are 'definitely not from Derry', I'm informed. 'People have been shot for less,' he adds, driving home the implications of, in IRA phraseology, 'collaborating with the institutions of state repression'. It takes time and work to gain an education in Northern Ireland's political semiotics.

I was initially bewildered by Northern Ireland. How was it possible that so much carnage could be inflicted with no apparent progress towards resolution? What was the process by which hatred and suspicion towards a group was passed on from generation to generation? Some of my friends back home in California spoke in hushed tones whenever they discussed Northern Ireland. Were they part of the 'American connection' perhaps, with secrets to protect? Others adopted an attitude of condescending indictment, pointing to the perils of religious irrationalism at its atavistic worst. In California, acknowledging the weight of the past only restrains you from laying hold of the future. In Northern Ireland, however, history is remembered, re-enacted, painted onto walls and paraded in the streets. The past is often a simpler place to live than the present.

I returned to Northern Ireland many times after my first visit, as I began writing about the peace process for the *Los Angeles Times* and other publications. I was an outsider trying to interpret — or reinterpret — the signs and signals of a society that seemed to change its rules and moral standards on a regular basis. I began reading standard and revisionist histories of Ireland, analyses of the Troubles, political polemics and cultural criticism. But I was most fascinated by what I experienced at first hand through interviews and observation: on the one hand, the dark side of human nature, the ability to justify and rationalise the most brutal of behaviours; and on the other, despite the common inclination to demonise one's enemies, the spiritual potential of transformation and redemption.

It is difficult these days for people in the United States to associate the term 'spiritual' with anything associated with politics. Despite the constant references to God and belief in American politics, there seem to be few Americans who regard either the conduct or the outcome of most of our elections as spiritually uplifting. What a nineteenth-century philosopher wrote about the ancient Roman gods during the height of that empire can be applied to American political institutions:

The temples are corpses from which the animating soul has fled, the hymns
are only words without belief, the tables of the gods without spiritual food
and drink.

For Hegel, the Roman statues had become just that — figures of
stone and marble, void of spirit and therefore no longer inspiring or
enriching.

It has become an axiom of political commentary that American
politics has become corrupted by money, captured by special interests, and that the core value of democratic participation — our civic
religion — has been ground down by the expediency of gaining and
holding power. It is fascinating then that President Clinton regarded his
three trips to Ireland as highlights of his presidential terms. I watched
him closely on all three, often standing amid a sea of Irish and
American flags. It was clear in his language and in his bearing that it
was in Ireland that he felt most at home.

President Clinton came to Ireland as a spiritual materialist, attuned to
the rôle that economics plays in the creation or diminishing of ethnic,
racial and sectarian animosities; but he was sensitive enough to know
that what was needed in Northern Ireland was a transformation, however
gradual, of the way that people defined themselves. Clinton seemed to
recognise that the spiritual realm, the way people symbolically orient
themselves in the world, was as powerful and important as the impact of
economics or the structure of political institutions.

One of the first places that Clinton stopped in Belfast on his initial trip
there in 1995 was the Mackie Metal Plant. The symbolism of the plant was
important as it reinforced the ameliorative effects of economic progress
and the attempt to break through the sectarian hold that the weight of
history had inflicted upon Northern Ireland. Introduced by two young
children, one Catholic, the other Protestant, Clinton told the integrated
group of workers and guests of honour that the economic rewards of
peace were clear for those who would look. The materialist Clinton
pointed out that his administration was the first to support the
International Fund for Ireland, which was 'becoming an engine for

economic development and for reconciliation', and that unemployment had declined and business and investments were flourishing.

On the evening of the same day, he spoke beneath Derry's historic walls and reminded the thousands gathered there that the day-to-day impositions of war, the shakedowns, the patrolling soldiers and the border stops were giving way to the ordinary daily flow of peace. As I watched the thousands of people, with the youth of Derry crammed toward the front near the stage, I sensed a physical, bodily yearning for peace. But I also remembered the comments of the bartender the previous night at the Telstar pub in the Creggan, a hard-core nationalist area of Catholic Derry: 'There are too many families with loved ones in the cemetery for healing to happen easily.' It was a sentiment I heard echoed many times in Protestant enclaves.

When he returned for his final visit as President in late 2000, Clinton travelled to the border town of Dundalk, where the Xerox Corporation had established a large factory. He again emphasised the tangible economic fruits of peace: 'Money isn't everything,' he quoted a young businessman as saying, 'but it's up there with oxygen.'

But during all of his three visits Clinton also acknowledged that all of the economic opportunities, jobs, inward investment and change in the material conditions of everyday life could not easily overcome the bitterness and mistrust derived from oppression, and the hatred and desire for vengeance that grows naturally out of violence. Clinton recognised that the psychological underpinnings of sectarianism — the inability to recognise the unique qualities of individuals or to see the other as completely human — did not disappear with an increase in the Gross National Product.

Fintan O'Toole had recognised the autobiographical background of Clinton's political initiatives. In one of his last public interviews as President, Clinton described the intensity of his opponents' anger towards him as coming from their sense of ethnic betrayal; he was a white Southern Protestant who rejected some of the dominant cultural values of white, male, Southern conservatism. Clinton's 'apostasy' (Clinton's word) was, according to O'Toole, 'breaking the rigid link between political ideology and ethnic identity'. In other words, Clinton turned his back on his own tribe. Coming from the South, Clinton experienced racial polarisation up close. He also studied the complex and liberating history of the civil rights movement. That background was the basis for Clinton's intellectual and emotional involvement with the issues of Northern Ireland and formed his belief that he might be able to play a productive role there. In his public comments throughout Ireland, Clinton tapped into the debilitating, but often psychologically comforting, dynamics of sectarian thinking. He asked the Irish people what they were willing to risk in a situation where the foundations of a spiritual life — the ability to allow both individuals and society to be transformed — were under tremendous pressure.

In Belfast, reflecting on the American Civil War, Clinton suggested that the beginning of reconciliation comes with a change of heart, but he acknowledged that there would always be those who could not psychologically let the bitter past become the past. In Armagh he told the crowd that by bringing people closer to each other they were also bringing them closer to God. And in Derry, referring to Brian Friel's play, *Philadelphia, Here I Come*, he asked that those in favour of peace sustain the faith and courage to 'leave one way of life behind in search of another'. He was either observing, or hoping for, a whole society's conversion.

One of Clinton's heroes, Martin Luther King Jr, knew about the liberating potential and the perils of crossing boundaries. His non-violent philosophy and his admonition to 'love our white brothers' did not mean that conflict was to be avoided. King knew that conflict could be clarifying and that the demands of love were also inextricably linked with the demands of justice. Central to King's view was that the end-product of violence was not social liberation or the promised land of revolution achieved by any means necessary, but that there was a critical psychological and political connection between means and ends.

It is not surprising then, that the Catholic civil rights campaign that emerged in Northern Ireland in the late 1960s was profoundly influenced by the theology that was embodied in King's life. King knew that means became ends and that the likely outcome of even the defensive violence being advocated by militant blacks would be defeat, dis-enchantment and the same squalor and deprivation. Influenced by the Protestant theologian Reinhold Niebuhr, King embraced the ideas of non-violent coercion and the spiritual discipline against resentment. Niebuhr made a distinction between the 'evils of a social system and the individuals who are involved in it'. On the practical side, Niebuhr believed that non-violent politics undermined the opponents' moral conceit that their interests were also identical to the interests of peace and order in society. King always insisted that the deep fissures of society could be overcome only by recognising your adversary's humanity and by renouncing the privileged status of victims. 'We must not let the fact that we are victims of injustice lull us into abrogating responsibility for our own lives,' King said.

Sectarian thinking is the antithesis of Niebuhr's and King's approach. In the sectarian mind there are no complex social systems; there are only groups, those who are trying to preserve or achieve good — 'us' — and those who pursue or embody evil and oppression — 'them'. To the sectarian, there is no opening for reconciliation or compromise; there is only victory or defeat. And there is only one victim — the self, never the other. It's a simplified schematic, but in the context of Northern Ireland the dynamic is all too apparent.

During my six years of reporting on Northern Ireland, I have seen the sectarian mind at work up close. In Derry, a Catholic activist sug-gested to me, straightfaced, that he could 'smell a Protestant'. While covering the Orange marches in Portadown, two Protestants, Victor and Angela, who had driven from Larne to support the right to march, explained to me that Catholics were a 'dirty tribe' and demanded to know why the United States was 'subsidising those bastards'. When I asked Victor what he did as a member of the Orange Order he laugh-ingly said, 'We hate Catholics.' What was particularly surprising was that he knew I was a reporter.

And a few hours after Clinton told eight thousand people at a new Belfast arena, in his last speech in Ireland as President, that 'you cannot be lifted up by putting your neighbour down', I sat in the Europa Hotel and watched a small gesture of reconciliation almost turn into violence. A Catholic 'nationalist' friend I was with was so impressed that a 'Protestant guy' bought him a beer at the bar that he wanted to sit down with him and his companions to talk. But when one of the Protestant's friends heard a Catholic name and a Republic of Ireland accent, a series of threats were made, followed by the rapid approach of the hotel staff, who proceeded to remove our erstwhile friends into the Belfast night. If they had not intervened, some physical violence would have occurred. On their way out, one of them told us to 'say hello to Veronica', a reference to Dublin journalist Veronica Guerin who was murdered by drug dealers involved with loyalist paramilitaries.

Later that evening, in an unrelated conversation, I asked my friend about someone he had introduced me to the night before and why he had spent eight years in Long Kesh prison. He explained that he had 'stiffed two Brits in a gun battle in Belfast'. We had talked for a long time before the altercation with the group of Protestants about the toxic impulses of sectarianism, a trait he insinuated was predominantly Protestant/Unionist, not Catholic/Nationalist. But after the altercation, in perhaps an act of unconscious bravado, the language became Orwellian. Individual human beings were transformed into collective 'Brits', and the taking of a life was made as easy as making someone a 'stiff'.

I'm not an optimistic man by nature, if optimism means embracing the facile dogmas of progress. But I do remember feeling a combination of hope and pride when I was driving towards the west of Ireland and a reporter on the radio announced the vote on the Good Friday Peace Agreement. My hope was for the people of Northern Ireland and the pride was for the rôle that the United States had played in pushing the process forward. I was with some non-political Irish friends from Dublin who didn't seemed as moved as I was, perhaps exhausted into numbness by twenty-five years of unremitting tragedy. Faith that things could fundamentally change was not part of their experience.

I also knew that this was just the beginning, and that the Good Friday Agreement was vague enough to gain endorsement by the pro-agreement parties. The difficult part would be filling in the details. But the agreement and the institutions set up under it acknowledged some profound realities. In the elaborate checks and balances of the Assembly structure, the group mentality was accounted for — both politically empowered and restrained, making sure neither community dominated the other. More importantly, there was an implicit recognition of the legitimacy of sharing power with those who had previously been demonised.

Radicals have always claimed they were advocates of alleviating root causes of oppression and conflict. For Republicans, partition and the British presence have been the problem. For extreme Unionists, the unwillingness of Republicans to accept their legitimate desire to remain part of Britain or repudiate violence has been key.

When I watched the day-to-day workings of the new Stormont Assembly — as a reporter and an outsider — I concluded that in the context of Northern Ireland, the mundane workings of government and the tedious grind of compromise and negotiation were what was radical. For democratic politics involves self-restraint and responsibility, qualities that sectarians seem to be lacking.

What I observed in my six years of travelling to Northern Ireland was a paradox. I met many people who justified the all too familiar brutalities with denial, rationalisation and history's sanction. Their spirits and hearts had become like one of Yeats's stones. And the dry material institutions of politics were infused with an animating spirit that seemed to represent, in Seamus Heaney's phrase 'a cure you didn't notice happening'.

I came to Northern Ireland looking for stories of individuals and communities, any avenue into the intimacies of Northern Ireland that could make concrete the abstractions of political rhetoric. I found the formal processes of elections and legislation, but I also heard the stories that the different communities told about themselves and the other. These truths are what supply a coherent narrative, a pattern to the seeming randomness of events. I believe the spiritual narratives of Northern Ireland are gradually changing and that each community will have to surrender a part of the powerfully unifying myths that have sustained twenty-five years of 'life waste and spirit waste'.

Politics is surely about positioning, advantage, group interest and power. But spiritual leaders like King operated on an additional level. In death, we now regard him as a visionary, somewhat tamed, but with the ability to see beyond the immediacy of the present and with the courage to risk challenging his followers. King knew that 'the evil in the foe is also in the self', and that the minutia of everyday life is where the most profound changes in society are reflected. There are leaders in Northern Ireland who understand this.

American civil rights activists have commented that when they eventually saw blacks and whites in the same hotel swimming pools, or when they observed a white waiter serve coffee to or casually light a black man's cigarette, was when they knew that the deeper meaning of their movement was taking hold. Exchanges of basic human decency between the races were no longer commented upon because they were no longer seen. They were simply taken for granted. When I left Northern Ireland after Clinton's last visit, I wondered how long it would take until a Protestant buying a Catholic a beer in a bar would not be worthy of mention.

That Realm Untenanted

Maighread Medbh

Maighread Medbh (maighreadmedbh@eircom.net) was born in Newcastle West, County Limerick, and is the author of two books of poetry: The Making of a Pagan *(Blackstaff Press), an autobiographical sequence plotting the development from womb through self-discovery to socio-political awareness and re-inventing of the self, and* Tenant *(Salmon Publishing), a narrative sequence following the fate of a fictitious Irish family during the years of the Great Famine. She wonders if one can write at all without touching on what many people call spirituality, but what she would call physical and psychic connectedness.*

In the first act of *Waiting for Godot*, Estragon asks for a carrot, but Vladimir gives him a turnip instead, which he doesn't like. After a search, Vladimir finds one carrot in his pocket and exhorts Estragon to make it last, as it is the end of them. In the second act, Vladimir produces nothing but turnips and a black radish and, as Estragon likes neither, he has nothing to eat.

If ever there was an allegory for hunger, it's this play. A tree, a country road, evening. Two men waiting for an eleventh-hour redemption that promises and does not come. They have no power, no will to act, nothing can be done. The state of starvation is a type of paralysis. You are too weak to save yourself from the rapid careering towards death, and obviously, even when you were strong, you were not in a position to save yourself from stepping onto the slope. This is Beckett writing from his creative perch on, as he once described Ireland, 'the last ditch of Europe'.

That Realm Untenanted

I was no stranger to ditches where I grew up on the outskirts of Newcastle West. My father was a labourer with Limerick County Council. We had very little money, but we were never hungry. My father dressed well on his days off, and my mother made sure that the house was well-kept and the children clean and warm. I had a new coat every winter. We would have denied poverty and never considered ourselves members of the working class. We had books and the intellectual confidence that comes from being academic achievers. With that confidence, though, was coupled a kind of fear. As long as we continued to achieve academically, we were guaranteed acceptance in society's various institutions. If we stopped, we had no fallback because we were economic and social mavericks, belonging neither with the poor nor the rich, neither farmers nor townies. To confound things, our home life was turbulent and isolated. The institutions became our greatest friends because they gave us a definite place and recognised our potential.

Education saved us from the will-less condition of the poor, but we were always only a slip away from it. It may have been some consciousness of this that made me ashamed of my origins for at least ten years after I had left home. Poverty, instead of radicalising you, can keep you conservative through its state of desire. The minute the single mother of two in a small council flat identifies with the society queen of a television soap, her enslavement is secured. I was a lot like that.

Only some of my poverty was economic. Mostly it was emotional. But its history was economic. My father had experienced hunger. He had grown up in an earlier and even rawer version of Frank McCourt's Limerick, in an area of abject deprivation, where his mother, the story goes, once had to sell pots and pans to the neighbours in order to buy food. When his fifteen-year-old sister died of consumption, his father carried her body to the cemetery on his shoulders. My father knew all about the various shades of want.

When I began to explore the subject of the Famine, I didn't immediately make these connections. My first feeling was exclusion. I like to delve beneath the skin of my subject and find the part of me that relates to it. 'Method Writing', others have called it. But with the Famine, I doubted that I could find a connection. After all, I had never been hungry or seriously deprived. One of my deprivations was itself a barrier: the fact that I had never had a sense of belonging to a community. The average Irish community of the early 1800s was a heaving, bouncing, careering animal of several symbiotic parts. The people were 'ar scáth a chéile'; one person's good fortune was everybody's, one person's need was everybody's. In the teeming rural villages, people lived a higgledy consortium of immediate and urgent close relationships, startlingly like aspects of inner-city life today. But I lived in a post-Famine, consumer-orientated Ireland of scattered rural dwellings, closed doors and reticence. Where was the possibility of empathy? I even had insufficient knowledge of the Irish language to comprehend their mindset, the labyrinthine psychic echoes that are corollary to language. I had little knowledge of farming. I wasn't sure that I was the right person to undertake this task at all, until I broadened my concept of history.

It is almost impossible for a serious poet to ignore history. When you look for subjects, or even for resonances and contexts, your most immediate store is your own past, and that past is entwined with and sculpted by the pasts of several others. What Irish child has not heard of the Famine by the age of seven? What Irish child is not aware of world famines? What Irish child has not listened to her mother's dissertations on the starving children in the world and their relevance to her own uneaten and wasted porridge? When visitors call, it is ingrained in us to offer them tea and food in the first five minutes for fear of being thought stingy.

While travelling with my brother once, I stayed in the family home of a casual friend of his in Clare. I was fed a large meal when we arrived at around nine in the evening, a mammoth fry-up at nine the following morning, and an epic dinner at one o'clock. I could hardly waddle my way out the door, such was the hospitality they demanded of themselves, and such the appreciation they expected of their guests. An ex-priest's house-keeper of West Cork provenance, who lived in a flat downstairs from me in Cork city, adored Bishop Casey because he was 'lovely and fat'. It must have made her feel that the country was getting somewhere if its natives could afford rotundity. She herself was bony as a bird. Whatever your disposition, your historical connections abide with you like the down on your skin, unshiftable.

Eavan Boland has described a stronger sense of exclusion than mine in her book, *Object Lessons*. She had not even grown up in Ireland, and, to cap it all, one of her ancestors had been the Master of a Workhouse in the 1800s, on the privileged side of the bóithrín, as it were. But then, which of us who walk now on this soil is not privileged — descended from the survivors, the lucky or better-off who did not emigrate and did not have to die? The dead and expatriated embodied the last vestige of a distinct native Ireland in their poverty-devilled lives. With them expired any hope of reinstating Irish as the first national language, as did the ancient system of land-ownership called 'rundale', with its complex determination of rights, its pre-industrial flexibility. By surviving, I could be said to share in some of the guilt of the oppressor, more so because I accept the system that made space for itself by wiping out the human resistance.

Eavan Boland stood her ground and claimed her territory. Her right to be a poet for this country did not need to be won. It was ancestral and made sweet by noble intention. Regardless of her socio-economic background, she could take an individual stance in the present, applying honesty to all of the conflicting issues. In one of her poems, 'That the Science of Cartography is Limited', she addresses herself to one of life's casual lies, evocative because it is very close to the truth — the lie behind the map. She remembers standing on an overgrown Famine road, one of those built under the Relief Works and left unfinished, and comments that, although the road is a physical and historical reality, the map does not show it. Even if it did, the flat representation of the landscape could not communicate the story of the people who have lived in it.

My feeling of inadequacy, in retrospect, was exactly the tool I needed in order to look at the Famine period. It was a direct legacy of it.

At the time, my dilemma ended in this logic: that I was Irish — however inadequately or impurely — and that I understood other types of hunger, such as loneliness, hopelessness, loss of faith, desire. That I walked the soil, that my ancestors had also used the ground of this country as their basic support. The objective facts of the Famine story could be read in a dewfall of history books, but the emotional memory must reside in the earth. I literally asked the ground to be my guide, came from my own clumsily tilled life to divine the earth for some of its secrets. I began the first poem:

> no matter how broken, the ground will transport me.

And I think it did.

Exploring the period of the Famine revived my relationship with the West Limerick countryside. The characters in the story had to have somewhere to live, so I placed them where I knew best. I re-discovered my love of the county's simple lilting greens, the cosseting demeanour of the roadside hedges and trees. I was alleviating my own hunger for identity.

It is difficult to pinpoint exact causes for social and cultural trends. At any given time, a multitude of events are taking place, all of which have been dominoed by previous circumstances. The psychological devastation described in Patrick Kavanagh's poem, 'The Great Hunger', was the diurnal legacy of the rural upheavals of the eighteenth century and the post-Famine phenomena of larger farms, sole inheritance by the eldest son and general depopulation. Religion is the last refuge of the deprived, diminishing in importance as a society gains more control over its economic life. I don't believe that it was the driving force behind the type of deprivation suffered by Kavanagh's character. I consider it the whip and not the hand. The real oppressor was a nation's fear in the face of its own independence, its desire to perform, and the very real spectre of penury. After all, Kavanagh's Ireland still remembered a time when obtaining sufficient food was a daily worry.

Ironically, the flesh that was so scarce in the early 1800s became the moral stalker of the following century. In order to survive, you now had to mortify and deny the flesh without the release of early marriage and the wild, salving social interactions that had featured in previous generations. You have only to look on William Carleton's *Traits and Stories of Irish Peasantry* for evidence of the social sanities of the early 1800s. Eithne Strong's character, Nance, in 'Flesh is the Greatest Sin', is in some ways the female counterpart of Kavanagh's Patrick Maguire. For Nance, natural body growth, which had been stunted in a previous century, is a dangerous corrupter.

On another level, what we know and have experienced as Catholic guilt may be a distorted remnant of shamanism. Listening to the environment, denying oneself certain loved things, suffering pain, may be ways of settling universal scores or increasing the potential of the mind, and fasting is a time-honoured route to spiritual enlightenment. Interestingly, John F. Deane has returned to the idea of suffering as ecstasy in his collection *Toccata and Fugue*. Seamus Heaney repeatedly conveys a sense of duty to the environment and to society, and the concomitant restraint. It is the tension between desire and restraint that opens his 'door into the dark'.

While starvation is the ultimate powerlessness and the antithesis of survival, hunger strike is a remarkable vehicle for gaining political clout. It is entirely disarming. The spectacle of a human being who is wasting away physically for the sake of an ideal is one that approaches the godly. The hunger strike, an ancient Irish form of protest, found a ritual expression in 1981, when ten men, in utter discipline, fasted to their deaths in a Northern Ireland jail. The way in which the fasts began, staggered as they were, felt like a silent procession up to a great door, one man standing to the side as the next was presented. This was the door of institutional justice, but became a door into the dark, a dark that the men seemed to illuminate as they entered. It was, for me, one of the most profoundly affecting periods of the Northern Irish conflict, and one that, when remembered, arouses feelings of admiration, annoyance and guilt.

Starvation always possesses an accusatory quality, whether it is in the face of a Kenyan woman who glares at the camera lens, or in the emaciated appearance of Lavinia Kerwick, whose anorexia seemed to me to be a form of rage against a system that would send the man who raped her back onto the streets before she had had a chance to recover. In Katie Donovan's poem, 'Strike', the aggrieved hunger striker will feed her community with the remains of her body. Her physical disintegration will give life to her sense of justice, will give flesh to her ideal.

A fasting person may deepen my faith in human transcendence; the first images I saw of early nineteenth-century Famine victims sent me into denial. I still remember the moment. It was in school, and I may have been around eight. I opened a page of my history book and saw a drawing of a starving woman and her child. Until then I had been under the impression that only black people died of hunger, and the only black people I had ever seen were small faces on the sides of charity boxes. They were black babies, half-toy, half-human, who lived in some land suspended between fantasy and the earth. Looking back, I amaze myself with the efficiency that I deployed in blocking all reaction to the picture. But when I sat down to write a poem called 'Easter 1995 — Hunger', it was the first image that returned.

> ... a woman and her daughter in a history book,
> their bones pointing out from their flesh.
> They weren't even black.
>
> And I don't want to see my face,
> I don't want to stroke the bones of my disgrace.
> That I could be the one to die
> that I'd not have the power to destroy ...

We have been reticent. In 1945, one hundred years after the Famine, there were no commemorations. We had to wait for more national confidence before we could look at it straight. Many communities around the country had had a culture of silence on the subject. Some old sores still ran, such as those connected with souperism in the west, where some Catholics took the soup the Protestants offered in return for their conversion to Protestantism. Nuala Ní Dhomhnaill in 'Plutonium' refers to this, and to 'radachur núicleach na staire', translated as 'the radioactive/Rain of History'. But in the past ten years we have been able to avoid little of the poisoned smoke of memory, the society turning inside out, vomiting up whatever has been sickening it. In 1995, one hundred and fifty years after the Famine, the whole country remembered, from every local library to a national commemoration in Millstreet, County Cork. We could finally voice our anger and pain.

Now that we have some national economic power, we no longer need to make a virtue of suffering; our children eschew suffering altogether. It hardly seems possible to write such a poem as John Swanwick Drennan's 'When Famine Was Sore in the Land', where redemption is seen as the flip side of destitution:

> And, lighted thus, misfortune shows
> The purpose of her earthly woes
> Pointing a meaning for our woes
> In every virtue they evoke.

We still take pessimistic stances though, as if we had a fear of returning to the dark days, as if we still weren't sure of our right to joy. I think we have that right, although it has taken me a while to reach that conclusion. I used to think that I couldn't be happy while somebody starved in the world.

Recently I did a reading where I looked at the work of Michael Hartnett, a poet who addressed the dark imagination if anyone ever did. I concentrated on his dark side, but found myself finally dissatisfied that I hadn't lightened the mood before I left the stage because the audience seemed to have lost energy, and so had I. The Irish tend to take sadness on board like water through a leaking hold.

Michael Hartnett walked his life with the mantle of the dispossessed poets of the seventeenth century on his back. While you can produce great art that way, I think you can also create great art in celebration. But then, if we didn't feel some lack, we might not speak at all. Our lack of political and economic power tuned us to produce a panorama of song. Existence itself is an odd number, is desire. There's a joke that goes like this: A man walks into a café and asks for coffee without cream. 'I'm sorry,' says the waiter, 'We have no cream; you'll have to take it without milk.'

Which hunger is it that moves you?

God the Father and the Empty House

❧

Linda McCarriston

A native of Lynn, Massachusetts, Linda McCarriston holds dual Irish/US citizenship. When she resumed writing poems in her mid-thirties, her work began to be published widely. Her first two books, Talking Soft Dutch *(Texas Tech Press) and* Eva-Mary *(TriQuarterly/Northwestern University Press) were both award-winners, the second a finalist for the National Book Award in the US. Her most recent collection,* Little River, *was published by Salmon Publishing in 2000. The mother of two grown sons, she teaches at the University of Alaska in Anchorage.*

Like her Daily Missal, they were gifts from my brother in seminary. Everything was justified by his studying for the priesthood: my mother's return to work wrapping meat in the market, my coming home alone afternoons to my father, who'd been drinking since the end of his midnight to eight a.m. shift, minding boilers at Amoco.

The two pressed profiles, each about the size of a hand, had compelled me since childhood: Sacred Heart and Blessed Mother, both with hearts thorn-encircled and flame-crowned. Wherever we lived, my mother arranged them with Jesus' face above and to the right of Mary's — superior and inferior, God and God's mother — for arranged facing each other, they could represent the unthinkable, Mother and Father God.

From a blue-collar family in a gritty immigrant city north of Boston, I went to Catholic grammar school, high school, and college, all designed to transform shanty Irish girls like me into marketable wives for Boston College boys. I call it my 'education in ignorance', and by graduation in 1965, I'd become the desired Catholic female product: a Diehard Battery looking for a life to power. All the sharp-edged ideas and practices that might have fostered ambition, autonomy, activism had been securely locked up in the Index of Forbidden Books. Dangerous for a girl, Marx and Freud, de Beauvoir. Especially dangerous for a poor girl with more than a nubbin of a brain, who had gotten the shit kicked out of her on a regular basis (including the sexual shit), and watched her mother, brother and dog likewise mortally threatened on a regular basis. Dangerous for her who'd observed what the priests, the doctors, the judges, the cops advised: Obey.

When I first met 'spirituality', in my late thirties, the word had its work cut out. It blossomed from the esoteric meadows of self-affirmation movements from which I could not have been more culturally estranged. Healing of injuries other than crude muscle and bone was new, as were self-realisation and human potential. This vocabulary beckoned to me from a crowd that made art and made love out of an ingredient that never flowed abundantly from the tap in my own kitchen: money. The closest I came to any of this was in my wood-fired automobile called religion.

I'd been long gone from the practice of Roman Catholicism, though I'd pitted myself against the anguish of my life trying to make it better by my own goodness, aspiring to sanctity, offering it up: First Fridays, the rosary, scapulae and the Stations of the Cross, my mother grey-faced in an arm-lock dragged backwards into their bedroom with his 'get her out of here' hissing into the kitchen and her attempt to keep a level voice and expression, telling me to go outside and play. My brother's hands gripping the inside of the third-floor window-frame, his knees barely hitched over the sill, his upper body dark out over the sidewalk, our father kicking at the knees, prying at the fingers, until I call him off and he hauls the boy back, knocking him backwards to the floor, straddling him with his hard beer gut, the ram he'd batter me with first, then unscrewing the Lucky Strike from his mouth to grind it down at his son's eye. My dog's dim rattle behind the bathroom door, after school, my opening the door to blood up to the top of the tongue-in-groove, pooled on the floor, spattered on the sink, the washer, mirror, everywhere signs of the struggle, the dog's terror-chatter in there between the tub and the corner, his tail stub tied in a rag, the long knife blood-sheathed dangling from the man's hand as he sat on the hopper, himself soaked in blood, wanting a dog that looked classier, making of the found mutt a member of the family more surely than any legal papers could.

There was no help for us because there was no help for any women and children like us, over the whole globe. A story such as Michael Collins's 'The Rain in Kilrush' draws a nightmare domestic world that is figurative and global as well as literal and local. Though the most recent wave of international feminism has made a dent in the scale of un-written male prerogative, Father remains the authority by which the parent or the prelate commits intimate crime. Father remains that very idea of order. Physically wounded and mentally duped, where does the child of such ideas begin to recover spirituality?

For me, the start was poetry. What else ever had been my own? Not my body, not my children, not my bed or my schoolroom, or confessional. Feelings had long been a luxury I couldn't afford. What I needed if I was to regain my soul was a field of ideas and language big enough to contain both the orthodoxy called Father and the shadow-realm cast by it, in which existed the Child of God who I knew myself to be.

Father did not speak for me. His speech in fact required that I and the shadow-realm did not exist. His utterance created that void and sustained it. Until I could make that space real in his language, words from it must remain 'backtalk', 'lip', insubordination.

It was to poetry that I brought that task, though the dilemma be-deviled me from the most quotidian of gendered exchanges to the depths of dreams. In these, over the years of this obsession, abstract patterns spiralled into abstract clarifications that defied even the language of the poem. Two opposing paradigms, both manifest in the same metaphor and icon — sexuality — they differed in only the conceptual arrangement of the requisite couple: horizontally or vertically: equally or inequally; justly or unjustly; 'The opposite of patriarchy isn't matriarchy,' Germaine Greer asserts on Sinéad O'Connor's CD, *Universal Mother*, 'it's fraternity,' the simplest and most elusive of conceptual shifts.

When I enrolled in an academic poetry programme, however, after years of not writing, carrying the consciousness of this dilemma, I found the field of intellectual inquiry there even more strenuously constrained than in the culture at large. As nowhere else, the United States defines art as that which marks the furthest reach from political social conscious-ness. A radical, atomising individualism, requisite for our upwardly mobile consumerist identity, finds its perfection in our modern and post-modern 'high end' poetry. In the name of such lyric primacy, idea languishes, because discourse languishes. In the name of lyric primacy, the voice arising from the shadow-realm, my voice, say, the voice of the fully ensouled child of God, lyric's fellow and answer, judge of and judged by, is cast beneath lyric's feet. American poetry's analogy for the Roman Catholic Church's dispatch of the female principle is the dispatch of the bardic principle. American poetry provides, in its lines, no just access to its lords. The bardic idea and witness are disdained as insubordinations.

How had these essential dyads — sex, parenthood, speech — come to mean the one standing over the other, a sword raised and a foot resting on the silent body? How had we, how had I, taken as the wafer of mystery this slick synecdoche in all its forms: Whole, the Half?

A dozen writing years later, the question was still alive. My mother, who would live another ten years, was seeing me off at Boston's Logan Airport, shaking her head, unable to fathom my intention to travel alone to Ireland and godknowswhat of a history that, with my father dead, was best left behind and forgotten. Why, the first in the family to return, did I feel I had left something someplace I'd never been? I would have told her if I could. A few years sober, I was guided by what seemed to be vestiges of a soul — a worn-down, faceless topography, but verified as authentic among countless other women likewise extricating them-selves from what Jung called 'a disease of the spirit'. To a woman, we had located the religious mystery in which we were raised and in which, walking deeper and deeper into alcoholism, we continued to seek goodness in self-abnegation. To a woman, we had brought to this effort bodies dazed by decades of abuse, most of it legitimised by Church and state, abuse we'd learned was our own fault anyway.

How striking to look back at those many lives in the acid-bath belly of the beast and remember how difficult it was to see our condition as warranting resistance. A mystery was, after all, God's unfathomable way. Years steeped in dogma such as Virgin Birth laid the conceptual foundation for the most gratuitous sleight of hand. Most of mystery, we had learned, flowed from the font of sexuality: the flesh of birth and death framed the central, empty pane of it in the Catholic triptych. Most of heresy, we began to see, was the reassertion of such blacked-out text. The world, the flesh, and the devil might have been the dangers from which the female was best sequestered, but the big risk for Fathers, we perceived in retrospect, lay in the consequence of exposure to these: spiritual custody of oneself.

Could we have lost our spirits if we'd kept our minds, we wondered? Could we have lost our minds if we'd kept our spirits? If our bodies' right to knowledge other than pain and degradation had not been denied, would we have lost the other two at all?

From Boston to the Liscannor Vat, therefore, in as straight a line as I could, I travelled to a well sacred to Brigid, about whom I knew almost nothing. A part of the material out of which I'd begun to rebuild a faith, she was patroness of poetry, smithcraft, healing. In someone else's guidebook I'd read the name, the place, a calendar of ritual. With the help of some Catholic women thinkers, I'd scraped away what felt like centuries of ash and manure to get here, whatever that was. Water. Its steady, private pulse. No middleman. No man. Fuchsia. Ivy. The dead.

Down behind a framed picture of the Sacred Heart I stuff a copy of my first book of poems, in gratitude and a slow-fermenting amazement. I inscribe it, 'To My Mother. From Her Daughter'. I know I am in the presence of what my lifetime of churches — of men in dresses and flowers in vases — have blacked out like the flesh-sex of the middle panel. In my hand is the manuscript of the second book, from which the publishers of my first, lyric poems have turned away. These poems relive the sanctified violence of my childhood. These poems utter that violence not in the lyric frame — not to arrive at forgiveness as a collision that transcends, not to present exquisite feelings exquisitely wounded, not to whisper lamentations to the likewise entrapped — but in the voice of one who judges the judge. With no name yet for this posture of address, for there is no name for it in the United States lyric tradition, I have invented the ancient public, Irish bardic mode, from necessity. 'Your Honour, when my mother stood before you,' the cornerstone poem begins, from the shadow realm, empowered, for the sake of the tribe, to speak to power as its equal.

'May these poems find their way powerfully into the world,' I implore, and kneel to drink from the water. It has been twenty-five years since I've entered any sort of tabernacle and uttered there any sort of prayer. It has been easily half again as long since I've expected anything good to come of it.

Outside the whitewashed arch of the passageway, the sky is kaleidoscopic greys shot through with bars of sidelong sunshine. Late autumn. There's no one around but me, and I know no one, have no family to find, no history to flesh out. My pilgrimage is accomplished. Ascending the steps to the road, I notice across it a pillar raised on a grand base, itself raised on a sizable bulwark. Both corners face the bay. I turn to close the small gate, a gesture of a gate, and listen a final time down the low, dark vault to the ancient trickle of water through slate.

For the rest, I wandered in my rental car over a small area of Clare and Mayo, pulling off the roads to walk in old churchyards, ruins and headlands, the Burren or Carrowmore, an ageing woman tourist caught on the outside of the Plexiglas screen that circles the real world. I felt as I travelled on ever more strongly that I was wasting time and money to follow a cornsilk-like tendril of question. Returning to the States, I felt I'd failed. Except for the well, I had nothing of the riches that other writers take from such journeys.

But messages had been blinking red on the phone for days before I returned. Two publishers wanted the poems that had boiled, unwritten, in me for ten years, and had boiled written, hidden in a drawer, another five. They were about to find their way powerfully into the world.

When was it that the iconography of the crumbling church grave-yards of the west of Ireland began to assert itself in my mind? Out of the palpable, dimensional landscape of my failure, the things I didn't do or see or understand, the places I didn't know enough to look for, rose ever more relentlessly the images of the Young Woman Mary and the Young Man Jesus, beautiful, a gaze balanced between them. I remembered their faces, framed large and small, crisp or faded, at the well. I saw them standing life-sized on graves, near one another, com-posed of the same stone, arms opened in the same angle, the same gesture, hearts aflame, thorn-circled.

These were not the images to which I was accustomed in these settings back home: the crucifix dominating ecclesiastical space, the son's body hanging by the gouges that lengthen as the hours do, with his weight. Thorns pounded into his head, his shoulders slashed and bleeding, the whips' signs, the almost auditory memory of the soldiers' malice. And where was the Pietà, that child again, dead across the lap of his crushed mother, the father — author and agent of all — absent, above, invisible?

Not long before my mother's death I was again in Ireland. It was a time when the predation of adults — males, with rare exceptions — on children was becoming a public subject. A painful subject. A subject still well beyond the willingness of most to entertain: savage stories that depend upon a secret but profoundly powerful prerogative long-protected in organisations world-wide as 'man–boy love' and 'father–daughter love' — sexual tourism and the child sex slavery it requires. In Clare, I listen to stories of how children, both boys and girls, were given to the visiting lord for the night. I hear the story of the pillar near Brigid's Well. Cornelius O'Brien, MP, son of Sir Turlough, renowned for improving his district, erected the ornament in his honour on the occasion of the birth of his hundredth child. Funds for the pillar were raised — extorted — from his tenants, just as those children had been.

Who do we think we are kidding when we insist that the human rights of women and children have been secured? In whose interest are the assertions that prerogatives so recently exercised as to create demands in the minds of living men have in fact been banished: property rights to women and children; rights to administer corporal punishment, rights to withhold or to dispense the basic needs of life? And how dare we, any of us, grow impatient with being forced to know of the intimate savagery with which our social and religious structures are hard-wired? How do any of us manage to set aside from the idea and practice of spirit this shaping root, this human paradigm?

One story from that summer will stay with me forever. *The Irish Times* courageously told it without euphemism. You may remember the little girl who had been routinely raped by her father, silenced by the textbook demonic threats, most rapaciously trashed by him at those times when her mother was in hospital delivering a new child to his hands. She had found a throw-away puppy and begged him to allow her to keep it. If she would submit without a peep to being sodomised by him, she might, he told her. Not only, of course, would such a puppy be probably the only gift her heart might treasure, and the only way in which she might exercise a tiny fragment of humanity in her world, or interrupt a loneliness and isolation so savage it carries a soul-sound like high wind at sea, but of course she would know that if she did not keep the puppy, it might be lost as she was lost. She was found, days later, hiding in a wheelbarrow in a barn, her puppy in her arms.

The last years of my mother's life, the Blessed Mother and the Sacred Heart remained on a wall in her dinette area. He still looked out over Her head blankly, and She gazed across into the space below Him. Not once ever had I offered to rearrange them, knowing my mother's response would be either fear of divine retribution or, in the converse mood and mode, contempt for the erotic idea. Yet I know that between those poles and along that declared axis was worn a figurative path as deep as that cut into stone across the American prairies. I watched her pace it in the small rooms of our lives together, and even when he was gone, she paced it out of habit and the unsatisfied desire to understand. The estranging placement of those icons was perhaps for her as much a woman's refusal of male privilege as it was a submission to the fact of it. In any case, I am sure it was for my battered, meat-wrapping, barely educated mother, last of sixteen children, a statement of idea, the best she could do under the circumstances.

How deep, how tenacious, how structural and invisible is this idea? How do others know and experience it? Do they know and experience it? How might such a question be asked? How might I have asked my mother? What percentage of people would exist on the planet today if women could not conceive unless they experienced orgasm?

What a wild encyclopaedia of responses! None, some will answer, with rue or sadness. Not many! Most respondents will laugh. Not me, I bet. Not my kids, too often. Why, all of them, of course! an occasional quick-witted man will retort, treating it perhaps as an interview question.

What a range of insights into the world we have made — of child rape and infibulation and the assumptions of the differences between female and male preconditions and capacities for gratifying sex — and the world as it might be, or have been: safety, autonomy, identity as conditions a woman brings to sex instead of entering sex to attain them.

Behind the sheerest scrim of Rome, of Roman Law and Roman Catholicism's property rights to women, resides the old principle of the bride and bridegroom. In these images of the lovers, in their gaze, which is neither the Pietà nor the Crucifix turning tables on the Father — flinging him to the bottom to raise up the Mother and Child in his stead — but the turning back of the vertical union to a just one, each blossoms into full half-ness and the longing for the other. The iconography of Christendom, of hierarchy, of autocracy, so at odds in fact with the words of the Christ, pales and fades in the graveyards, eradicable as graffiti across the old justice of sexuality: what we know about the position of women before the coming of Patrick. What I saw when an unprepared pilgrim was an idea of spirituality, an ancient New Idea, justice made flesh in the act of love.

Into the walls at the corner of my bedroom — in which are collected the numinous oak leaves and snake skins, horse chestnuts and chestnut tree chestnuts, and a few Hail Marys' worth of my mother's old rosary — I hammered two nails and arranged those plaques at the same level and close together, allowing, now that my mother and father were dead, the gaze to stream between them. A morning prayer to that towards which I'd started long ago and which now had its icon: Great Mother and Father, in your sweet embrace of desire, delight, and surprise, that brought me forth and brings me forth each morning....

Abuse: A Love Story

Lucy Dolores Moore

Lucy Dolores Moore is the pseudonym of an award-winning novelist from New York who lives part of the year in the west of Ireland. All the names in this memoir have been changed.

You might have seen him around Dublin. He's fifty and handsome — boyishly so, despite his thinning hair and thickening girth. He carries himself with an exuberant carefree vigour that makes people use words of him like 'magnetic' and 'charming'. He's massively intellectual, a real hound for information about anything and everything. His precise memory and his childlike delight in wordplay make conversation with him memorable. No, more than memorable: unforgettable.

And nice. 'Nicest man in Ireland,' the friend who introduced us assured me. Polite, attentive, concerned. Ever the gentleman. Never more than two drinks of an evening. Doesn't smoke. Not a bad habit in sight.

For three decades before his retirement to the countryside, he was a fixture at Dublin's political and cultural events. Pressed to run for office more than once, he instead devoted himself to industry, building his company into an international presence and making himself a tidy fortune in the process. Honours and offices, committees and awards — all were part of his life.

But not women.

He is the kind of man about whom you ask your friends, 'Why hasn't he been snapped up?' He was linked romantically with one woman, then another. He would squire them about, dance with them, travel with them. But he kept them at a distance.

I was a widow when we met. My marriage had been a classic love-match; five years after my darling's death I was lonely, but not looking. I wrote, I travelled, I taught. When I met the man I am describing — he has a common Irish name, so let's call him Seán — I found him engaging and intelligent. Our many shared interests brought us together and, after a time, I found myself opening up to him. And he opened up to me. He told me he had not shared his thoughts and feelings so deeply with anyone.

I came to depend upon him for companionship. Then, ever so slowly, I realised I was falling in love. But I did not speak of it, unsure of his feelings, aware of his lack of interest in romance. It was Seán who took the first step beyond friendship. When, shaking with emotion, he professed his love for me, I thought I would dissolve with joy. It was like opening a door to find it was suddenly spring. My life had been barren for so long, I had forgotten what happiness felt like. We were not lovers, not then; indeed, we had not even kissed when Seán told me he wanted to build a future with me. I was the one he had been waiting for, he said. We were destined for each other. He was glad he had waited, that he had not wasted himself on other women. I was swept away by Seán's devotion. He gave me a gold ring and declared us betrothed. We set off on a honeymoon to Connemara.

It was dreamily perfect, more perfect than I can bear to remember. I felt upheld and sustained by love. One night, I told him about my near-drowning as a girl and how frightened of water I remain. He responded with a tale of how he had once rescued a drowning man in the Liffey. As usual, his story was entertaining and dramatic, punctuated with imitations of bystanders; details about the time of day and the heavy traffic and the weather were woven in with amusing anecdotes about other watery near-disasters ... 'What,' I finally interrupted him, 'is this all about?'

Seán took my face tenderly between his palms. 'What I'm trying to tell you,' his voice was shaky, 'is that if I would do all that for a stranger, what would I do to save you, no matter how far out at sea you might be?'

That was the sort of thing he would say, words that would shake my soul with their tenderness and compassion and love. 'I have been thinking,' he said suddenly one evening, 'that I'm not afraid to die any more.'

'Whatever are you talking about?' I demanded, my widow's heart frozen with fear of another loss.

He shook his head. 'I'm fine, I'm fine. It's just that when I look at you, I know that any God who could make you has to be a good one, and I'm not afraid of going to Him.'

That time we spent together was the happiest I had been in years. We danced in the streets of Clifden while he sang in Irish. He chatted up a publican in Oughterard while I admired how readily he befriended strangers. We took the ferry to Inishbofin to spend a soft day there, and I slept with my head on his shoulder as we plied the waves back to Cleggan town. We had outrageously exuberant dinners with my friends, we walked hand-in-hand on the beaches, we heard music every night, everything was perfect.

No — not quite perfect. He was uneasy when it came to sex. Kissing, hugging, stroking, all those fine preliminaries, caused him no problems. But he was unable to have satisfying intercourse. He apologised profusely, continually, endlessly, blaming his age, his lack of experience, the long time since he'd been with a woman. To me, it was not a problem. I loved him; we would work things out.

All too soon our vacation ended. When we arrived at my cottage, Seán was unusually tired and went directly to bed. He slept deeply, so deeply it worried me. His body was leaden. He did not stir, not even to adjust his body to mine when I moved in the night. The next morning, he could not awaken. Fifteen hours in that coma-like sleep, and it was as though he had not slept a wink. He was exhausted and restless, unable to focus. He tried to read but nodded off over his book.

I asked him what was the matter. Was he ill? 'I dunno,' he shook his head. 'I just don't know.'

Seán went home. I did not hear from him for days. When I did, he was curt and distant, made excuses about his absence, would not say when we would see each other again.

My heart raced painfully. I understood he might have difficulty with the suddenness of our love, I told him, but I was willing to wait while he sorted things out. I twisted the gold Celtic-knot ring on my hand, our betrothal symbol, while I awaited his answer. Finally he said that he would call again the next day. He hung up without speaking a single tender word.

That was the beginning of the nightmare. When we saw each other, anything more than superficial chat provoked strange accusations and peculiar jokes. He grew wildly jealous of other men, claiming I rose late at night — after he phoned at eleven — to sneak out for secret assignations. He grew furious at the mention of a gay artist friend and denounced him as a probable rapist. He made frequent coarse comments and suspected that strangers we met on the street practised private perversions.

Sex became even more fraught with difficulty. He refused to see me naked, demanding that I keep my clothing on while we made love. He especially liked a long black dress, and when I wore it his lovemaking took on a disturbing intensity; he touched me in hurtful ways, his eyes empty, his face twisted. I kept hoping the nightmare would end, that our dreamy happiness would be given back to us. But things only got worse. One day Seán suddenly demanded, 'Were you sexually abused as a child?'

I was nonplussed. No one had ever suggested such a thing.

'You were,' he told me adamantly. 'I feel this very strongly. It's like a presence in this room. You were definitely sexually abused.' But he refused to discuss the subject more and left in haste.

If things were not easy when we were together, it was infinitely worse when we were apart. He was frequently incoherent when he called. He would announce plans to see me, then an hour later would cancel those plans. He would send me letters protesting that he was 'my 'lover', calling me 'precious', and then another would follow saying that he would never see me again. I fell into the darkest despair and left for America, my heart shattered.

Confused and exhausted and hurt, I went to see a friend who is a gifted psychoanalyst. Jane listened in her calm, attentive way while I unwound my tale. 'Did anything odd,' she asked, 'happen during the honeymoon?'

'Not a thing,' I said. 'We were blissfully happy.' Then I remembered the deep sleep, how strange it had seemed, how heavy his limbs had been, how he had been unable to waken.

'Was Seán sexually abused as a child?' Jane asked.

I was startled by her question. Seán described his childhood as idyllic, his family as loving and secure. But in mid-life he had suffered a complete physical collapse. When no physical reason for the ill-ness could be found, he was sent for psychological evaluation and told he had been 'interfered with sexually as a child', as he quaintly put it. But the diagnosis, he claimed, was in error. 'Everyone in Ireland has been sexually abused by a priest,' he claimed. 'If you believe the therapists. It's the flavour-of-the-month diagnosis.' In disgust, Seán had left the psychologist's office. His physical symptoms, he said, had instantly abated, his proof that the diagnosis was laughably incorrect.

Why was Jane suggesting the same possibility?

It was the deep, coma-like sleep that prompted her query. Many, if not most, abused children survive by splitting off portions of their psyches, escaping their abuser by disappearing down a rabbit-hole of consciousness. Dissociation, it is called, this tearing apart, this psychic dismemberment. The child endures the experience by vacating the premises. Once the psyche's integrity is breached, dissociative states can recur, especially under stress. When memories threaten to surface, a deep coma-like sleep often occurs.

'No one can say from a distance,' Jane ventured, 'but I suspect that the original diagnosis was correct. Seán may have repressed memories of abuse for most of his life. Being intimate with you caused the executive personality to lose its grip.' When Jane said that, I remembered another oddity of our honeymoon — the fact that, on our last day in Connemara, Seán had begun to lose things. Always an in-charge person, he became confused and obsessive when his sunglasses, his jacket, then his wallet, all unaccountably disappeared — losses that betokened a deeper loss, loss of that fierce control over his memories he had kept for a half-century.

Seán is probably not a multiple personality, a rare psychological mutation that can result from childhood trauma. In such extreme cases, separate personalities form that act autonomously of each other, each without the other's knowledge. Less rare — indeed, relatively common among victims of abuse — is the dissociation that Seán apparently suffers from. He buries his painful memories so deeply that they are not even available to his normal consciousness. Such a psychological strategy is effective until the hidden memories seep out. I do not know what happened the first time, what triggered his breakdown, but Seán is a strong, even wilful soul who responded with a 'flight into health', an apparent miracle resulting from the psyche's denial of distressing information. I was another such trigger for memory. Loving me — and I believe he did, perhaps still does, love me — Seán see-sawed back and forth between desire and desperate fear.

Many child victims are threatened with violence, even death, by their abusers. Their splintered personalities include, in addition to the silenced child-self, a fierce protector whose job it is to ensure that the truth is never spoken. Whether these forces are seen as individual personalities or as contending parts of the same personality, the results are the same. Seán could not directly share his inner pain with me, not only because he had spent fifty years keeping it from his own awareness, but because to speak the truth would put him in danger. So that mute silenced child spoke in the only way he could: Seán dressed me in black and attempted to rape me as he had been raped. I am saddened to realise that his violent assault may have been a dumb show of love, a signal of the depth of Seán's trust in me.

Seán must have been a lovely child — brilliant, eager to please, physically beautiful. There is still about him a radiance, a childlike buoyancy that is endearing. It is as though some part of him is frozen in time, always offering itself to the world as though perhaps, this time, he will not be hurt, will escape undamaged, will win freedom by his charm and his pleasantness and his delightful mind.

But he did not escape undamaged. He was hurt in ways I cannot begin to imagine, in ways he has not begun to heal. Seán told me that it had been the heartbreak of his life that he could not find a partner, that he wants more than anything to love and be loved. Yet intimacy endangers him; sexual joy weakens the vice-grip he has placed on his memories. When the horrors begin to leak out, he does not — cannot — recognise what is happening, so that when he lay in my arms that day and felt that someone in the room had been abused, he had to believe it was me.

I believe Seán's abuser was a priest: Seán's wild homophobia, his desire to have me dress in black while we made love, point in that direction. Fifty years ago, a man who had pledged himself to God had taken that small child's body and hurt it for his own pleasure. The rage I feel at that man is almost beyond expression. Not only that he used a child in that way — but that the child he raped grew up to be a man I loved, a man who cannot love me back without risking the destruction of his psychic defences against the pain of that memory.

Seán writes to me sometimes, still. Sometimes he expresses puzzlement at why we are apart, 'after the good times we had'. Sometimes he writes as though nothing painful ever happened between us. Sometimes he writes in what seems to be the voice of an eight-year-old. 'Are you mad at me?' he pleads, 'Was I so bad?' Only he writes 'bed' instead of 'bad', the memories still bleeding through. He writes self-justifying letters to friends, expressing his disappointment that I left Ireland abruptly, 'just because I had work conflicts and couldn't spend as much time with her as I wanted'. I do not write back. I do not know what to say.

I still sometimes wear the ring Seán gave me for our betrothal. My friends demand, 'You're *not* still in love with him?' and I cannot answer. I wish I could swim out to save him, the way he promised to swim out and save me, no matter how deep the waters, no matter how far from shore I had been carried. I wish I could undo the hurt, could offer that small boy the protection no one ever offered him, so that his little garments would never be lifted by that brutish hand.

But I cannot. Seán may live out his life as a celibate, keeping the vows of a man who broke them. Or perhaps he may collapse again, if the pressures from within grow too strong for his powerful will. Or, most horribly, he might harm himself, assuming the role of the punisher because he dared to pantomime his fearful truths. All of these possible stories are so sad that it pains me to write them. But a happy ending for Seán's life's story seems unlikely. Even with psychological help, these savaged children face hard lives as adults. Without it, they can survive, but never thrive.

How many men are there in Ireland like Seán, beautiful wronged beings who hurt others in order to protect themselves? How many women have been baffled and hurt by their intense love and swift rejection? How many children wonder over their father's rages and mood shifts? How many lives are lived without joy, because joy is such a strong solvent that the rigidly constructed outer personality dissolves and the terror reveals itself?

When I think of the pain Seán inflicted upon me, I shudder. If I could go backwards in time, knowing what I know now, would I refuse his dumb-show of pain, refuse to put on the black cassock-like dress, so that I would be spared the cruelty I endured? I think so. But then I think: perhaps someday that silenced child will remember that, once, he showed someone what happened, and that afterwards he was not hurt or maimed or killed. And perhaps then Seán will have the courage to seek the help he so desperately needs.

And the joyful times we spent: if I could unlive them, would I do so, in order to avoid the painful aftermath? Sometimes I think so. But more often I think — I pray — that it will ultimately have been worth it, that the memory of our honeymoon will rest in Seán's memory until one day, knowing himself capable of such delight, he will find the strength to fight past his demons and claim the happy life he so desires.

Irish Spirits

❈

Mary Teresa M

Mary Teresa M is the pseudonym of an Irish-American poet who has been in recovery from alcoholism and co-dependency for more than a decade. While her poetry does not centre around this subject, she draws strength for the creative struggle from the spirituality of recovery.

*F*riday, pay-day. We pull up to the rear entrance of the pub. The back of the pub is full of laughing men, relaxing after a hard week's work. The pubs like Ye Olde Mill Grill that dotted the neighbourhood were gathering places. The men were always good to me as I came in and sidled up to my father who loved me and knew what I wanted. I was always successful. He would not say the things to me he would say to my mother. Many of those men knew what was happening for they too did not go home until very late in the night. They too did not want to face their wives. They too could not deny their children. Those weekly rituals initiated me to the life that centres on the god, alcohol.

There were also the seasonal rituals. Ash Wednesday is the day you go to Monsignor O'Brien to take the pledge. For the forty days of Lent my father suffered from alcohol detoxification with its almost unbearable cravings as his penance and ours. His black mood lessened as Lent progressed. But the tensions of Holy Week in our home were thick, as his demon chased him into submission and our hopes plunged into despair. On Easter Sunday he would rise like the Lord Jesus, in an ecstasy like Saint Teresa, surrendered at last to his lover. And a whole predictable cycle would begin of drinking and family problems arising from drinking.

My father died of cirrhosis when I was twenty-one years old. His mental functions had deteriorated. In his last years he suffered from alcoholic dementia and delusions that produced erratic and bizarre behaviours, as if his own spirit had been stolen from him and a counterfeit walked around in his skin. At his last admittance to the hospital before he began slipping in and out of coma, with blood drooling from his mouth, he yelled at me, 'You and your mother are lying to the doctors again, telling them I have a drinking problem. I can stop any time I want to.' Indeed he could. He stopped many times. He just couldn't stay stopped.

We were a small family of five — my father, my mother, my brother, myself and alcohol. We lived in an Irish-American community saturated with feastdays, weddings and funerals, celebrated with alcohol. We told jokes on ourselves. 'Whenever you meet four Irish Catholics, you know you will find a fifth.' I once thought alcoholism was the Irish curse. Although it has been observed that displaced and colonised people are frequently at risk, statistics show that alcohol is no respecter of persons, culture, education, wealth or status. Whether alcohol takes its root in genetics or the biology of psychosocial stressors, its effects are the same.

In America we call it the elephant in the living-room. It sits there bigger than life yet no one mentions it. We tiptoe around it, afraid to cause a scene, a binge, a shameful public display. Oh, when someone loses a job or ends up in jail, or dies young from cirrhosis, cancer of the pancreas or oesophagus, words are whispered, 'The booze. It was the booze that did this.' The pain, the grief, the shame in my family and the families of many of my friends were swallowed over and over in those muted whispers. Living with this powerlessness takes its toll in fear, anxiety and control. For the alcoholic the booze has its own will. It takes food out of the mouths of children. It plants a harsh word or a fist in somebody's face. It shrivels the capacity for love like it literally shrivels the brain.

I determined to build a life for myself that was free of alcohol and its effects. I did not know that, even without alcohol, I carried the alcoholic family system of shame, fear, grief and hypervigilant control within me right into the family my husband and I would create. I tiptoed around my social-drinking husband as if he were ripe for a binge or a rage. I governed my actions by watching his moods. I made choices based on his desires not mine. All-other-oriented, controlling my environment. Anxiety and fear ruled me, for no apparent reason. I found that an occasional drink helped me control this anxiety.

I did not take my first social drink until I was twenty-four, and I drank rarely for ten years. At forty, I walked into my first Alcoholics Anonymous meeting. It was difficult to walk into that room, even to consider that perhaps I might have become what to me was the unthinkable. I was not a party person. I did not go to bars or pubs. I liked a quiet drink after work before dinner, then gradually at dinner, then gradually after dinner, then gradually before sleep. I did not act out. I did not make a fool of myself. I simply eased myself through the evening. I liked to drink in solitary stillness like a meditation. Alcohol loosened my tongue at social gatherings. I never got really drunk. I could hold the booze. I was bright and sometimes witty. I was not an alcoholic like my father, or like my uncle Joe with the broken blood vessels all over his face. I was not like the people who live on the streets or the guy that gets into fights, or the woman who drinks herself through the day — the stereotypical alcoholic, the end-stage alcoholic.

What was it that brought me to that first AA meeting and initiated me into the spirituality of the Twelve Steps? Fear. I was terrified. I knew something about my drinking that other people did not know. I knew I had a relationship with wine. Wine was with me in the good times and the bad. Wine seemed faithful when life was not. At first it fooled me. It said, 'I am not beer, whiskey or stout. I am what sophisticated, in-control people drink.' I particularly loved fine, dry Chardonnay or deep, red, rich Merlot. After a while I just bought the gallon jugs on sale. Wine said things like, 'You need to relax' or 'You deserve some fun' or 'Make sure you save enough money for me'.

There was a strong impulse within me that had a will of its own. I fought with that impulse, making little rules. I will not drink before five in the afternoon. I will drink only at weekends. I will not drink unless others are drinking. I never did drink before five, but as with my father, the exercises in control failed. I was terrified. Even when I was not drinking, I was thinking about drinking.

Fear brought me to that first AA meeting. By the time I got to AA, I had reached a demoralisation and hopelessness because I believed that I could not be free of the drink. I knew I was powerless. I knew the road I was on was insane. Through my father's life I had seen where that would eventually lead me. But I was also terrified of not drinking again. I liked wine. I did not know if I could live without it. I wanted to keep it close to me. I listened to story after story of people who shared the very same relationship with alcohol. Some were like me, at the beginning of the addiction. Others had lost everything. Yet the people who told these stories were free of the call of the inner demons. They had something they called serenity, a deep peace of spirit. Through their stories I came to believe that was possible for me.

The words about serenity and owning your own spirit again implied a freedom I had never really known at the core of my being. I was always driven between the poles of fear and desire. These people pointed at the Twelve Steps as a way to attain this freedom. I looked at those steps and said, 'Nothing new here.' They laughed at me and told me to get a sponsor to teach me how to use them.

I experienced difficulties when I came into Alcoholics Anonymous. Although I did not want to be enslaved to alcohol, I still wanted to maintain a relationship with it. I could not imagine a happy life without it. I was a religious person. To ask a self-admitted drunk to give me advice on what they called a spiritual programme was humiliating. The sense of shame I felt at admitting I had such a disease was overwhelming. To admit the truth — that I was powerless over anything — seemed a weak moral failure. To admit it publicly was a great shame. What of the very real possibility that I could not maintain abstinence after that? I would be even more ashamed.

I have learned that humility is not humiliation. Humility is not afraid, does not have to prove anything. It is like humus, of the earth, a balanced sensuous earthiness out of which freedom of spirit flowers, full of humour and delight. The recovering drunk I found for my first sponsor moved me through the Twelve Steps like a mechanic teaching an apprentice how to use tools. These tools maintain the spirit, free from fear, resentments, false pride, blame and shame. I will be forever grateful to her.

Alcoholism is a biochemical condition that affects the mind, the emotions, the social, psychological and spiritual life of the individual and his or her family. Whether alcoholism is genetic or biochemically induced through use of alcohol, alcoholism is considered a disease. It exhibits the criteria for a disease — predictable, chronic, progressive deterioration. Alcoholism is not curable, but it is treatable and manageable like diabetes. I accept that I have a disease and that I am not morally culpable for having the disease. However, I am responsible to manage it.

'Have a drink?' For some people it is relaxation, freedom from ordinary states of mind, camaraderie and a little bit of ecstasy. For others it is a demon with a voice, a slavery whose symptoms dance in the body, the mind, the heart and the spirit. Recently I found old cheque receipts with regular entries to Tommy's Liquors, The Brown Jug, and Party Time Liquors. I laughed not only because I am free, but because those tiny pieces of paper broke through another layer of denial. 'Mary Teresa, you haven't had a drink in over ten years. You don't have a problem with alcohol. You deserve a little relaxation.'

Sometimes I grieve for my father and my brother who died in addiction, their own strong spirits stolen by the spirits in the drink. If I could hold my dying father in my arms now, I would say, 'It's okay. It's okay. It's been a long, hard time, hasn't it?' I would rock him and I would rock the denial that was killing him, the denial that was desperately trying to protect him from the horrid truth of what had happened to his life, his family, his freedom, his own soul. I would soften the fear and soften the shame to break through to his own strong heart.

But I cannot. I never could. As it is, I only have today to soar into freedom, breaking the chains that bind me. I have the hope of healing the cross-generational chains that bind my children.

The Ancestral Bequest

Caitlín Matthews

Caitlín Matthews is the author of thirty-six books, including The Celtic Spirit, Singing the Soul Back Home, *and* In Search of Women's Passionate Soul. *She teaches practical applications of ancestral and Celtic spirituality world-wide and has had a shamanic practice in Oxford, England, for the past twelve years. Her forthcoming book,* Troytown Dances, *is about the unravelling of the ancestral bequest. She is currently at work on a major study of the ancestral bequest,* Remembering the Ancestors: The Art of Transgenerational Healing. *Her website offers details of courses, books and events: www.hallowquest.org.uk.*

Within every family, there is an old, old story circling round. We hear it when past triumphs and good times are remembered: times when relatives and ancestors made good, won through, achieved their hour of greatness. But there is also a story that we don't hear: the things that never worked out, the skeletons in the closet, the black sheep, the hidden shame.

The ancestral bequest of each person is different: no one is exempted. It can inspire and profoundly influence our emotional and vocational development, leading us to use the ancestral gifts of our family lines in wonderful ways. It can also, like the dead hand of a will, reach out of the realms of death to squeeze pleasure out of the living, a mysterious restraint upon the spirit that is never fully understood. This legacy is a form of transgenerational transmission that cascades from generation to generation. This bequest can be seen within both countries and individuals, where it can be seen as a national or collective bequest. This is often borne by and perceivable within the lives of individuals, as I hope to show in the case of Ireland and its peoples.

Dysfunctional family patterns manifest the ancestral bequest in many ways. We have only to look at the genealogy of the Kennedy family to notice profound similarities and coincidence — premature deaths and tragedies, plane accidents, car accidents, drug-related incidents, to relate only the most obvious. Yet the qualities of this notable and gifted family still shine through. When the ancestors cry out through us, they need our help. We are given many opportunities to experience the ancestral bequest in our lives, but fewer opportunities actually to sort it out. This cannot be done by one person alone; rather, it needs an alliance or collective to assist it.

Ancestral healing is currently being addressed in many therapeutic ways — through psychotherapy, gestalt and community ritual. But the most effective healing happens when three things are established: when we begin to respect the ancestors as having existence, rights and needs of their own; when we recognise and separate our individual life-motivations from those of our ancestors; and when we invite spiritual help to transform the bequest.

This has been made clear to me in my shamanic practice, in which I see many cases requiring ancestral mediation. Shamanism is the servant of all spiritual traditions, a way of reaching into areas that other methods cannot touch because it goes beyond time and space, able to readjust spiritual imbalances and bring ancestral mediation to long-rooted problems. The shaman, with the help of personal ally-spirits, journeys in spirit into the unseen side of reality to discover the cause of imbalance and to enable a spiritual transaction that will affect the whole pattern of a person's life. The ripples of this healing touch everything in that person's life-field, including their family, work, talents and environment. Deeply held attitudes change at a soul-level. By this means, the ancestral bequest can be clarified.

A shaman, like a midwife who attends births and deaths, is continually crossing thresholds to bring power and life or to remove and transfer stale and used-up factors across the divide by which we differentiate this manifest world and its unseen counterpart — both sides make up reality. Ignoring reality's other side causes displacement, disorder and disease.

Because our society is both rationalist and post-religious, many people are sealed off from spiritual channels of healing. We have denied the existence of any life except that which we perceive with our five senses, living in a time-bound and debunking culture from which the saving myths, stories and rituals have been excluded. We need these now if we are to heal the ancestral bequest. We do not have to hold them as rationally true, only to observe that their mythic truth can throw light on what each of us undergoes. Let us look at one such story where the effect of the ancestral bequest can be seen in the context of Ireland and its people; it is a particular form of transgenerational transmission that can and does cripple future generations.

According to the place-name myth books known as *Metrical Dindshenchas*, which relate the myths of place in Ireland, we read that Mag Slécht in Cavan was once called 'the plain of adoration or prostrations'. Here stood the statue of Crom Crúaich, an ancestral deity whose worship was instituted by the early High King, Tigernmas. Every Samhain (Hallowe'en), the first-born of every family and the first-born of all livestock were sacrificed to Crom Crúaich. It is told that Saint Patrick overthrew that custom and demolished the idol. The reasons why families colluded with this practice were about survival:

> Milk and corn they especially asked of [Crom Crúaich] in return for a third part of all their first-born; ... great was the horror and outcry about him.... They stirred evil, they beat palms, they bruised bodies, wailing to the demon who held them in thrall, they shed showers of tears, weeping prostrate.

This horrific story seems to echo the biblical account of Moloch, the idol to whom first-born children were sacrificed: the kind of practice that Saint Patrick would have been keen to terminate. But before the reader discounts this as merely legend, I would like to compare a recent case from my practice.

Joanne was a pretty young Protestant woman from Northern Ireland. But she held herself in a wooden, ungraceful manner and looked away frequently from a too-direct gaze. She wanted help with a long-term problem that no one had been able to help alleviate. She had come to me because the physical and psychological therapies she had tried bore no fruit in her life. She had reached beyond therapy towards a spiritual transaction that would remove an insoluble burden. Joanne's self-esteem was very low, and, though her qualifications were off the scale in terms of excellence, she was frustratingly powerless to act for herself or to reap the fruits of her long studies.

When I started to check out Joanne's bodyfield — which is where much of the client's psychic baggage can be experienced — my hand registered the cold hardness of a wall or block of masonry, rather than the warmth of a human being. This was the first instance of how a strict family upbringing had shaped my client. She told me that, in her family, children were expected to be both obedient and successful in every-thing they undertook: any failure was punished by blows, words and curtailments of liberty. Her brother and sisters were as dysfunctional as she was — highly educated but out of work through a total inability to motivate.

That there were ancestral issues feeding off Joanne was soon appar-ent. I made a shamanic journey for her, in which I was led by my spirits to the source of the problem and shown solutions. They showed me a well that had been capped so that water couldn't be drawn from it. With the spirits' help, this cap-stone was pushed off. The smell that came from the well was one of overpowering rot and decay. From deep down, there stirred other presences. I stood back as a flock of birds flew out of the well in a long skein. Confused, I asked my spirits what action should be taken — I had come to rescue Joanne's soul fragment, not to release many souls. I was told to watch and wait. Gradually the birds came to earth, transforming into children holding hands. In a long line, they spiralled the well striving to draw water from it. It was like a scene from the Irish legend of the Children of Lir, when Finola and her brothers transform; the difference was that instead of turning into wizened beings, the birds in my vision shapeshifted into the forms of innocent children.

I asked my spirits what I was witnessing and was told that this was a well from which living water once flowed, but that, in Joanne's family for many generations, there had been a long pattern of elders harnessing the vital energies of children to their own ends, a pattern that had been passed down over and over, so that the souls of subsequent generations of children succumbed to this deathly imprisonment.

Joanne, by asking for help, had incidentally caused the release of the trapped soul-parts of children in her extended ancestry and her immediate family caught in this spiralling pattern. One of my spirits indicated which of the children was the soul-part of Joanne, and we drew her gently away from the line. In anguish for the pain of these other children, I asked help for them too, acknowledging that this was too much for me to deal with unaided. From a long way distant, I saw the spirit-helpers of those children come to bear away the trapped soul-parts, while other spirit-allies cleansed the well of neglect and decay. The well was cleaned, and all the children drank their fill before leaving.

I was told that this living water had been stale and without power to quench deep thirst because of the ancestral bequest. The questing minds and ardent hopes of generations of children had sunk into neglect, but these were now movingly released. Some of those children were now dead, some of them still living. I was told that their soul-parts would wing to the appropriate places. Those who were still living would begin to live their lives with the power to use their innate gifts and skills without hindrance.

It wasn't until after Joanne had gone home, restored to herself, that I remembered the Crom Crúaich story. Joanne's was a family that had offered up its first-born, generation after generation, upon the altar of self-abnegating hard work for the sake of the family honour — those who failed to measure up to this sacrificial syndrome were the ones who evaded imprisonment; those who had complied and co-operated, in the spirit of the Mosaic commandment to honour father and mother, were the ones who had become enmeshed, their young lives fettered, their hopes and liveliness crushed.

Such patterns are not necessarily instigated by some evil ancestral perpetrator; they often begin as a temporary survival measure in hard times or as a coping strategy. Once such patterns are established, however, they are next to impossible to eradicate by ordinary means. Like a tiny mistake in the early part of an equation, the distortion factor becomes gross, the ancestral burden grows heavier through succeeding generations until someone decides that enough is enough.

We should be careful not to demonise the ancestors. They thought of us, loved us, left secret caches of wisdom in our cells and memories, wisdom that we could use in our time. Our ancestors were no better nor worse than ourselves: they were human beings too. In their ongoing life on the other side of reality, some may be stuck, or as the Christian world would hold, 'in limbo', needing regeneration and release. But some ancestors, distant and unknown to us perhaps, may be so regenerate or wise that they act as teachers and helpers for us here and now. I believe we can not only recognise and heal the negative bequests but also access and understand their corresponding gifts.

Each family and each person has a unique set of gifts or skills that are usually recognised some time before adulthood. But every gift has its corresponding responsibility — it is not free. Every violinist knows that to produce sublime music, four to six hours a day must be spent in practice. Similarly, each gift we inherit or possess comes with its own contract or set of conditions. The more gifts we have, the more complex the contract.

The concept of this contract was known to ancient Irish society as the *geis*. A geis is a binding obligation to observe the contractual small-print of one's gift; it is inextricably bound up with one's honour or face in the community, as well as being a gauge of one's spiritual integrity. Geasa (the plural form of geis) are set to guard the boundaries of our gift. They can be either positive or negative — enjoining or forbidding certain acts.

Geasa were most often recognised at birth and proclaimed by Druids — a form of gifting-augury that perceived the nature of the new-born's gifts. A similar augury is seen in the European stories of fairy-godmothers who proclaim the gifts of the new-born. Some geasa are imposed upon the taking up of a rôle in society, such as when a king became ruler of Tara. From those to whom more is given, more is required.

The most notable example of a geis-bound individual is Cúchulainn, whose prodigious abilities in heroic combat were bound by multiple geasa. Some of his geasa concern his manhood name, which he earns by slaying the hound, or Cú, of the smith, Culainn; his deed causes his name and nature to be recognised. He thus gains an additional geis: that he is forbidden to eat dog. Later, geis collides with geis when he is invited to a feast at which dogmeat is served, thus contravening another of his geasa, never to refuse a feast. This incident heralds his early death.

The act of naming often imprints recognition of the gift and its geis. The name given at the nexus of childhood with adulthood confers its own fixative; in our society it is often in the nickname conferred by peers. The gift that goes with the conferring of a name becomes part of Irish tradition as the personal names of ancestors became adopted as patronymics.

We can see this demonstrated in the American-Irish novel by Henry Morton Robinson, *The Cardinal*, which follows the career of a young priest, Stephen Fermoyle. After he is consecrated as bishop, Stephen falls ill with a mysterious infirmity that afflicts his legs. His old father, Dennis, sits at his bedside and relates a Dublin legend, by way of consolation and to help grant understanding of his son's illness. The story goes that every clan along the Liffey bore its special mark of God's favour: the O'Donnells were blessed with beautiful hair; the Desmonds were strong. Their own clan, the Fermoyles, relates Dennis, 'were marvellous at games of leaping and running. A proud way of walking they had, too.' But 'there was a penalty attached to the possession of these gifts'. The O'Donnells suffered premature baldness, the Desmonds ran to fat and the Fermoyles were smitten in their legs. Although this is a work of fiction, such a legend serves to remind us of the kind of remembrances passed down in families over the generations.

We each inherit gifts and skills as part of our ancestral bequest: they are resident in our bloodlines. In ancient times, the Gaelic family model was that of clan; within each clan were septs whose descendants were the proud bearers of a skill or craft that served the chief and the clan. The mysteries of such skills were once passed down the family from generation to generation, but in our own time such conscious transmission of skills is rare. The ancestral bequest and family gifts impact not only upon individuals but also upon culture and land. In the text called *The Settling of the Manor of Tara*, the ancient sage, Fintan, tells us about the five provinces of Ireland and their qualities: 'knowledge in the west, battle in the north, prosperity in the east, music in the south, kingship in the centre.' This extraordinary Middle Irish text gives an accurate, if idealised, catalogue of how the gifts of the land imparted to the people who manifest its qualities: the stories, eloquence and learning of Connacht; the wars, conflicts and endurance of Ulster; the treasures, customs and prosperities of Leinster; the music, fertility and poetry of Munster; the sovereignty, bounty and supremacy of Meath, the ancient sacred centre of Ireland.

In these ancient traditions, the spirit who represents Ireland is Flaitheas or the Goddess of Sovereignty, a personification of Ériu or Éire. In the earliest king-making stories, she appears as a loathsome hag whom the rightful candidate for king treats with respect and acclaims with a kiss, whereat she turns into a beautiful young woman who, in turn, acclaims the candidate as rightful king. In later poetic tradition, Sovereignty becomes the aisling or vision-woman, found in some misty mountain pass by the poet, mourning the lot of Ireland and pleading for a candidate to come forward. The urging of the Goddess of the land of Ireland has brought forth champions of varying talents over the centuries — heroic, literary, reforming, liberating and administrative heroes and heroines who have attempted to align themselves with the ancient gifts of her land.

Flaitheas, or Sovereignty, is the voice of the land, but there are other ancestral voices who speak out of a chequered struggle for a restored Irish sovereignty. In ancient legends and stories, the severed head, revered by the Celtic peoples as the seat of the soul, becomes an oracular head, which informs the living. In its most regenerative aspects, the severed head serves as a sacred oracle of ancestral wisdom, as a reminder of the continued ancestral presence; in its retributive mode it becomes a voice of vengeance, a spearhead of internecine feud.

Premonitions of the Irish ancestral bequest appeared to the novelist George Moore who, during the civil conflict for Irish independence, had a nightmare in which he saw Ireland as a God demanding human sacrifices. and woke to the cry coming from many lips: 'Take me, take me, take me, I am unworthy, but accept the burnt offering.' The legacy of Crom Crúaich is not just a pagan bogey-man set to scare off decent Christian folk; it is a potent living entity. The ghost-haunted corridor of Irish consciousness echoes with resounding memories and precedents that keep old stories fresh and long-dead ancestors alive. The health of a nation is seen in the way in which these memories are handled.

On the walls of Derry and Belfast the heroes of Ulster led by Cúchulainn (as earlier the host of the Fianna led by Fionn mac Cumhaill inspired the nineteenth-century Fenians) can so easily elide, by mythic association, into the figureheads and martyrs of modern Irish terrorism. As I have written in *The Celtic Spirit*,

> Many of the popular myths and fantasies that have been woven around the Celtic peoples — some self-fabricated — have been designed largely to mantle the unpalatable facts of conquest, colonisation and cultural diminishment.... The minute we listen to romantic traditions, with their victimhood and inadequacy thinly veiled by bombast and boast, we mire in a quicksand that will suck us out of reality into a jealous cauldron where bitter nationalism and retributive terrorism can be brewed.

The unwholesome legacy of the Celtic Twilight was borne in brutally upon W.B. Yeats, whose own myth-weaving played its own part in heralding heroic rebellion. In contemplating the horror of civil war, he wrote:

> We had fed the heart on fantasies,
> The heart's grown brutal from the fare;
> More substance in our enmities
> Than in our love.

Tales of heroism may fill up the emptiness that hurt and pain have excavated in the soul, but they can also become vehicles by which the ancestral and national bequest is borne forward only to reanimate future generations. For we should not forget that the Irish bequest extends to all parts of the diaspora world-wide. With what can they be replaced? Who lifts the burden, who lays the ghost? How can the gift flood back into daily use?

It is only by returning to primordial methods of spiritual healing and transformation that the ancestral bequest can be lifted from the shoulders of those who come after us, both family and nation. We need to remember that everyone living and dead has a bequest. For when we release blame and recrimination, submerging both in unconditional compassion, we gain space in which our *gneart*, the strength and power of life, can reassert itself, and our natural gifts well up once again. But by retaining resentment, blame, vengeance, we merely allow the old bequests to riddle us through and live on, in and through us, allowing them eventually to seed in our children. Ancestral healing affects not just the ancestors or ourselves, but also our descendants. Our common future may be seeded within the past, but it is transformable in the precious present moment of life today.

Pearls: The Spirit of Story

Corinne Lally Benedetto

Born in Cambridge, UK, of Irish-American parents, Corinne Lally Benedetto received her PhD in sociology from the University of Chicago in 1994. Her Irish roots are concentrated mainly in Mayo and Cork. This essay is her first foray into creative academic writing, cracking open the dry husk of scientistic narrative and spilling forth a poetry of reason. Her current book project, The Integrative Classroom, *marries academic theory and personal experience. She teaches at DePaul University's School for New Learning in Chicago, Illinois.*

Irish-Americans experience their Irishness indirectly. The meaning of the culture has, over time and out of the same necessities that first began to sever the ties of the emigrants to land and memory, shifted into the realm of legend. Cut off from the land, we are forced to remember ourselves. Faced with the daunting task of inferring our families from the once-treasured debris of the dead, we often settle for lineage.

We research family names and draw out anthropological links in fancy family trees, but these are roadmaps to the Land of the Fairies. None can visit except in dreams. It is the hidden heart of my Irish family tree, rather than a depiction of the interlacing branches in fullest view, that I conjure. This heart beats like a far-off sacred drum with the rhythm of story.

Along with music, the given-down stories in an Irish family contain an emotional legend of feelings. The twin acts of listening and story-telling free the sensuous experiences that seed each tale, and as we tell stories and listen to them, family members across the span of generations make body-to-body contact. The stored emotional memor-ies charge like synapses across time. The spirit of a whole family can be formed out of the individual experiences relayed by narrative. To my Irish family, spirit is one thing and religion another. It's spirit that tells you who you are and where you've come from, religion that tells you where you're going.

For the Irish in America, the landscape of memory is inextricably linked to the holy ground of Éire, and many immigrant families crafted narrative out of the experience of leaving this home. Irish family stories preserve the record of these farewells. Though imperfect, sketchy and fraught with every problem plaguing oral culture, the emotional amber of story is superior to the preserved written word or document.

My Irish family, its past swathed with lacunae, nevertheless swirls with the passed-down spirit of these stories. They function as bridges between self and ancestor, linking memories and feelings in the body, and staving off the lethean nature of time. I've re-created some of these bridges across time by imaginatively entering into the lives of my three grandmothers, using recreations of the very stories each one told to her family. The first set of stories focuses on the emigration stories of my stepfather's mother, Mary Lydon, who left Ireland in 1910 as an eighteen-year old girl. My paternal grandmother Margaret Corcoran's wry warnings and life lessons form the next group of tales. The last section contains a slice of the wealth of family stories given to my siblings and me by our maternal grandmother, Eileen Dalton.

Each of my grandmothers, or theirs, left Ireland for America, running from conditions they found intolerable towards those more easily borne. Memories of their last hours at home must have stayed sharp inside each woman until her death. Those preserved in story would fill a thimble.

In the only studio portrait ever taken of her, Mary Lydon wears a string of pearls and a modest-necked white dress. She seems to be struggling with all her might to look serious and grown-up for the camera. In her eyes hides a mighty laugh and her mouth shows just a hint of the lip she's biting for the sake of appearance.

Although she arrived from Ireland in the last blush of girlhood, Mary spoke with an Irish tongue all her life. As children, we delighted in its sound and often tried to imitate her whirring pronunciation of each other's names. During the years we knew her best, she spent much of her time sitting in a grey-and-black-tiled kitchen telling tales and brewing her strong, dark tea ('I won't have any of that weasel-piss!' she'd declare of any pot holding less than four steeping bags).

She had come to America in 1910, bolting from the prospect of an arranged marriage to an oldest son who had, at long last, inherited his farm. To reach the ship, she had ridden the night train from Castlebar to Dublin. Her father, John, bereft by her sudden announcement, purchased the seat next to hers and spent the entire ride pleading with her to stay.

'They wanted me to settle on an old man and stay on the farm with him. I knew I'd be trapped if I did that. There wasn't any real future I could see in Castlebar, though I did love the place. I loved the college, too, and the dances. What would I do for fun out in the country? I left then, I just bought the ticket and told Mam and Pa I was going for the Dublin train. Pa came all the way with me, both of us crying. He knew I was set on it, but he still tried to get me to come back home. I wanted to stay with them but not with the old man on the farm. I didn't want to get married at all! Pa went back alone on the train and I got on the boat. I never did see them again. My brothers came over after awhile, but Mam and Pa stayed at home.'

The fact that Mary did leave, despite her father's entreaties, gives me a clear sense of the steely resolve in her character and leads me to believe that the proposed match with the eldest son was merely the catalyst for a move plotted long before. As I listened to them, her tales of leaving always pointed to a seeker of fortune and freedom. She was feisty and feminist long before it was fashionable. Mary got on that ship and held onto the rails or her steerage bunk or her mess tin for dear, dear life.

By the time she grandmothered us, Mary was a slow-moving, nearly apartment-bound woman whose stolid presence made fantastic the stories of her dancing days. I found it incredible to consider her as the newly American working girl who threw an engagement ring at the man she eventually married because he voiced his objection to her entertaining other beaux. Before she finally accepted his terms, she worked for ten years as a maid and governess in Chicago. She lived with her several employers (the salt-monied Mortons among them), and sent most of her wages back to Castlebar via an aunt who had come to Chicago years earlier.

'I got along well with all the children and their families. It was ten years that I worked with them you know, and the older ones would come home from their colleges and come find me right away to tell me their stories and other things they wouldn't tell their parents. They all were sorry, and I was too, when I left to get married. Michael had fixed up an apartment with all new appliances, a frigidaire and furniture and all, and kept it as a surprise for our wedding night. He was tickled to open the door and have me see what he'd done, but I went in and saw it and knew right then my fun was over. He must have known I felt awful seeing it all there. I'd always had my own private rooms with the Mortons, all my friends would come and we'd have a grand time. Now this seemed more like work to me!'

Soon after her marriage, Mary had bad tidings from home from a newly arrived older brother.

'All the time I worked, I sent the money home through Aunt Mary. She was in Chicago when I got here and I asked her to help me send the money to Mam and Pa. A long time after, I found out from my brother that she'd never sent any of it. Not a penny. By then, they were dead and she was dead and it was too late for anything. I felt terrible about it and so angry! I still do.'

This story of her aunt's betrayal was told often at tea-time, and served, I think, as an illustration of the perils of freedom. She wanted all of us to know the price she'd paid to craft at least a portion of her life's story. As it turned out, her life after marriage conformed exactly to the mores of working-class respectability. Mary grudgingly accepted and then grew gracefully into her domestic role, leaving the wild Irish rose fondly but quite clearly behind. Yet, she never completely abandoned this earlier self, choosing to preserve the youthful Mary in the selection of stories she offered to us as we sat sipping the thick tea together.

Mary told most of her stories to my mother, wife of her youngest child, and my mother gave them voice in the family. Almost every one was a tale of her high-stepping youth and few shed light on her transformation from working girl to working wife. She bore six children and kept a household that included several immigrant brothers. She allowed neither bitterness nor regret to colour the stories of her early days, and she never allowed any of us to forget there was more to Mary Lydon than met the eye.

If it weren't for the moll's toughness in the eyes of its subject and her ever-so-slightly mocking lips, Margaret Corcoran's photograph might reflect only a glorified moment in the life of a young Irish city girl with her first flapper haircut, in a dress-up outfit of pearls and diaphanous chiffon. As it is, she's impossibly young, with off-camera hands whose fingers clench impatiently. Much later, she explained her lifelong insomnia to me as a result of this hatred of sitting still or waiting: 'I can't fall asleep because I always have the feeling I'm going to miss something!' I knew her long after she posed for her coming-of-age picture, of course. That Margaret, whose voice rose strong among the chorus of my childhood, offering tales tinged with sarcasm over solitaire and a dwindling pack of Kools; she flung off those pretty pearls and the fancy dress the moment the shutter clicked and got back to work. For her, the palace clock was always chiming midnight.

She'd grown up surrounded by work and by the moral significance of working. Her father, born in County Carlow, was a union organiser of sheet-metal workers in America. This was a dangerous role at the time, and touched Margaret's heart with a strange blend of idealism and cynicism, leaving her longing for a life she wouldn't care really to live. Her stories always seemed to me like tales of longing. The conflict-ridden sanctity of workers' labour that she imbibed in her parents' household allowed Margaret to claim the right to rule inside her own home as a married woman, but also prevented her from ever being truly at peace there.

Her own working life began early. Her mother's death, when Margaret was nine years old, propelled her into the roles of surrogate mother and housekeeper for many years. She often told me of the morning her mother died, and the strangely spiritual events of that day always remained a sure and true link to life's meaning for her.

'I took care of my mother when she was sick. She'd been really sick for a long time. One morning, she seemed to be feeling better and she asked me to get her some strawberry pie. She said she had a craving for it. I had to go down to the corner store for the pie — there was a store where you could buy it by the slice. I left her alone in the apartment while I went there. I really wanted her to have something she could enjoy and that tasted delicious, like strawberry pie. But, just as the man at the store put the pie in the brown paper bag and handed it to me, all of a sudden I felt an icy cold hand touch my left shoulder. I knew right away it was warning me. I dropped the pie on the floor and ran back home. I was a fast runner, you know. I always won the parish races. But, I knew she was dead and I'd be too late. And she was. I tried to get back in time but I knew what the hand had told me and she was dead in bed when I came back to the apartment. I felt the hand again when Jim was a baby. He was having convulsions in his bed upstairs and I was downstairs vacuuming, but I saved him because I knew what that icy feeling meant.'

I don't believe Margaret ever bought any kind of baked dessert in all the years I knew her. She made all of her own pies from scratch and without assistance — although she allowed my grandfather to cut up the apples. Inside our small universe, her pies were famous. She usually made apple, lemon meringue or chocolate cream. She'd put her hands in the serious-looking mixing bowl, even as the blades scraped back and forth, adjusting the crust (lard, egg yolk, vinegar and flour). Her baking, cooking and cleaning were all done with a single-minded fury whose intensity belied the satisfying outcome. She cleaned and cooked, planted zinnias and roses, stripped the wood-work much more often than necessary and fixed sweet-smelling beds that were heavenly to sleep in. But she never made strawberry pie.

She loved her five boys with the same kind of hard-driving intensity, ruling them with a velvet fist and planting in them the new seeds of longing.

I watched her closely when I was a girl. Her contradictory blend of gentleness and fury must have fascinated me; I only recall wanting to be close and listen to her. She decoded the family for me, and I listened avidly. The two of us would play Kings in the Corner and Gin Rummy until early morning hours and she'd talk to me of family intrigue. She hated sentimentality, yet conveyed a depth of warmth and security only a child could appreciate. Her tales were true-to-life and I wore them inside as badges of our great intimacy.

'You know, when T married J, I was so nervous about the rehearsal dinner because her family were snobs, rich snobs who didn't think T was good enough for her. Grandpa was really nervous, too, and drank too much liquor. They had the party around their pool and Grandpa went around and grabbed all the bridesmaids and threw them into the water. They'd already had their hair done for the wedding and nice dresses on! I could have killed him. Later, I felt sorry for him but I never let him know that. It was just too awful. He was really sorry the next day, and T was so angry. Now, I'm glad that he did it!'

Her stories were often braced against this love him/hate him frame-work, and gave me a way to view my grandparents' marriage without judging it. Many years later, I brought both of them to visit the University of Chicago on what turned out to be their last major excursion together. It was the kind of autumn day that perfectly fits an old-stone university quadrangle, and they were enthralled with the splendour of the gothic stone structures and their deep, dark, chandeliered interiors. At one point during our walk, they moved slightly ahead of our little group, and Margaret took his arm. 'Well, Dad,' she said, making it sound like an intimacy and an announcement at once, 'next time maybe we'll get to go to school in a place like this.' I pray for that.

❦

In her photograph, Eileen Dalton models a tailored black dress for Marshall Field & Co., white gloves and box handbag clutched with just the right amount of muscle tension in her right hand. Her left wrist is bent, fingers lightly touching her hip and allowing her pearl bracelet to show alluringly. On the picture's back she has written, '36-30-36? You try and beat it at age 65! Don't you like my ankles?' She's proud and sure of herself, looking off to the right of the camera and into the future. Her modelling career began in middle age. She was a matron model, offered more work than she could accept. She often used the story of her refusal to move into the big-time modelling world as a way to illustrate her belief that decisions affected many people and were never to be made solely on the basis of one's own desires.

The tales of loving that Eileen Dalton gave to us were hardly tales of romance. These would have been as likely in her home as saloon legends. Her stories were something a person could count on; thinly veiled life lessons meant, as I now see, as a kind of moral inheritance, and they placed decisions made for love of family at the summit of a life well-lived. Eileen carried her imposing cache of nearly formulaic tales always at the ready. My brother, sisters and I never knew what might prompt one to the surface for telling, as they appeared in response as equally to error and misfortune as to the stirring of brown sugar into our morning's oatmeal. The four of us longed for them, begged for them and dreaded them, too. If we fidgeted or resisted with the claim that we knew the story already, she'd stand tall at the head of our kitchen table, irises widening fast within their blue crystalline rings and exclaim, 'Well, you'll just hear it again! And, do you know why? Because, This-Is-Your-Heritage!' And so, we listened, and now we know the narrative structure of those life choices so well it's as if they spring fully grown from our own memories.

She'd play the ukulele and sing 'That Old Gang of Mine' with my grandfather, always finishing off with a soft sermon on the importance of singing together and making music as a family. She'd learned this value from her mother and father.

'Oh, we had such fun! The seven of us, when Papa was alive, would gather around Mama at the piano and sing. Mama had a lovely voice. We were always singing. We had to find a new apartment every two or three years because the neighbours would complain to the landlord. We'd take that piano with us to the new place and start singing again. Never let anyone make you feel ashamed of what the good Lord gave you. I just hate a person who thinks so highly of himself that he won't get up in front of a group and sing or do a recitation.'

Eileen's parents, brother and four sisters were continually invoked at the family table as our grandmother made it very clear where her loyalty to us had first grown. 'We weren't rich, dear, but we had class. I've known rich people and they always wanted what we had — love. I had a beau whose family was from New York and they had a lot of money. He came to visit me here in Chicago and he treated Mama like a servant. He looked down on her, can you imagine? He didn't treat me that way, but as soon as I saw how he acted to my family, I let him know I wouldn't marry him for all the money in the world. I met your grandfather later and he loved Mama so! We were the family that his own people — and they had money, ooh la la — never were to him. I knew he'd be a good husband and a good father and that's why I married him.'

Over and over, she brought the point home: decisions are made out of need, not desire. Sometimes the needs of one family member had to be addressed at the expense of others, although the unintended consequences might be tragic (and had sometimes been for her). When her son, Tom, was nine years old, his chronic asthma became life-threatening. She sent him straightaway to school in Arizona, and forever after suffered in the knowledge that he'd felt abandoned. But she told the story (one of her favourites) without any visible regret.

'Tom was missing so much school and living in a big oxygen tent here at home. I wrote to our friends in Tucson, and they got him in at Saint Joseph's. I had to put him on the train alone. He thought I was sending him away from us to be mean, but I had to do it. He would have died here. I found a Chicago family that was moving out there for the winter and he rode out there with them. Later, I found out he was making liquor in his dormitory and living the wild life. I had the Oak Park house re-done so that we could rent it out as apartments and told your grandfather we were moving the whole family out west. And we did. Your grandfather, such a good man, went back and forth, keeping his newspaper agency running. We stayed out there for three years so that Tom would have his family around him.'

When I was young, I believe I heard that tale as her plea for understanding and benediction. We children granted that to her whole-heartedly, nodding agreement with mouths full of meatloaf and stewed potatoes (don't-you-even-think-of-wasting-that-food!) Now, I hear it differently. I've had to make my own difficult decisions, hurtful to some, with the greater good of the family in mind. It is she who offers benediction to me through that long-ago story of love in action. I'm given the means to understand my own life through her stories of family struggle, confusion and strength. And, in the background, softly tinkling, is Mama's piano music wrapped around each scene and holding it tightly.

I am the storyteller now. My children mix up the protagonists and sequence of events and roll their eyes if I've told it too often, but they're always drawn back to the tale. Some day, the memories will set and new minds will be ready to receive these gossamer threads of life lived as family. Is this a particularly Irish way of sharing family memories and creating bridges backwards in time? I only know that it's our way, and that stories have always been connective forces in this family, channels of its spirit and, ironically, silent healers of its pain and tattered edges.

Part Five

Global Green

When the Celtic Tiger was born in the late years of the twentieth century, many predicted it was just a matter of time before Ireland became utterly absorbed — californicated, the most cynical warned — into contemporary materialistic culture. Outfitted with new duds and a handy cellphone, Ireland would surely roar into the new millennium shed of old superstitions that had stood in the way of progress.

The economic boom has indeed had impressive effects. Where grey ruins once tumbled, spanking new bungalows stand. Sleepy villages demand bypasses to handle weekend traffic. Exiles come home to get jobs in the new post-industrial economy. New golf courses need new airports. Everyone seems in a hurry to make it in the new economy — or just in a hurry. At the same time, widespread disaffection with conventional religion has made churches seem like slow-leaking tyres, gradually but steadily deflating. Will the upward economic trend finally cross the downward spiral of church attendance, leaving Ireland fiscally powerful but spiritually destitute?

There is another possibility. Irish history (and prehistory before that) suggests that spiritual challenges are best met by mining the past while embracing the future. The Celts did not kill off the ancient Goddess but installed her in their pantheon. Christianity did not persecute pagan beliefs but wrapped itself around them like ivy on strong trees. Even the troubles that plague Ireland now and in the past have been turned to spiritual use, as when the recovery movement grew out of the spiritual challenge of addiction.

In a new global culture, Irish spirit must be invented anew. And if that new global culture presents special challenges to ancient ways, those ancient ways also challenge and illuminate emerging paradigms. In a virtual world, what is the significance of place, of the body? Irish spirituality, never dualistic, both demands a rootedness in space-time and acknowledges an Otherworld beyond. In a global economy, what are the requirements for true prosperity? Irish spirituality, like that of other indigenous cultures, offers a complex vision of reciprocity between human, animal and vegetative spheres. In a democratic society, what constitutes power? Irish spirituality encourages a subtle balance between the need for strong leadership and the requirement to impose limits upon it.

There is much to mine from Ireland's rich spiritual past: balance between masculine and feminine energies; humble commitment to service; love of the word and the powers beyond the word; belief that a leader's integrity is vital to the people's health; extraordinary sensitivity to place. And perhaps most importantly, awareness that this world is not all there is, that there are mysterious realms that affect us and that we, in turn, affect — worlds just beyond range, out in the western sea, at the dim meeting of sky and cloud. It is such eternal visions that draw people, Irish and otherwise, to Irish spirit.

The Quantum Celt

Robert Anton Wilson

Irish/Austrian American Robert Anton Wilson is a descendent of the O'Lachlanns of the Burren and the Wilsons of Dublin; now resident in California, he lived in Dublin from 1982 to 1988. He is the author of many books, both fiction and non-fiction, that elude genre categorisations and push against the walls of conventional reality-tunnels, including (with co-author Robert Shea) the renowned Illuminatus! *trilogy and, most recently,* Coincidence *(New Falcon Press). A Buddhist-agnostic, he can be found at http://www.rawilson.com.*

The reality of metaphysics is the reality of masks.

Oscar Wilde

The day in 1982 when my wife, Arlen, and I arrived in Ireland we tried her battery-operated radio to hear whatever we might find — our way of dipping our toes in the new culture before plunging into its alien waters. By the kind of coincidence I don't regard as coincidental, we found an RTÉ interviewer discussing with a Kerry farmer local legends about the púca. As a long-time púcaphile, I found the conversation spellbinding, but the best part came at the end:

'But do you believe in the púca yourself?' asked the RTÉ man.

'That I do not,' the farmer replied firmly, 'and I doubt much that he believes in me either!'

I knew then that I had found my spiritual homeland, wherever I may otherwise roam, and that Yeats and Joyce and O'Brien had not risen out of a vacuum. We had planned to stay six weeks; we stayed six years.

Anthony Burgess once argued that English English, American English and all the other varieties of Anglophonics have become rational and pragmatic (closure-oriented), but Irish English remains ludic (open-oriented). While I see some truth in that formulation, I would prefer to describe all-other-English as belonging to what neuro-linguistic therapist Richard Bandler calls the metamodel (statements we can logically judge as true or false) and Irish English as belonging to the Milton-model (statements not containable in true–false logic but capable of seducing us into sudden new perceptions).

The Milton-model, named after Milton Erickson — 'the greatest therapeutic hypnotist of the twentieth century', in the opinion of his peers — contains no propositions subject to proof or disproof, uses language the way that the Kerry farmer did, and can cause both intellectual and physiological transformations. Because of his many successes in curing the allegedly incurable, Erickson often became proclaimed 'the Miracle Worker'. Oddly, most of Erickson's patients did not think they had undergone hypnosis at all. They just remembered having a friendly chat with an unusually sympathetic doctor.

According to the Korzybski-Whorf-Sapir hypothesis, the language a people speaks heavily influences their sense perceptions, their 'concepts' and even the way they feel about themselves and the world in general. 'A change in language can transform our appreciation of the cosmos,' as Whorf stated the case. The clinical record of Erickson and his school indicates that language tricks can even make us ill or make us well again. The Irish neurolinguistic system illustrates these theorems uncommonly well.

Whether you call it ludic language, Ericksonian hypnosis or the verbal equivalent of LSD, Irish English — even in the professional hands of Ireland's greatest writers — shows the same non-Aristotelian 'illogic' or Zen humour as that Kerry farmer. Witness:

Death and life were not
Till man made up the whole,
Made lock, stock and barrel
Out of his bitter soul

W.B. Yeats

'Men are born liars.' — Liam O'Flaherty, in the first sentence of his autobiography. Logicians call this an Empedoclean paradox. To an Irish stylist, it does not appear Empedoclean nor paradoxical but merely another pregnant bull. Since O'Flaherty belonged to the class of all men, he lied; but if he lied, his statement does not carry conviction, so maybe he told the truth.

'Are the commentators on *Hamlet* really mad or only pretending to be mad?' — Oscar Wilde

'Durtaigh disloighal reibel aigris dogs' — Myles na gCopaleen. (It only makes sense if you pronounce it as Gaelic, and then it becomes ordinary English, expressing a typical English attitude toward their Hibernian neighbours.)

'They shall come to know good.' — James Joyce. (Read it silently, then read it aloud.)

'There is in mankind a certain ********************************* Hic multa ******************* disiderantur ********************* And this I take to be a clear solution of the matter.' — Jonathan Swift (all expurgations Swift's own.)

'I considered it desirable that he should know nothing about me but it was even better if he knew several things that were quite wrong.' — Flann O'Brien.

Or, to take a few examples that lend themselves better to condensation than quotation:

Consider Swift's pamphlet war with the astrologer Partridge, in which Swift claimed Partridge had died and Partridge vehemently insisted on his continued viability. Swift won hands down by pointing out that just because a man claims he's alive does not compel us to accept his uncorroborated testimony.

Or: Bishop Berkeley, proving with meticulous logic that the universe doesn't exist, although God has a persistent illusion that it does.

Or the scandalous matter of Molly Bloom's adulterous affairs in *Ulysses*, which number between one (Hugh Boylan) and more than thirty (including a few priests and Lord Mayors and one Italian organ grinder), depending on which of Joyce's 100+ narrators one chooses to believe. This grows more perplexing when one realises that some of the 'narrators' seem more like styles than persons: styles masquerading as persons. Or maybe the ghosts of departed stylists, in the sense that Berkeley called Newton's infinitesimals, the ghosts of departed quantities.

Colonised and post-colonised peoples learn much about text and sub-text; and Yeats did not develop his mystique of mask and anti-mask out of Hermetic metaphysics alone. In my six years sampling Dublin pubs (1982–88), I overheard many conversations in the form:

'I saw your man last night.'

'Oh? And?'

'All going well there.'

Who the devil is 'your man'? Does this concern hashish from Amsterdam for the punk rock crowd, gelignite on its way to Derry, or just the ingrained habits shaped by eight hundred years of foreign occupation? Maybe, but the speakers might simply refer to tickets for a soccer game. (You will find a similarly oblique dialogue in the second section of the 'Wandering Rocks' montage in *Ulysses*, except that 'your man' has become 'that certain party'.)

I do not claim that Sassanach conquest alone produced Ireland's elusive wit and ludic poesy, but it sharpened tendencies already there as far back as Fionn mac Cumhaill. Yeats says somewhere that Ireland was part of Asia until the Battle of the Boyne, but that dating merely represents W.B.'s reactionary romanticism. Joyce knew that Ireland remained part of Asia; *Finnegans Wake* explicitly tells us it emerged from 'the Haunted Inkbottle, no number Brimstone Walk, Asia in Ireland'.

You can test one level of truth in this by simply asking directions in both Tokyo and Dublin. In either place you will encounter old-fashioned politeness and friendliness unknown in most of the industrial world, and you will get sent in the wrong direction. Hostile humour? I think not. Asiatic languages, including Irish English, simply do not accommodate themselves to Newtonian grids, either spatial or temporal.

Arlen and I used to play a game in Ireland: whenever we saw two clocks we would compare them. They never agreed. In Cork, the four clocks on the City Hall tower always show four different times; locals call them 'the Four Liars'. The sociologist may class this as post-colonial syndrome — based on the baleful suspicion that the English invented time to make a man work more than the Good Lord ever intended — but Joyce noted that the only three world-class philosophers of Celtic genealogy, Erigena, Berkeley and Bergson, all denied the reality of time (and only Berkeley lived under British rule.)

A Dublin legend tells of an Englishman who, noting that the two clocks in Pearse Station do not agree, commented loudly that this discordance 'is so damned typically bloody Irish'. A Dubliner corrected him: 'Sure now, if they agreed, one of them would be superfluous.'

Even more in the Taoist tradition: Two Cork men meet on the street. 'Filthy weather for this time of year,' ventures the first.

'Ah, sure,' replies the second, 'it isn't this time of year at all, man.'

Compare the Chinese proverb, 'Summer never becomes winter, infants never grow old.' Einstein's relativity and Dali's melting clocks belong to the same universe as these Hiberno-Chinese eccentricities.

In Clare and the west of Ireland generally, one often hears the grammatical form, 'My uncle was busy feeding the pigs one night and I a girl of six years ...' (One also hears this in Synge's plays — all of them.) Elsewhere in the English-speaking world one would hear, 'My uncle was busy feeding the pigs one night when I was a girl of six years ...' The Irish English retains the grammar of Irish Gaelic, but it thereby retains the timeless or Taoist sense of a world where every now exists but no now ever 'becomes' another now.

Nor does this neurolinguistic grid, or reality-tunnel, only manifest in Irish speech and literature. William Rowan Hamilton, probably the greatest of Ireland's great mathematicians, made many contributions, but two have special interest for us here.

1. Hamilton invented non-commutative math, which I shall try to
   explain. In arithmetic, 2 x 3 = 3 x 2, or they both equal 6 (if you
   haven't raised too many pints that night.) Ordinary algebra, the only

kind most of us ever learned in school, follows the same rule: a x b = b x a. Everybody knows that, right? Well, in Hamilton's algebra, a x b does NOT = b x a.

More 'Asiatic' influence? More of the Celtic Twilight? In Pure Mathematics, you can invent any system you want as long as it remains internally consistent; finding out if it has any resemblance to the experiential world remains the job of the Applied Mathematician, or the engineer. It required about one hundred years to find a 'fit' for Hamiltonian algebra, and then it revolutionised physics. Hamilton's maths describes the sub-atomic (quantum) world, and ordinary maths does not.

The reader may classify Hamilton's feat as a variety of precognition or maybe just as more of the Hibernian compulsion to challenge everything the Saxon regards as unquestionable.

2. Physicists of Hamilton's day endlessly debated whether light travels as waves, like water, or as discrete particles, like bullets. He supported both totally contradictory models, although in different contexts. Among fundamentalist materialists, they call this the heresy of 'perspectivism', but again, after one hundred years, it became part of quantum mechanics, although usually credited to Neils Bohr, who only rediscovered it. Perspectivism also haunts post-modern literary theory, cultural anthropology and especially the Joyce Industry, as more and more Joyce scholars realise that all of the narrative 'voices' in *Ulysses* seem equally true in some sense, equally untrue in some sense and equally beyond either/or logic in any sense.

Quantum mechanics owes a second huge debt, and a perpetual headache, to another Irish physicist, John Stewart Bell. Bell's Theorem, a mathematical demonstration by Bell published in 1965, has become more popular than Tarot cards with New Agers, who think they understand it but generally don't. Meanwhile it remains controversial with physicists, some of whom think they understand it, but many of whom frankly admit they find it as perplexing as a chimpanzee in a Beethoven string quartet.

In a (hazardous) attempt to translate Bell's maths into the verbal forms in which we discuss what physics 'means', Bell seems to have prove that any two 'particles' once in contact will continue to act as if connected, no matter how far apart they move in 'space' or 'time' or in space-time. You can see why New Agers like this: it sounds like it supports the old magick idea that if you get ahold of a hair from your enemy, anything you do to the hair will affect him.

Most physicists think a long series of experiments, especially those of Alain Aspect and others in the 1970s and Aspect in 1982, have settled the matter. Particles once in contact certainly seem connected, or correlated, or at least dancing in the same ballet. But not all physicists have agreed. Some, the Anti-Bellists, still publish criticisms of alleged defects in the experiments. These arguments seem too technical to be summarised here, and only a small minority still cling to them, but this dissent needs to be mentioned, since most New Agers don't know about it.

The most daring criticism of Bell comes from David Berman of Columbia, who believes he has refined the possible interpretations of Bell down to two: (1) non-locality ('total rapport') and (2) solipsism. We will explain non-locality below, but Berman finds it so absurd that he prefers solipsism. He says the moon, and everything else, doesn't exist until perceived; Bishop Berkeley has won himself one more convert.

Among those who accept Bell's Theorem, David Bohm of the University of London offers three interpretations of what it means: 'It may mean that everything in the universe is in a kind of total rapport, so that whatever happens is related to everything else (non-locality); or it may mean that there is some kind of information that can travel faster than the speed of light; or it may mean that our concepts of space and time have to be modified in some way that we don't understand.'

Bohm's first model, 'total rapport', also called non-locality, brings us very close — very, very close — to Oriental monism: 'All is One', as in Vedanta, Buddhism and Taoism. It also brings us in hailing distance of

Jungian synchronicity, an idea that seems occult or worse to most scientists, even if it won the endorsement of Wolfgang Pauli, a quantum heavyweight and Nobel laureate. You can see why New Agers like this: it means atomic particles remain correlated because everything always remains correlated. You will find it argued with unction and plausibility in Capra's *The Tao of Physics*. I suggest that physicists often explain this in Chinese metaphors because they don't know as much about Ireland as they do about China, and because they haven't read *Finnegans Wake*.

The strongest form of this non-local model, called super-determinism, claims that everything is one thing, or at least one process. From the Big Bang to the last word of this sentence and beyond, nothing can become other than it is, since everything remains part of a correlated whole. Nobody has openly endorsed this view but several (Stapp, Herbert, et al) have accused others, especially Capra, of unknowingly endorsing it.

Bohm's second alternative, information faster-than-light, brings us into realms previously explored only in science-fiction. Bell's particles may be correlated because they act as parts of an FTL (faster than light) cosmic Internet. If I can send an FTL message to my grandpa, it might change my whole universe to the extent that I wouldn't exist at all. (For example, he might suffer such shock that he wouldn't survive to reproduce.) We must either reject this as impossible, or else it leads to the 'parallel universe' model. I'm here in this universe, but in the universe next door the message removed me, so I never sent it there. Remind you, a bit, of that Kerry farmer?

Even more radical offshoots of this notion have come forth from John Archibald Wheeler and Jack Sarfatti. Wheeler has proposed that every atomic or sub-atomic experiment we perform changes every particle in the universe everywhichway in time, back to the Big Bang. The universe becomes constant creation, as in Sufism, but atomic physicists, not Allah, serve as its creators. Yeats again wakes?

Bohm's third alternative, modification of our ideas of space and time, could lead us anywhere, including back to the Berkeleyan/Kantian notion that space and time do not exist, except as human projections, like persistent optical illusions. (Some think Relativity already demonstrates that ... and some will recall Mr Yeats again, and that Kerry farmer ...) All particles remain correlated because they never move in space or time, because space and time exist only 'in our heads'.

Meanwhile, Harrison suggests that we may have to abandon Aristotelian logic, that is give up classifying things into only the two categories of 'true and real' and 'untrue and unreal'. In between, in Aristotle's excluded middle, we may have the 'maybe' proposed by von Neumann in 1933, the probabilistic logics (percentages/gambles) suggested by Korzybski, the four-valued logic of Rapoport (true, false, indeterminate and meaningless) or some system the non-Hibernian world hasn't found yet. The Kerry farmer would handle all of this better than the typical graduate of any university outside Ireland.

And so we see that two Irishmen, Hamilton and Bell, have the majority of physicists arguing about issues that make them sound like a symposium among Berkeley, Swift, Yeats and Joyce. Through their literature, speakers raised in Irish English have transformed the printed page; now their mathematicians, raised in the same neurolinguistic grid, have revolutionised our basic notions of 'reality', which in the light of what we have seen, badly needs the dubious quotes I just hung on it.

Bridey in Cyberspace

✤

M. Macha NightMare

M. Macha NightMare (www.machanightmare.com), when not on her broomstick, is Aline O'Brien. Her grandmother came as an orphan to Moorestown, New Jersey, from Galway. She is the author of Witchcraft and the Web: Weaving the Web in Cyberspace (ECW Press) and, with the ecofeminist Starhawk, of The Pagan Book of Living and Dying (HarperSanFrancisco). She rides the broomstick circuit as ritualist, presenter and organiser. She calls herself a circuit Priestess of the Reclaiming Tradition.

The websites of her Brigit cell are www.ordbrighideach.com and www.laurels.uni.cc

A blue moon shines in the sky over northern California as witches gather in a large room lit only by the candlelight from four altars in each quarter. In the centre stands a table dressed in lace, greenery and fresh white flowers. Upon the table sits a brass-trimmed stainless-steel bowl shining in the firelight — Brigit's well. Inside the bowl is a cauldron. Surrounding the bowl are three large white pillar candles, and nearby are an anvil and hammer.

Three priestesses of Brigit, one wearing red, one gold, and one white, embody her and speak in her voice. Tonight, I wear red. As I speak of her, then speak to her, then speak in her voice, I feel my heart open. I walk around the circle and look into the eyes of each person. I feel her smiling through me, feel her palpably when I touch the hands or heart of every celebrant.

I listen to Bridey's words spoken by my sister priestesses and myself. We speak of the year just passing. We all — celebrants and priestesses — review our lives last year. We return to the present with our plans for the coming year. The priestess in gold lights the cauldron, and as its flames arise, she invites each of us to approach Brigit's altar and make a public pledge of our goal for the coming year. What promise will we make to Brigit? What blessing will we seek? What service will we do? What creative project? What inspiration or powers or healing do we ask of her?

We may commune silently or we may speak our pledge aloud in community. Most of us speak aloud. As each pledge is spoken, Brigit of the forge strikes her anvil to seal it.

I approach the altar and feel the heat of the fire. I reach my hands into the warm waters surrounding her flaming cauldron, draw them out and anoint my face, neck, arms and chest. I ask Brigit to bless my writing with her inspiration. I ask her to guide my fingers on the keyboard. I hear the ring of metal striking metal as I take a little yellow glittery birthday candle from a small basket on the altar and light it with the flame from one of the pillar candles, taking Bridey's light back into my life, into my work.

On the World Wide Web I have found a shrine called Ord Brighideach, an online sister- and brotherhood of people who honour Brigit. This unique devotional order came about by way of a website created by two women in Oregon. The order comprises nineteen cells, like the nineteen priestesses of Brigit at Kildare, with nineteen people in each cell. Each cell is named for a tree and each day, beginning at sundown, one of the nineteen tends her flame; on the twentieth day, as of old, Bridey herself tends it. Some of the cells also maintain a Web presence, by creating a website, or setting up a listserve to share experiences, insights, recipes and stories, or both. There is also a listserve for the entire order, subscription being optional. All websites are linked to the main order.

When a dedicant joins the order, she or he sends a small donation to the keepers of the flame in Oregon, that is, the people who created the website and set up the order. In return, she receives a Blessing for Flame-Keepers, a prayer, and a candle lit from the Kildare flame with which to start her flame-keeping.

I had known of the order for a few years, visited the site, and reflected on whether I wanted to join. The site invites those who hear her call to join in shared devotionals. 'If she speaks to you — as poet, healer, smith, storyteller, musician, craftsperson, midwife, mother, hearth keeper, land steward, tender of herds, seer, woman of fire, lawgiver, deity of the home, lady of the sun, or simply as goddess or saint — you are welcome to walk among us.'

I contemplated for a while, going back to the site from time to time and listening for her call. Brigit is a goddess I can relate to — she's brilliant, powerful, compassionate, tender, and easy to approach. She displays strength, skill, industry and artisty in ways that don't threaten men and don't restrict women. To the strong woman, she models righteous strength. To the independent woman, Brigit needs no partner to make her whole. Many people all over the world can hear her singing.

My reservation about joining was that I travel erratically and I wondered how I could maintain my watch in airports, buses, cars and wherever I was lodging. I knew that I was expected to tend her flame once every twenty days, for as long as possible, taking safety into consideration. The principle is that the longer we are able to tend, the more energy we will be able to generate: an offering to this world and the otherworld, as well as to Brigit — 'She Who Gives Energy'.

I set aside my reservations, confident that I could somehow maintain my pledge and keep my watch. Dedicants are asked when we apply to join to swear an oath to Brigit as a flame-keeper the first time we tend the flame as a member of the order. The oath includes a statement of dedication to Brigit and to our commitment to tend her flame faithfully, but reflects our own path to her service.

Often my life is such that I feel my knowledge of what Brigit has to offer me comes from time spent dancing in the heat of her forge. She powers the blows that shape me. She is the annealer of my soul. Yet I see her in the greening earth after winter's dark. In the coastal hills where I live, I see wild iris spring up in her footsteps. She pours the waters of healing. She stirs the cauldron of compassion. She keens in grief for the dead and whistles up the wind. She is balm to my soul.

These are the things I spoke of when I first pledged myself to the order. I chose an all-women cell and thus became a sister of the Laurel, a member of Cill Labhras. I tend the fourteenth shift. One of our cell, Tiffany Lavendar, designed a Laurel Cell website to help establish our group identity. My cell sisters are witches, pagans, Christians, liberal and conservative, conventional and unconventional. What we share is our dedication of maintaining the sacred flame of Brigit bright throughout the world.

In the firelit room in California, we have stood before Brigit's holy well and sacred flame and spoken pledges to her. We've felt on our skin the healing waters of her well and the waters of the world. We've taken small candles, lit from the altar candle, which had been lit from the Kildare flame. We've heard the ringing of hammer on anvil.

Now we come together singing a chant. I take up a woven grass Bridey doll, dressed all in white lace and flowers, and hold her aloft in my left hand. I reach back my right hand to grasp the left hand of the next priestess. One by one everyone joins hands, and we chant and dance the spiral. We follow the Bridey dolly inward to a tight spiral in the centre, then turn and face each person, one by one. Looking at the fire of Brigit in each pair of eyes, we spiral outward to the perimeter of the sacred space. Then turn and in again, seeing each face, tightening into a corkscrew near the centre, turn and out again. We dance the spiral in and out and in again, all the while chanting Starhawk's chant:

> We will never, ever lose our way to the well of her memory
> And the power of her living flame, it will rise, it will rise again,
> Like the grasses, through the dark, through the soil to the sunlight,
> We will rise again.

When the time is right, we raise our arms aloft and change the chanting to a wordless sound coming from deep in our hearts through wide-open throats, louder and higher as our collective energy builds, until it crests and showers back down upon us. We slowly sink to the floor. We touch our hands and foreheads to the ground, imbuing our pledges with the energy we raised in the dance, as we seal the spell with these words:

> What we have received tonight has been held in our keeping.
> What passes now flows out of our hands and into the earth,
> Trusting in time and right season,
> Let us go on.

✤

Every year in early February I renew my connection to Brigit and I make a pledge to her in the presence of my sisters and brothers in the Reclaiming community.

Now, once every twentieth day, I join with others who hold Brigit dear in keeping her sacred flame. Beginning at sundown, as in the Celtic counting of nights and days, we light a candle to her. All three hundred of us flame-keepers do this from wherever we live in the world, in twelve countries — Australia, Brazil, Canada, Finland, Greece, Ireland, Netherlands, New Zealand, South Africa, Spain, the United Kingdom and the United States of America. We honour our heritage as we take it into the age of the Internet.

In our annual ritual in honour of Brigit in California and in our keeping of her sacred flame, we reconstruct the ways of our ancestors in our high-tech, multicultural, post-modern world. We carry Brigit's light of consciousness through the darkness and into the future.

Meetings with Remarkable Sheela-na-Gigs

✣

Fiona Marron

Fiona Marron is an Irish painter born and raised in Clane, County Kildare, living back in Clane since 1996 after thirteen years in the US. Her work has been exhibited on both sides of the Atlantic, most recently in a one-woman show of mythic landscapes of the Liffey River. Mother to Gordon, Jack and Julian Dunning, she is interested in issues of women's spirituality. Her artwork can be seen at www.silenagig.com.

I am not sure where I first heard the term 'Sheela-na-gig', but I do remember trying to find out what it meant. Most explanations I came across were colourful but derogatory towards women. My favourite was 'a crazy hoor that might leap out at you showing her gee', that last being the slang word in Ireland for the female genitals and not a million miles away from 'gig'. I was enthralled when I heard that there were actual stone carvings called Sheela-na-gigs, hidden away in the National Museum because they were regarded as the pornography of our ancestors. I was curious and determined to see ancient stone carvings of naked women exposing their genitalia.

It was in the early 1980s, when I was a student at the National College of Art and Design in Dublin, that I started what the great archaeologist Marija Gimbutas, author of *Language of the Goddess* and *Civilisation of the Goddess*, called my 'Sheela odyssey'. Along the route of that odyssey, I looked, touched and painted stone carvings that inexplicably linked me to something greater than I. The Sheela-na-gigs inspired me to paint them, when I never regarded myself as a figurative painter, then affected other people through my interpretations. Even though much about the Sheela still remains a mystery, I have come to enjoy and celebrate that mystery and my hope is that you may do so too.

Sheelas have been known by many different names in different parts of Ireland. They have been called the 'idol', the 'evil eye stone', the 'devil stone', the 'witch on the wall' and the 'hag of the castle'. The earliest literary references come from John O'Donovan's ordnance survey letters for Tipperary in 1840, where he mentions a carving at Kiltinan Church. (When the figure was stolen in January 1990, the publicity did much to popularise Sheelas again.) James O'Connor, who made a marvellous replica of the stolen figure, quotes O'Donovan's description of the Sheela as:

> the figure of a woman in bas-relief, rudely done, but whose attitude and expression conspire to impress the grossest idea of immorality and licentiousness. (It) represents a woman who was known by the name Sile ni ghig, a person described as having plunged herself into all kinds of excesses and having precipitated herself by her follies into the depth of destruction.

Sheela, as well as being a woman's name, means femininity and also a special kind of woman: a wise woman, a spiritual woman. Some say the name originates from Macroom, County Cork, where it was used to describe old women. 'Na-gig' is more obscure. Barbara Walker speculates that the term means 'vulva woman', with 'gig' or 'giggie' meaning female genitals and related to the Irish 'jig', which in turn comes from the French 'gigue', in pre-Christian times an orgiastic dance. In ancient Erech (Iraq today) a 'gig' seems to have been something similar to a holy yoni (a symbol of the female genitals venerated by Hindus). The sacred harlots of the temple were known as 'nu-gig'. Who can say if the word could have travelled so far?

Laurence Durdin-Robertson declares that 'Sheela' means the image of a woman and 'gig' is the name in Norse for a giantess — the oldest of the goddess races. He also suggests that Sheela-na-gigs are a derivative of the frog goddess, symbol of the vulva as opening to the underworld. Gimbutas said that my representations of Sheela from Carn Castle, Westmeath, which I titled 'The Hag in the Iron Wood', reminded her of the frog goddess of Catal Huyuk, an ancient temple city of the Anatolian plain in today's Turkey.

Other squatting goddess figures, almost identical to the Sheelas, guarded the doors of the temples of India where all who entered would touch the gaping yonis as an act of self-blessing. Sheelas also have distinguished breastless ribcages similar to the Indian goddess Kali in her corpse aspect. Kali is the goddess of death and destruction but also the creator and giver of life. When I thought about this, I saw a connection between Kali and the Cailleach, the Irish crone or hag, known under many names and thought to have been a goddess who married a series of husbands and passed from youth to old age more than once. She still survives today as a lively figure in modern Irish folklore. I see her as the creator and devourer of the world, a symbol of the great mother in continuous cycles of life, death and rebirth.

Eleanor Gadon remarks that Sheela-na-gig is remembered in Ireland as the old woman who gave birth to all races of people and that her function as a decoration on the church was similar to the gorgon on Athena's shield — to protect and to ward off evil. The Sheelas that are still *in situ* today — many, unfortunately, badly damaged by being exposed to the elements for centuries — are placed over the entrance archways of medieval Christian churches, castles, gateways and bridges as symbols of protection and fertility. Indeed, I believe that the Sheelas served as a bridge between pagan and Christian cultures in Ireland, Scotland and Wales and even England and France.

How old are they really? How many have been lost, stolen or buried? Could they be the continuation of goddess imagery that Marija Gimbutas discovered from 35,000 years ago? It's all a wonderful mystery. Jorgan Andersen in his magnificent book, *The Witch on the Wall,* writes about the recent evidence of a Sheela-type carving from the neolithic period found in Grimes graves in Norfolk, England. This would suggest that the Sheelas as we know them today may be reproductions of older carvings.

For me, they are a celebration of life, the power of female regeneration, the cycle of life, death and re-birth. Back to my own discoveries: I'll never forget the day one of my teachers arranged for me to have access to the crypt of the National Museum, where several examples of Sheelas were stored. I was accompanied by a security guard. He told me to walk quickly as I had only twenty minutes. I remember walking down a large stone stairway, at the bottom of which was a long corridor. The smell of antiquities filled me with anticipation and excitement. There were hundreds of artefacts stored there. I wanted to look at everything but knew I had to keep focused on the mission at hand. Eventually we came to the area where the Sheelas were. The guard pulled the string of the lone light bulb and, as the light flicked on, at least twenty Sheela-na-gigs in all their vulva glory stared at me.

I gasped in awe and probably fear. It was the most incredible sight. I didn't have time to be frightened, but I was. I remember a sort of buzz in my head. Was I getting one of my dizzy attacks? Was I going to faint? I attempted to start drawing, but my hand was shaking. There were so many carvings, all so different, carved out of various types of stone in various shapes and sizes. I decided to try to focus on just one at a time. It took longer to do some than others because their stones were eroded and the image unclear. My eyes kept being drawn to the vulvas, those dark secret caves.

I asked the guard if I could stay a little longer. Kindly, he gave me a few extra minutes, even though he said he had better things to do than stand in front of 'those horrible yokes'. Then my time was up and I had to leave.

Back in my studio space in college, I reworked several of the drawings, putting in details of light and shade I remembered. Those amazing hags started to take shape, and I was so excited. About a week later, I decided to make new drawings — but all the original drawings had disappeared from my portfolio. I couldn't believe it. I searched everywhere. Where had they gone? Who would ever want them? They never turned up.

But a bigger disappointment and mystery was ahead: I was denied access to the Sheelas in the museum when I looked for a second visit. Perhaps I didn't plead hard enough; perhaps I gave up too quickly. But it would be almost a decade before I would be in the crypt of the National Museum again, renewing my acquaintance with Sheela-na-gigs.

I gave up on the Sheelas, but they did not give up on me. While I was living in Oregon and pregnant with my eldest son, Gordon, Sheelas re-visited me in my dreams. They were strange and wonderful dreams, all with amazing colours and intense feelings. I remember one where I was the foetus in the womb, and a Sheela was yelling with her mouth as big as her vulva. I was always extremely emotional when I woke up. I started to draw Sheelas again, using my dreams as reference, but I knew instinctively that they were just not quite right. One night it became clear to me that I just had to see those carvings again.

On my third trip home, I was successful. The dean of antiquities at the museum referred me to a person who remembered me from the time ten years earlier, and I was invited to draw two Sheela-na-gigs that were in this person's office. It was fantastic to have all day to draw and absorb every detail of these two marvellous and wonderfully pre-served Sheelas. I got to know Sheela Ballylarkin/Kilkenny and Sheela Cavan very well indeed.

A few days later, I returned to the crypt, and this time I had as much time as I wanted. I will always be extremely grateful to the people who made this possible. The ancient smell was the same, but the Sheelas were now stored in a different area and there were only nine of them. They looked lonely and neglected as they rested on their dusty shelves, but even in the dim light they still had a very powerful presence. I got to work.

As I was drawing, I experienced that buzz in my head again. This time I was not afraid but allowed myself to tune into it. Various images of Sheela's female form became more definite as I studied the carvings. It was as though they were emerging from the stones. It was easy now to see the details I had missed before. Each Sheela had her own distinct personality.

As I gained confidence in my drawings, and familiarity with each Sheela, I felt ready to touch the carvings with my hands. It had not felt right to do so without getting to know them first. Touching them, I learned more intimate details — a nipple on a breast, scars or tattoos on a forehead, the same around the incised ribs. One of my most amazing discoveries was to touch the vulva of the Burgesbeg/ Tipperary Sheela and discover she had a dropped cervix or else a giant clitoris. I decided it must have been the former, as it was common for women to have a dropped cervix after many childbirths. This Sheela became my 'Soul Carrier', a title I chose because practically all of her had eroded except for her vulva, which she held preciously with her fingers. Her vulva became her soul-centre for me.

In the dim light and quiet calm of the crypt, I meditated on the mystery of these incredible carvings and the effect they were having on me. There was so much to explore and find out about. One thing I was definitely sure about was their connection to the goddess and her culture, her manifestations of life, death and rebirth. The Sheelas were the embodiment of all three aspects — the triple goddesses if you like.

I spent three days down in the crypt of the museum. The security guards had got to know me and never bothered me as I sat doing my drawings. They had a little room nearby, where they had breaks and made tea. I could hear their footsteps when they walked around.

I decided to attempt some photography. I timed the flashes for when the guards were out of sight. I felt that they would surely disapprove of me taking photographs and quite possibly confiscate my film. I took deep breaths to stay calm, but my heart was beating so hard I felt it could be heard. I gradually photographed all the Sheelas. The brightness of the flash illuminated them like never before. I got glimpses of more detail and texture on the stones. I prayed the photos would come out and be in focus.

As I reached the end of the roll, my camera made its loud rewinding noise. Out of the corner of my eye I saw a guard walking close to the area I was in. I threw my jacket over the camera and held my breath. Suddenly he stopped and turned the other way. I wondered if he knew what I was up to. Had he heard the whirring noise of my camera? Not taking any chances, I extracted the roll of film and hid it in my bra. Then I reloaded the camera in case I had to hand over the film. As it turned out, I didn't have to hand over anything, but it was exciting playing spy for women of the world who love the goddess and her symbols.

Later, as I worked in my studio in Portland using a variety of media and colour, I found each Sheela wanted her particular aura of colour that represented and expressed different feelings. Sheela Carne Castle — 'The Hag in The Iron Wood' — is charcoal grey with subtle flecks of gold and pink. Her background is red, orange and yellow. She is sexy and nasty with her defiant hunched-up shoulders and strong squatting legs. I believe she is one of the most powerful of all my Sheelas. 'Raising Her Voice' from Seirkiernan, Offaly, has a red-ochre body. Her stone, unusually red in colour, stayed with me when I went on to paint her. She is the only one of her type with her vulva holes that resembles a cribiform hymen. Flashes of green, blue and gold fill her vibrant background which sings joy and strength and also quiet endurance.

Professor Etienne Rynne has put forward the idea that Sheelas have a definite pagan background. He quotes examples from Germany in the fourth century BCE and first century CE. He claims that they are associated with a fertility cult, which merged with the male god Cernunnos, lord of the animals, and that this would account for the medieval protection aspect.

One of my favourite theories on Sheelas is put forward by Brian Branston of Stratford-on-Avon. He says that 'Sheelas represent the earth mother waiting to be fertilised by the sky father. This is the reason why the pudendum is being so invitingly held open ... the sacrament of fertilisation took place each morning at sunrise when the sun shone on and covered the goddess in her original position.' I really like this idea, a possible explanation for Newgrange on winter solstice, if one views the entrance as the opening to the womb/temple inside. Mary Condren makes another lovely womb association when she talks about the Killinaboy Sheela from Clare — the congregation enter the womb of the church through the arched entrance, above which a wonderful Sheela is perched.

Killinaboy was the site of the next part of my odyssey — seeking out Sheelas still *in situ*. I arrived with my husband, Brian, and my son, Gordon, to see the Sheela above the arched entrance of the ruins of a church built in the eleventh or twelfth century on the site of an early monastery founded by Saint Inghean Bhoithe. The Sheela is known locally as Baoith. Saint Inghean Bhoithe would have been a very important saint since her name is derived from the cow goddess, Boand — one of the greatest of the prehistoric goddesses. Boand is sometimes linked to Brigid, often portrayed with a cow as in the wonderful stained-glass window above the altar in Clane Church — my home village in Kildare, of which she is patron — which depicts Saint Brigid with her cow.

The Killinaboy Sheela was barely visible, there was so much ivy covering her. Brian helped me up on to his shoulders and, with the aid of a long stick, I managed to beat back the encroaching ivy to expose this wonderful Sheela exposing herself. I made drawings and took photographs while Brian and Gordi explored the ruins. I remember feeling it was a perfect day. On a break, I lay down on the ground underneath the Sheela and adopted her pose. As I lay like this, staring up at her, I was overcome with sadness. I began crying. I couldn't help it, and I couldn't stop. I cried for women suffering everywhere, my sisters all over the world.

The vagina is a sacred entrance, but how do we regard it in this day and age? Unfortunately not with respect and honour. Too many women and young girls are daily used and abused and raped all over the world. Too often this part of a woman's body is looked upon with shame. We can even be ashamed of it ourselves. The way of the goddess is almost lost to us. I wept deeply, with all of my body, for my sisters — past, present and future.

Our menstrual blood is regarded as a curse — a dirty inconvenience — as we moan and groan about this most precious and wondrous of substances. But Vicki Noble, an American shaman who was a guiding inspiration for me, says that menstrual blood under certain scientific microscopes gives off a white light, the only substance from our bodies to do so. Sheela's message to me was 'look to where you came from' — a mother's womb — 'know where you came from'. This is what I heard in my head, so I attributed it to Sheela.

Back in Portland with photographs and dozens of drawings, I began to study each Sheela-na-gig and interpret and represent her as she dictated. I relinquished control and absorbed this ancient icon as she emerged both from eroded stone and centuries of silence. I had an incredible amount of energy, and there was a wondrous calm and balance in my life. I felt I was doing what I was meant to do. In my own way, I was setting the Sheelas free.

And then it was time for them to meet the rest of the world.

My many women friends, who were aware of my adventures, were patiently waiting to see the paintings and drawings. I was very protective of these images which had come to mean so much to me. So I had an 'opening' at my studio and invited about twenty women to come. Our ages ranged from twenty-something to sixty-something. We were maidens, mothers and crones and we celebrated our womanhood.

There were gasps, shrieks and tears to shouts of anger and joy and laughter. Everyone was very emotional, and we couldn't stop talking. Every woman had so much to say; I loved that our talk was so free and open. We talked about our bodies but especially about our vaginas. We talked about our sexual feelings and experiences — about childbirth and stillborn babies, about sexual frustrations and sexual fears, about religion and repression and, of course, about the goddess and the legacy she has given to all of us.

The energy that night was something we could all feel as we danced to it and acknowledged it as our collective female power. And I offered it up to Sheela-na-gig and thanked her.

Since that night there have been many openings and many celebrations, with exhibitions, talks and slide presentations. Women from all over the world have come up to me and said how much Sheela-na-gigs have affected their lives and how good it was to meet soul sisters. Many expressed how they moved from being ashamed of their bodies to being confident and proud of them. But that first night will always be particularly special to me. I'm so glad and grateful to my dear friends who encouraged me to move forward with my work, helping me to make more people aware of Sheela.

In her glorious mystery, Sheela-na-gig has a lot to answer for. May the dance continue.

The Fairies vs
the Money Economy

�֎

Eddie Lenihan

*Born in Brosna, County Kerry, and a resident of Crusheen, County Clare, Eddie
Lenihan first became aware of the treasure of Irish lore and stories when doing his
MA in phonetics. He began collecting then what is now the largest archive of taped
folklore material in private hands in Ireland. Author of fifteen books for adults and
children, including* Rowdy Irish Tales for Children *and* In Search of Biddy Early,
*he is also a seanchaí who visits schools, libraries, prisons, and hospitals telling Irish
traditional stories. In 1999 his successful efforts to save a fairy bush from road-
builders attracted world-wide attention. Lenihan teaches English and Irish in an
Irish-speaking secondary school in Limerick.*

*T*wo very simple (or seemingly simple) yet important questions
confront us today in Ireland, those of us who wonder what in God's
name kind of black hole the country is spinning into: Where has the
Otherworld gone? And, more specifically, where have the fairies gone?

To many at the beginning of the third millennium, these questions
might seem childish. After all, stories about the fairies are for children,
aren't they?

Wrong. Many sensible Irish adults today would be glad to admit that
they still believe. But they won't do so. Not openly. And why? Because
they're ashamed to. And they're ashamed because they've lost confidence. In who they are. In what they believe. In fact, they no longer even
wonder, most of them, what they're doing in this world.

There is a slippery slope here that should have been foreseen by
any of those wise pontificators who, for so many generations, were in

charge of our spiritual sanitation. If they'd had any imagination, that is. But they hadn't. After all, what had imagination to do with religion or morality? Religion was facts. Religion was rules. Religion was obeying, not questioning. And morality meant fitting into the prevailing world-view. With the result that now, in a land of ever-increasing fact, detail, rules and management, religion and morality have only a marginal place. Religion, especially, has lost its way, its true function — which is surely to raise people above this miserable factuality of the workaday, slaveaday world.

Where is the connection between religion and the fairies, you ask. It is a very clear, though much unseen one: the fairies are of the Other-world, just like God, angels and saints. Yet not a single clergyman had the wit, in 1999 when I was trying to save the *sceach*, the fairy-bush at Latoon, County Clare, to see that here was a case that deserved — no, demanded — his intervention. Why, one may ask. For the utterly simple reason that if you allow a unique fairy-bush to be uprooted and thrown aside so that yet another modern highway may be built, then you can have no logical objection when the same road-builders decide that they have to bulldoze a church, graveyard or other equally sacred place.

The reason? Because such places represent the Otherworld. Certainly the destruction of the graveyard would cause protest. But so would the destruction of such a bush a mere generation ago. Could any of us then have foreseen the use of churches as office-buildings? Yet it has happened. Despiritualisation is a progressive, insidious cancer in our society and I feel that every individual who cares for the kind of Ireland the next generation will inhabit has a duty to stand up and say, 'Enough is enough'. Unfortunately, the institutional churches have been far too timid in this regard — with inevitable consequences for themselves and society alike.

The Otherworld is all around us, whether we acknowledge it or not. And most of us do, in a hazy, unthinking, conventional religious way. The majority of us don't (not yet, anyway) knowingly mock other people's religious beliefs. Yet those same civilised people think, for the most part, that a seriously held belief in the fairies is somehow outlandish. Quaint, maybe even culturally desirable, but certainly not to be taken seriously. But why not? Better that, surely, than the new Irish Famine — no belief at all, except in money and possessions.

And what about the hundreds of examples of injury and misfortune that have followed interference with fairy places? I have personally interviewed scores of people with such tales to tell. The remarkable thing is that up to about forty years ago all this respect for, and fear of, things fairy co-existed in Ireland quite comfortably with a sincere belief in Christianity, whereas today both are far less a part of daily life for most Irish people. Why? One of those simple, complicated questions to which I have no conclusive answer. But I do know that anything that reminds us that we are not the sole owners of all we see can only be beneficial. Environmentalists, Greens and other assorted friends of the earth find no difficulty with this part of my argument. But they, as well as most other Irish people, don't take it that step further — that there are things in this world we have no claims on, no rights to. They are already owned by others — the Good People, the Fairies, Them, The Other Crowd, call them what you will. Our so-called simple, primitive ancestors knew this well enough and made very clear allowance for it.

A land-reclamation contractor of my acquaintance — a man usually plastered with oil, happiest when dismantling bulldozer engines, one far removed from anything extra-terrestrial, it might seem — put it very succinctly for me when I asked him whether he would bulldoze a fairy fort:

'I wouldn't. An' I'll tell you why. First of all, I have my business to be thinking of. An' as well as that, the fuckin' world is big enough for Them an' for us.'

His exact words. A civilised man's answer, an answer perhaps born of painful experience. The now world-famous *sceach* at Latoon, between Ennis and Newmarket-on-Fergus, would have gone the way of many similar landmarks had I not been lucky enough, seventeen years ago, to speak with and record an old cattle-drover, since dead, of that locality, who knew a great deal about it. He told me that he had listened to his elders describe how the fairies of Munster, on their way north-ward to fight the Connacht fairies, would gather round that bush, wait there until the various contingents had come across the Shannon from all corners of the province, then set off to do battle. In these encounters they would sometimes win, other times lose. But whatever the outcome, on their way back to Munster, dragging their dead and wounded with them, they would gather again around that bush, wait there until the last stragglers had come in, then depart back across the Shannon to their homes.

Many a morning, he told me, he arrived in that field early — maybe four or five o'clock in the morning — to collect cattle for a fair in Ennis, Sixmilebridge or wherever. And within a radius of fifty feet of the bush he saw lumps of 'stuff' (as he described it) with the consistency of phlegm, or liver, but whitish in colour. He knew at once what it was — the fairies' blood. And each time he saw it, he knew that there had been a battle the previous night.

And no folklorist will contradict him in this matter of the colour of the fairies' blood!

One morning in May of 1999, on my way to work in Limerick, I noticed earth-moving machinery in the field close to where the *sceach* grows. That evening, I stopped, enquired what was happening. I was told that the new £20 million Ennis relief-road was to pass here. But what of the bush, I asked. Those in charge of operations had no know-ledge of any bush. I told the engineer what I knew, then wrote to a local newspaper as well as contacting Clare FM Radio. They were sym-pathetic, and both gave me space to explain.

And from there events snowballed, first to national radio, then to the *New York Times*, and after that to radio, TV and papers all over Britain, Europe and the United States. And it was this international interest that saved the bush. Many of the reporters and television crews who came to talk to me were there to be amused, of course — this was a colour-story about Irish whimsicality and such.

But I made clear to one and all that to me this was anything but an 'Oirish' story, and that I would co-operate only on the basis of its being approached seriously, since it was nothing less than a matter of life and death: if this bush were destroyed and a road built over where it had stood, there would be accidents, deaths at that spot. I was convinced of this because I knew of two other places where interference with fairy forts in the course of road-widening had led to inexplicable accidents, both in number and type, accidents that unbelievers in fairy influence can account for only in terms such as 'unfortunate coincidence'. Also, of course, I was thinking very much of myself in this case, since I would be passing this way twice a day, to and from work, and I might well be (probably would be, since I knew the true nature of the place) one of those casualties.

I'm glad to say that there has been a sensible resolution of the matter. Clare County Council and the National Roads Authority have changed the course of the new road slightly, leaving the *sceach* in its rightful place. In so doing, they have displayed a flexibility that can only be saluted and welcomed. They have shown that, even in this harried, technological age, some respect remains for a world that is different from ours but very close to it, one that may have disastrous consequences for us if we fail to take it into account.

Would that Christianity could say the same for Hell nowadays!

The Lost Are Like This

❈

Paul Perry

Paul Perry was born in Dublin in 1972. He moved to the US to study at Brown University where he wrote his bachelor's thesis on the new urban voice in Irish poetry. In 1998 he was awarded the Hennessy Prize for Irish Literature. He has been a James Michener Fellow in Poetry at the University of Miami, a C. Glenn Cambor Fellow in Poetry at the University of Houston, and is currently serving as Writer in Residence in County Longford, Ireland. His book, The Drowning of the Saints, *is forthcoming from Salmon Poetry.*

Every poet is essentially an emigré. An emigré to the Kingdom of Heaven and to his own home.

Marina Tsvetaeva

A badly lit sacristy. The pungent musk of incense.
Words, mysterious and alluring, like 'tabernacle'.

Before this the walk on the narrow path from Sandyford Road to Dundrum and its church. A winter twilight. Friends. Girls. Sitting and kneeling and pacing towards the altar where the Eucharist waited for your tongue.

As altar boys you vied for the paying gigs. Funerals and weddings. One funeral, I was asked to leave off the lights. People strayed from the cold into the dark. At a wedding, a bride could not stop herself from tittering throughout the service. The vows were peppered with giggles and infected us, the altar boys.

I remember the moving crib at Christmas, the gaudily coloured eggs at Easter and an outing with the priests to the ice rink in Dolphin's

Barn. I remember fighting over who would get to ring the bells during Mass. And the wine, generic and tempting, the priest swishing its ascetic aroma around the silver chalice and licking his thin lips.

'Chalice', the word sensual and cold on the tongue.

I remember the priest making a visit to my house. My poor mother mortified, brewing up some tea and shuffling biscuits onto a plate and slicing sandwiches, wondering why he was coming, what I had done. Perhaps he thought I might make a decent initiate into the priesthood, or perhaps this was simply part of his social rounds. The truth is I had done nothing but follow my duties as an altar boy. The priest left. My mother cleaned up, relieved, but still a little confused.

I also remember the jittering men across the street waiting for the pub to open, and my father buying stacks of print-smudging Sunday papers outside the church. A ritual of his to gather the news after the Mass.

The priest never called again. My father continued to buy the papers. I grew out of the altar boys, stopped for some reason as arbitrarily as I stopped going to Mass itself. My father said he'd pray for me.

When I stopped going to Mass, I started writing poetry. Poetry became a form of prayer. An agnostic's prayer. An atheist's prayer.

The obvious correlation to my creative endeavours is to say that they were a response to the lack of religion in my life, filling some kind of void, spiritual or otherwise. I looked at my habits and beliefs critically for the first time and decided they weren't sincere. I suppose some of the motivation, some of the impetus to write was to offset this rejection of religious habit. I wanted to believe, but it just wasn't in me. I had no confidence in the religious beliefs handed down to me, and I wasn't prepared to make any kind of Kierkegaardian leap of faith.

The Word turning to poetry in its grief, Derek Walcott writes.

It occurred to me though that there might be something contradictory in what I was doing — writing poetry without belief, that is without a religious belief. I am not sure whether this was because of my Irish Catholic upbringing, but I seriously doubt it, because I had

had a non-denominational education. So here was my dilemma: how to write, or discover, or make something of metaphysical value, something of spiritual value, when I had no definite religious beliefs of my own.

In other words, how to know whether there was a poetry in the world where there is no evidence of God. I wanted to find meaning and beauty — to celebrate, commiserate, and wonder in things in themselves rather than as an expression of anything divine. Poetry was my effort to discover a divine world that did not necessarily include a deity.

The sublime in the everyday.

When I conceived the title behind my first collection of poetry, *The Drowning of the Saints*, I was thinking about the ships from the Spanish Armada wrecked off the west coast of Ireland. I was thinking of the actual ships and of the metaphoric resonance of such a catastrophe. Ships with the names of saints: The *Santa Marie de La Rosa*, for example. Ships carrying Irish and Spanish alike. It was a physical, material drowning, but I also appropriated the image to mean a spiritual drowning, my own and others. It was a conclusion, less logically and more associatively made. I felt that the culpability of the Irish in the Spanish deaths made a kind of spiritual death.

Niall Fallon writes in *The Armada in Ireland* that no blame can be attached with certainty to the native Irish who undoubtedly witnessed the wrecks, the captures and the hangings, except to point out that no attempt was made to aid the Spaniards, none of whom survived. At first I was simply disappointed with my Irish forebears. But, the more I thought of it, the more the act of negligence on the part of the Irish, the wreckage, the war itself came to represent a spiritual kind of crisis in myself and in Ireland too.

Chilean poet Pablo Neruda comments that poetry is a deep inner calling, that poetry came from liturgy, that the poet confronted nature's phenomena and in the early ages called himself a priest, to safeguard his vocation. Today's social poet, he writes, is a member of that earliest order of priests. Neruda was one of many — many authors who had used poetry to explore what Mallarmé calls the mystical meaning of existence.

I went on pilgrimage.

I went along the west coast of Ireland and imagined the scenes of wreckage. Cnoc na Crocaire, or Gallows Hill, in Clare. I tried to re-imagine the spirit of their journey. I said to myself: tonight, the sea calls out. Tonight, the sea calls out to all souls, shipwrecked or not. Over distances of geography and time, urging you to imagine an armada of drowned sailors, to witness a barrage of ghosts smouldering upwards into the bruised halo of the moon. Tonight, the sea calls out and you are here circling Cnoc na Crocaire, poor witness, belated exile, watching the shadows ride the dark tracks of night and the rain shoot down into a scaffold of grief, listening to the lament of the waves working the past into a frenzy of surf, envisioning the fear the mariners felt.

I said to myself, 'But really, what can you do? Stand, shiver on the shore and ruminate? Is there anything to salvage from this sea? What did you expect to find, or hope to do? To reach across time? And what? This is all a gesture of longing, but again for what? Surely, nothing as portentous as forgiveness? Imagine the fear they felt, Spanish and Irish alike.'

So, I did what the sea told me to do: took the words like loot and wrote of a carved cabin door from the *Santa Maria de la Rosa* that became a carved cabin door in O'Connor's farm or an oak table with a mahogany top from the *San Juan Bautista* that found its way into Dromoland Castle. Wrote about small bounties of loss, how saints and sinners went down with the elemental pull of calamity. Witnessed the sea and watched as it lowered the sky, pulled down the clouds and made a symphony of cliff and stone with its briny absolutions, its declarative waves, its voices and chants, its swallowed anchors and quilted face of nets and pots and sinking stars. Be here tonight, listen as the sea calls out to all souls shipwrecked or not, stand accounted for, watch while to the sea's aid like a thousand wrecked dawns a storm hurries.

'Spirituality' is not a term you hear bandied about by the youth of Ireland. It's not like so many other holy cows in the new Emerald Isle, a broken taboo, but rather remains a shibboleth of an older generation, of elderly women with headscarves entering their dotage and going to Mass every day, or alternatively of New Age hacks and religious pundits. You don't think of Irish Gen. Xers worrying about spirituality; not in the age of the Celtic Tiger.

'Spirituality' — it's a big clumsy word like all the other abstracts that we fumble around with. There's a vagueness about the term, a shadowy insubstantiality. There's something suspect about the word which comes perhaps from its historical vagaries in meaning: 'In the name of the father, the son, and the holy ghost' became 'In the name of the father, son, and holy *spirit*' not long ago. A small point perhaps, but one that reveals the close alliance between religion and magic through the ages, and one that emphasises the reliance of both on language and words themselves. In this way I believe that, among other things, poetry can dispel the dubious semantics of spirituality and create a space where its metaphysical musings can be better explored.

For me, Heaney's characterisation of Yeats — as always passionately beating on the wall of the physical world in order to provoke an answer from the other side — is a kind of poetic motto, something I think poets do even if they don't believe they'll get an answer. Poems are prayers sent in hope. In vain? Maybe. With doubt? Yes. Poets are hopeful atheists. Poems are prayers sent by the descendants of Saint Thomas.

There were no magic wells in my childhood. The life of the spirit, I suppose, can be inherited. But it can also be made or discovered. Paul Valéry in 'A Poet's Letter' writes that poetry comes from 'spiritual surprises and accidents; or in a sort of oblivion and frenzy, or in a truly admirable outburst'. But then he goes on to dismiss the idea of inspiration, writing that the naïve conception of an extraneous force or an all-powerful soul suddenly taking the place of our own may be sufficient for the ordinary mythology of the mind. It satisfies most poets. Indeed they will not hear of any other. But I have never been able to understand why one should not delve as profoundly as possible into oneself.

Contemporary poetry is compelled by doubt. It is provoked into answering the technological age. What does it mean to write with doubt? A doubt of what? One's own medium? One's own self? The world and the existence of God? When we struggle with such issues, when we doubt the accepted beliefs that have been handed down to us, we can produce poetry. Edward Hirsch, in *How to Read A Poem and Fall in Love with Poetry*, laments the loss of 'soul culture'. He writes that the lyric poem rejuvenates the capacity for wonder in us, which instils the culture of the soul back into us. I wholeheartedly agree. What poetry allows one to do is to contemplate the spirit, the ineffable part of humankind, or the essence of one's being and how it interacts on a non-material plane, a metaphysical level, and within that contemplation, if faith is lost, it does not necessarily constitute a loss of spirituality.

Poetry brings us to the contemplation of the spirit, of things unexplained through language. It is, like the contemporary Polish poet Adam Zagejeski's last collection of poetry, a search, life-long, eternal, and, for us who are not among the initiated, a course in Mysticism for Beginners.

Many poets talk of poetry as a vocation, which it is. It is a calling. It is up to us to decide who or what has made such a calling.

God's absence usurps the muses.

Seeking the Source

Patricia Monaghan

Patricia Monaghan is a member of the interdisciplinary faculty at DePaul University, in Chicago. Her first book, The Book of Goddesses and Heroines, *is the standard reference work on the world's feminine divinities. She has published more than a dozen books of non-fiction and poetry and is currently completing* The Red-Haired Girl on the Bog: A Celtic Spiritual Geography *(New World Library, 2002), from which this is excerpted. With ancestral roots in east Mayo, she has been travelling to Ireland for more than 25 years.*

'Dowra?' my Connemara friends said when I told them. 'Whyever would you want to go to Dowra?'

'To look for the source of the Shannon,' I said.

It's easy enough to find in myth, that bubbling pool where magical hazel-bushes drop nuts into the mouth of a speckled one-eyed salmon. Because the nuts contain wisdom, the salmon is the wisest creature in the world. Anyone who catches and eats it — like the hero Fionn mac Cumhaill and the goddess Sionann — can absorb all that wisdom. Even to catch a glimpse of the salmon of wisdom, the old stories say, brings good fortune.

But myth tells more than maps. I had tried without success for several years to find the Shannon's source. Most maps of Ireland fail to mark it. I have two that do, but each puts it in a different place. Once, several years earlier, I had followed one map to Keshcorran, where people apologetically shook their heads. The source was not there, despite the little red star on the map I held. Then I found mythic geographer Michael Dames's citation of 'a field near Dowra', a little town on the borders of Leitrim and Cavan, as the Shannon Pot's location. It was enough to launch another expedition.

The day before I set off, I ran into Roundstone's bodhrán-maker, Malachy Kearns. Like everyone else, his response to my planned excursion was, 'Whyever do you want to go to Dowra?' But unlike anyone else he added, 'I just bought a farm there.'

He scribbled down the cellphone number of his estate agent. If anyone knew his way around Dowra, it was surely Tony.

Thus prepared — no need for rod and creel, I would be content just to see the salmon leap — I set off one spring morning in search of the source.

I travelled the familiar road north from Connemara into even more familiar terrain, my mother's family home near Bohola. East of Sligo, I turned onto roads I had never travelled. I told myself to relax, enjoy the scenery, this could be another wild-goose chase, there was no guarantee I would reach Tony, much less that he would know the way to the Shannon Pot. The towns shrank, the stretches of wild land grew, my heart expanded.

At Drumkeoran, I found a phone at the community centre. One ring, then an answer. Perhaps luck was with me, perhaps this time I would indeed find the mythic Pot.

'Hello,' I shouted into the bad connection. 'Malachy Kearns told me to call; he said you'd know how to find the source of the Shannon.'

'Tony did not know, but he knew who would: 'Go into the town, cross the bridge to McGrail's, ask for Oliver.'

I thanked Tony profusely. But my hand was still on the receiver when I thought: Oh no. Should I have asked for more details? I recalled wandering back and forth on a road in Cork, looking for the Maxol station at which I was to turn. Finally I stopped at the only station I could find, an Exxon — which had a few years earlier been the Maxol in question. Or how about that hour I spent in Galway looking for 'the green house', the one painted blue decades before? Or the time in a midlands village when I was to turn at a pub called Rooney's? There it was, plain as day, and a road to the right just as described, but nonetheless I stopped to check.

'Ah now,' a helpful farmer said, pointing up the road, 'this is a narrow little town that stretches some way, and there at the other end is another pub, also called Rooney's, with a road to the right beside it. Turn there.' He winked. 'Same family.'

A decade ago, Rooneyville would have driven me distracted. But Irish directions no longer distress me. They are like coded spiritual messages reminding us that the journey is more important than the destination, that not all places are meant to be found, that not all times are right for the finding. That sometimes what you find will not be what you sought.

But this time there was no problem: Tony's directions brought me straight to a bridge, across which I saw a drygoods store called McGrail's. Eternal hope sprang. But the store was closed, shuttered tight. I peered in the windows and peeked behind the building. A fine new house stood beside the store, not physically attached but close enough to seem a unit. I rang, and Oliver appeared. He regretted that his brother was not around — the teacher, he would know so much more. But Oliver could direct me, indeed he could. I was near enough, just follow the road towards Cuilcagh Mountain, I would see the signs for the Shannon Pot soon enough, I would indeed.

I set off again, this time confidently. I had directions, hadn't I? But no matter how far I drove, every sign showed seven kilometres from Dowra. Was I going in circles? It was a perfect spring day, with sweet sunlight and fragrant air, white maybush and greening grass. Ah well, I said to myself, at worst I was having a lovely drive. Then, suddenly, a directional sign. A few turns, the road narrowing with each one, then a cattle gate. A small hill. An empty parking lot. No interpretative centre — what Connemara mapmaker Tim Robinson calls an 'interruptive centre' — just a path.

Would there really be a bubbling pool, or was that just metaphor? Had I driven all day to see a sodden marsh? Not knowing what to expect, I started down the path. A bit of a stream ran beside me. Was that the Shannon? I followed the streamlet downhill.

A cow lowed. Insects buzzed. The creek bubbled.

At the bottom of the hill, a little bridge. A tiny river flowed under it, perhaps three feet wide: the Shannon, soon joined by the stream I had been following. Close to the source, the Shannon was already acting like a river, pulling tributaries into itself. Across the bridge, I turned left and took a few steps, then stopped dead in my tracks.

Before me was the most archetypal landscape I had ever seen. A round mountain belly rose above me. Two long flanks of hills reached out to the sides. Where they joined was an almost perfectly circular pool, the lifesource of the goddess. The water moved constantly, bubbling from springs fed by rain from swallowholes in the white chalk hill above. The pool's sloping sides were green and slick. At the one place I could approach, bright primroses bloomed beneath the surface. I leaned down, holding my breath. Was the salmon there?

I have known salmon all my life. As a girl in Alaska, I watched them in the shadowy river banks, waiting for the tide to turn, great looming urgent presences, their gills bloody, their skin torn into shreds by their headlong migration. My father fed us on salmon he caught in the churning Kenai River or the placid grey waters of Lake Louise. Later I fished Prince William Sound for red-fleshed kings and bargained with native fishermen on the Yukon for huge, pale, dog salmon. Alaska's salmon are a different species from Ireland's, but they share a homing instinct that leads them from the ocean where they lived amid whales and dolphins, back to the river mouth they exited as fry, to the exact spot they hatched years earlier, there to spawn, there to die. Who is wiser than one who knows the way home?

In Ireland, the salmon run begins just as the mayflies — their Latin name of *ephemeroptera* captures the brevity of their lives — hatch, mate and die, all within hours. It was spring; scores of mayflies added agitation to the Shannon Pot. Were I a salmon in that bubbling pond, I would surely rise to feed. I sat on the green hillside and waited.

Were those silver fins beneath the water?

I had come without a map to a place where slant light gleamed on the undersides of slim willow leaves. To a round pool that bubbled softly. To an opening beneath a mountain belly from which wisdom might be born. I had failed in my first attempts to find the source. Might it not take several visits to win the eye of the salmon of wisdom? But after all, I reasoned, this was no longer the age of myth; anything I saw would just be a fish, a migrating fish that had swum up from Limerick, past Killaloe and Portumna, through Lough Ree and Lough Bofin, past

Carrick-on-Shannon — just a fish, no mythic being with the power to impart wisdom, just a fish after all —

Still I stared at the pool and waited.

Sitting on the green slope, I pondered the persistence of my search. I was not from the region; I had no special devotion to the river's tutelary goddess, Sionann; yet the image of a circular pool from which a great river rises held some compelling power to which I responded. And the Shannon Pot had repaid my persistence, for on that splendid day in May it was uncannily beautiful, a place I could credit with nurturing wisdom.

The Apache people of the American south-west say that 'wisdom sits in places' and tell their children to 'drink from places'. Apache sage Dudley Patterson once described wisdom as 'water that never dries up'. He articulated the connection of place and soul this way: 'You need to drink water to stay alive, don't you? Well, you also need to drink from places. You must learn their names. You must remember what happened at them long ago.'

The Apache are a desert people, but their idea of wisdom strangely echoes that of rainy Ireland. It is important, both say, to repeat the names of places, for in doing so we evoke their stories. *That* happened *there*: place and story are deeply tied into both Apache and Irish wisdom traditions.

I remembered listening once to the great novelist Salman Rushdie talking on the radio. He was praising the post-modern world as one in which place has become unnecessary. 'The roots of the self are no longer in places,' he said. He proclaimed that the city is our place now, not separate place-bound cities but that exciting, multicultural, global cities where we will find our stories from now on. But must this denationalised world, I wondered, be denaturalised as well? Where is the place now for storied places of the past, places created by nature but filled with storied wisdom by humans?

But things also happen *then*. A story makes then and there into here and now. Past, whether mythic or historical, connects to future in the momentary present. Story revivifies place, brings it alive with people and events, with tears and blood, with tragedy and hope. And some places draw to themselves more powerful stories than others. Such a place is the Shannon Pot, where the maiden Sionann devoured the salmon of wisdom, then dissolved into Ireland's greatest river. Philosopher Mikhail Bakhtin called such places 'chronotopes', 'where time takes on flesh and becomes visible for human contemplation; space becomes charged and responsible to the movements of history and the enduring character of a people.' At such places, the beauty of land and the mystery of myth come together so precisely that it is impossible to tell where one begins, the other ends.

Place-stories — from myth, history, rumour, gossip — have been told and retold for millennia in Ireland, a story for each name on the map. The traditional poetry called the *Dindshenchas*, where we find the tale of the maid Sionann, was devoted to such place-name narratives. Within such stories, wisdom lived like a salmon in a secret pool, for narrative is an ancient way of preserving human knowledge.

Great places, argued W.B. Yeats, were like great books, and perhaps even more lasting: 'in a little time, places may begin to seem the only hieroglyphs that cannot be forgotten.' But I wonder if we will continue to read those unforgettable texts. So much of what anthropologist Clifford Geertz calls 'local knowledge' is being lost, in Ireland as elsewhere, and with it, a certain kind of wisdom. Not a universal, abstract wisdom, the same no matter where you stand, but wisdom expressed and embodied in specific places. We still say we 'come from' a place, as though we were birthed by the earth at a specific spot. Yet who among us knows that mother place? Who could, like the salmon, find the way back?

My grandparents came from a pre-global village. When economic exile drove them from Bohola, they left brothers and parents, cousins and friends. My grandmother never returned; my grandfather only once, in his eighties. Occasional letters carried vital news across the great water, but everyday news went unexpressed. Did the old dog die? How was the weather? What colour was the shed painted? We might dismiss such matters as trivial, but in doing so we would be deaf to the word's meaning, for Trivia was the Roman goddess of crossroads. Every trivial exchange leads us towards or away from deeper relationship. Without witnessing the trivia of each other's days, even kinfolk become strangers.

Unlike Rushdie, I do not warm to the post-modern city, for I love wild nature in salmon streams and hedgerows, the weedy corners of my garden, the mating of mayflies, all those huge and tiny mysteries. I do not yearn to lose myself in a stream of humanity, rich and diverse. For that richness, that diversity has its base in beloved places of some homeland, without which we become homogenised into those new beings so aptly dubbed 'airport people', people whose stylish corporate surroundings look the same in Tokyo or New York or Dublin.

Instead of Rushdie's beloved City, I want the village. I already live in a global village, albeit a virtual one. I am in daily touch with a dozen people, weekly with scores. I hear about Dawn's accident in Iowa and the bad weather down Maggie's way in Florida. I hear about Fiona's art opening in Laois, my cousin Mike's dog trials in Australia, the marching season in Bob's Ulster town. My siblings send around jokes (usually groaners), reminders of birthdays, grievances and peeves, song lyrics. I love this ever-widening pool of relationships and wonder how, just a few years ago, I lived in a narrower, more constricted world.

Once we knew our homeplaces, physically, viscerally, by sight and sound and smell. But we increasingly share a world for which we have no accurate map, where place is supplanted by site, homeplace by home-page, the tactile by the virtual. What is the wisdom of this village where we can be intimate with people whose laughter we cannot hear, whose tears we cannot dry? It would be easy to deny that the virtual world can be sacred as the Shannon's source. Easy to demand that we return to a simpler time when only the tangible was real. But human connection has always transcended the physical. We have always touched even when our bodies are separate. How many stories have we heard of mothers who have known the instant their children were hurt? Of people who saw a relative just at the moment he died in a distant city? Is not the ultimate virtual reality the soul?

As we learn to navigate this new world, mythic wisdom becomes more, rather than less, important, for, as Michael Dames has pointed out, myth does not follow a binary 'either/or' logic but employs 'both/and' terms. The salmon of wisdom is named both Fintan and Goll; it has two eyes and only one; it was once a man and has always been a salmon; it was captured only by one person, Fionn and Sionann; the Shannon Pot is a cauldron and a womb — all and only some of these things are simultaneously true. To sustain both our literal and our global villages, we need to learn to think like that, holding apparent contradictions as equally true.

I sat on the wet grass by the Shannon Pot, pondering its past and its future. The willows swayed. The cow lowed. The insects buzzed. The pool bubbled.

Then, a flash of silver.

And gone.

Just like that.

Irish Spirit Now and Then

❧

Seán Kenny

Born in Dublin, Seán Kenny lived in Kinsale, County Cork, before moving to California, where he currently lives. A born-again pagan, Kenny's novels and children's books — The Hungry Earth, Celtic Fury, D-RAM *and* Fast-Wing, *all published by Wolfhound Press — collectively show his views on the problem of spirituality today. Kenny is also a filmmaker whose one-hour documentary,* Kinsale 1601: The Turning Point, *captures the defeat of Gaelic civilisation. He can be reached at www.seankenny.com and www.firbolgfilms.com.*

*L*ike most of my generation who grew up while the Catholic Church still controlled all of the schools, and teachers began every class with a prayer, on peril of their jobs, I cannot reconcile the sadism and bitterness of that establishment with its stated philosophy of love and forgiveness. I saw none, through a succession of the Presentation Sisters, the Marist Brothers and three Christian Brothers schools, with a total of thirty or more teachers. What I can say now is that, while I know my spirit is wounded, I also know that these people do not and never did have a monopoly on the supernatural, and that it is possible to find a sacred path through life without becoming like them.

What I was entirely unaware of at the time was that I was growing up in an Ireland undergoing wrenching change. By the end of the 1950s a century of unremitting emigration had taken its toll, emptying the country of most of its rural population, who could neither be sustained by the land beyond a feudal lifestyle nor absorbed by the depressed towns. But large families were still the norm — I am the oldest of five — and their housing needs created the drab concrete suburbs that now surround every major Irish town.

None of these, of course, were new towns or villages. I spent the first ten years of my life living in Clondalkin, now a suburb of Dublin, separated from the city back then by miles of farmland. But the pattern of its expansion was the same as everywhere else — new people coming to live in existing, and indeed ancient, communities. Clondalkin, typically, had its own parish church, an attached convent, various priests' houses and a couple of monasteries. And it fell quite naturally to the existing religious powers to build and manage the new schools that would educate all of these new children.

The Catholic Church's orders of nuns and brothers owned the only available land on which such schools could be built within the ever-sprawling mazes of houses. But this new migratory population did not bring with it its own vocations, and schools that had once been 'all nuns' or 'all brothers' now found themselves with lay-teachers as the majority of their staff. Into these institutions my generation trudged to be inculcated in traditions that held no relevance for us, and out of it we emerged with no clear ideas at all.

I am possibly one of the last of those who grew up in a world where everyone went to Mass every Sunday. That was the absolute minimum acceptable behaviour. Some people went to more than one Mass, some people went every day. Sometimes we went to Mass in Walkinstown or Inchicore for variety. Ten o'clock Mass was a quick Mass with no sermon. But that meant waiting till after Mass to have breakfast if you wanted to get Holy Communion. Let me restate this. Everyone went to Mass every Sunday. It was an unalterable fact of Irish life.

Except, of course, for the Protestants. But in the world I grew up in there were no Protestants. As in most Irish towns, Clondalkin had a small Anglican church but, whoever those people were, we never saw them. And the dwindling Anglo-Irish population was not a part of this enormous migration I am describing.

Ireland was continuously inhabited for thousands of years before the birth of Christ, and architectural remains such as celestial observatories, passage graves, and even the early Christian beehive huts and round towers attest to its insular development. And its history is unique too — invasion, conquest, subjugation, famine and loss are all a part of it, but equally important are the influences that are absent — the Romans, the Renaissance, the Reformation, the Enlightenment, the Industrial Revolution. The premise of my first novel, *The Hungry Earth*, is that the contents of our unconscious minds are handed down over the generations, and this is a belief that has only grown stronger for me over the years. But if this is so, and if our experiences as a people are quite different from those of other nations, then it is those very differences that must define us and bestow on us our Irishness. This is one of those ideas that makes sense momentarily, yet slips away if not given the fiercest concentration. Why is that? Why is it so difficult to come to terms with what must surely be the very thing this book is about — the Irish spirit?

Why can we not become aware of some or all of these differences? I believe there are two huge obstacles in our way. The first is our adherence to an imported religion. Christianity is a foreign religion whose symbolism and origin myths are entirely at odds with the environment in which the Irish developed their own pagan ideas. Judeo-Christian beliefs are patriarchal, which is consistent with a nomadic people always in search of the next oasis; the bull must take control of the herd and keep it all moving in the same direction. Then there is the Christian obsession with water as a holy substance; that makes sense in the desert, but not on a rainwashed island where it is the sun that is the unpredictable arbiter of life. Water sources may all have their own peculiar magic and would later be pronounced holy wells, but it is light and heat that are in short supply in our environment.

Pagan Ireland would much more likely have been matriarchal, which is borne out in many ways, such as the triune goddesses, including Ériu herself, the succession of female metaphors in story and song — Sean Bhean Bocht, Dark Rosaleen, Cathleen Ní Houlihan —

and by the devotion to the actual mother and to the mother of god, to the point that it is always the Virgin Mary whose statues are suspected of supernatural powers. I should mention too that this overlay of later Christianity on the earlier beliefs is the theme of my second novel, *Celtic Fury*.

In every possible way, Christianity has blocked our view of the pagan past. Of our three mythological cycles, two have been corrupted to the point of giving them Christian endings — Oisín returns from Tír na nÓg to meet Saint Patrick, and the Children of Lir, after nine hundred years as swans, are baptised. Christianity subsumed Celtic festivals, made saints out of goddesses such as Brigit, built churches and monasteries in places that were already sacred.

The second obstacle to knowing our spiritual core is surely the loss of our original language. Language is consciousness. And language evolves to give us the means to raise each other's consciousness through communication. The Irish language is the consciousness of the Irish mind. It is a language in which every noun is masculine or feminine, endowing all objects with animism. And it is a language that has no word for 'yes' or 'no', wholly appropriate to a society that has not yet reduced itself to an abstract moral rigidity, but allows for emotional flexibility, essential in the search for one's own sacred path. And Irish is a purely oral language, awkward to symbolise but with intonations that make it much more powerful than English as a spoken tongue.

So what if we were all to become Irish-speaking pagans again? Would that be the road to spiritual re-awakening? Such studies, undertaken in the right context, might be hugely beneficial to reinvigorating the Irish spirit, but we have been led down that path before in our quest for an identifiable national spirit. Gaelic games flourish today as never before — they are Ireland's biggest sporting events. The Irish language is alive and well, as are Irish music and dancing. But they are re-invented versions of what was there before, not a route all the way back to our spiritual beginnings.

Therein lies the agonising truth. Were you or I to eschew all the trappings of modern life — to live in a thatched stone hut on some remote island or peninsula, eking out an existence without coinage — we might still be no closer to understanding it all. Because we would still be separated from the ideas of our ancestors by having *chosen* such a life when they knew no other. We've bitten the apple of post-modern global high-technology. It is impossible for us to go back.

Not only can we not go back ourselves, but it is not even possible for us to rub shoulders with people who represent a tradition handed down unconsciously over countless generations. No such Irish people exist any longer. Even the people who live in Gaeltacht areas today are in no way cut off from the same ideas and culture as the rest of us. Inis Meáin, the middle island of Aran, is today dominated by a pink hotel, with plans for a wind farm. There is no lost rainforest tribe to be studied by anthropologists.

A hundred years ago the situation was less gloomy. A person alive then, if he opened his mind and learned to speak Irish, could meet and discourse with people continuing a way of life relatively unchanged, so far as they themselves could tell, from when their world began. One person did do this. He recorded in his journals what he saw and heard, and transformed it into some of our greatest drama. His name was John Millington Synge.

Synge remains an enigma to this day. He died very young, aged thirty-seven, before some of his plays had even been performed, with what fame he had achieved resting on controversy over the accuracy of his portrayals of Irish peasant life. It was left to his fellow-writers to defend his reputation. Yeats was forever indebted to him and said so at his Nobel prize acceptance speech. Joyce translated *Riders to the Sea*, a play he had earlier derided, into Italian, and tried unsuccessfully to have it performed. And even the most ardent nationalists, notably Pearse and Griffith, who had done their utmost to discredit Synge in pursuit of their own noble-peasant notions, were far more tolerant of him in death than in life.

There is a huge irony to Synge's success, which is that he came from the very opposite side of the social spectrum to the people he was studying. He was a Dublin Protestant whose widowed mother kept up their middle-class household with rents from an estate in Galway, a fact of which she never tired reminding him as he used his stipend to travel around Europe and ultimately to support his unwholesome writing habit. All of his family were deeply religious and utterly disapproving of their youngest's artistic leanings. His three older brothers were more practical: one was a colonial adventurer who borrowed against the Galway lands to invest in a ranch in Argentina, one was a Protestant missionary to China, and one was a professional land agent.

When Synge became engaged to a Catholic, he kept it a secret from his mother for as long as he could. None of his family ever attended a performance of any of his plays. They did not co-operate after his death in releasing his papers for study, nor would they allow Yeats to have a death mask made of him. And his friends from the literary and theatrical world were excluded, without exception, from his funeral procession. I mention all of this because it is testimony to his perspective. Synge's point of view and his artistic purpose were not just extraordinary, they were unique.

Synge was a solitary person. Sickly as a child, his only physical pursuit as a man was walking. He hiked the Wicklow Mountains, the Blaskets and Mayo. But the place that would transform him as a writer, from mediocrity to genius, was Aran. He visited the islands four times, spending most of each visit on Inis Meáin, where, as he put it, one is forced to believe in a sympathy between man and nature. Later on this first visit he would also write:

> Some dreams I have had in this cottage seem to give strength to the opinion that there is a psychic memory attached to certain neighbourhoods.

And on his second visit he wrote:

> There is hardly an hour I am with them that I do not feel the shock of some inconceivable idea, and then again the shock of some emotion that is familiar to them and to me. On some days I feel this island as a perfect home and resting place.

Seán Kenny

Growing up in Ireland in the 1960s, I was exposed to 'the theory of evolution' as it was called. But my teachers and my more devout relatives hastened to point out that the 'missing link' had never been found, whereas archaeologists — they told me — had discovered the actual Garden of Eden. Two generations earlier, young Synge had read and been converted to Darwin's ideas and consequently abandoned his own organised Protestant religion. Interestingly, his first exposure to the Irish language at Trinity College, Dublin, was the result of that establishment having a department whose aim was to proselytise to the natives in the west — to convert them to that very faith. Synge's prowess at speaking Irish has been the subject of scholastic debate over the years, but there is little doubt now that he did speak it well and, perhaps equally importantly, knew that the English idiom of the bilingual Aran Islanders, and of the poorly educated country folk in general, was derived from the native tongue.

Armed with this and his broad exposure to European culture, Synge would pursue the opposite strategy of every other great Irish writer: he would abandon exile, seek out the most isolated of all Irish communities and use the universal ideas he brought with him to discover the Irish soul. This is what sets him apart and why I single him out as a guide for those of us in search of a lost sense of who we are. He took the opposite tack to fellow Paris exiles, Joyce and Beckett. And while Yeats enjoyed the largesse of his wealthy patronesses, Synge weathered weeks at a time in a stone cottage among the most primitive people in Europe, of whom he said:

> It is hard to believe that those hovels I can just see in the south are filled with people whose lives have the strange quality that is found in the oldest poetry and legend.

The plays he later produced offer the most uncompromising look at the thoughts of simple Irish people, unconsciously revealing their innermost feelings, unconstrained by Church or state. They were dangerous plays in their time, so much so that one of them, *The Tinker's Wedding*

— 332 —

— about a couple of travelling people who tie a priest up in a sack when he reneges on a promise to wed them for half-price — was not produced in Ireland until the 1970s.

The Shadow of the Glen, which begins with a Wicklow sheep farmer who pretends to be dead to catch his wife out with a younger lover and ends with the wife leaving both the husband and lover, to roam the country with a tramp, is a near-perfect distillation of the hard choices that faced so many thousands of Irish people in the twentieth century — marry late and stay put, or pack your bags and take your chances — and yet it is based on a story he heard on Inis Meáin. Synge's greatest play, *The Playboy of the Western World*, is even more pointed in its criticism of an Ireland that values land and security over individual freedom. At the end of that play, the heroine, Pegeen Mike, laments the loss of the eponymous hero, knowing full well that with him went her only hope of escape from the dreary, predictable monotony of Irish life.

Synge's last play leaves us in no doubt that he believed he had arrived at the heart of the Irish condition. Censured by his co-directors of the Abbey Theatre, W. B. Yeats and Lady Gregory, for his 'peasant plays' as they had come to be known, he stated that he would write his version of Deirdre of The Sorrows. This legend was already the subject of both an A.E. and a Yeats verse play and had been translated into peasant prose by Gregory, so they can hardly have been wildly enthusiastic about Synge taking on this story too. Synge's stated motivation for choosing this particular myth within the genre of pagan mythology was to have his fiancée, Molly Allgood, to play the lead role. But he was now interpreting Irish myth through his own observations, lending his version a new authenticity.

In this play, the Irish royalty of ancient time — Conchobar, Fergus, Leborcham — speak in the same idiom as the characters in the so-called peasant plays. Synge could, of course, have given them any voices and it is highly significant that he chose to show us that we are the lineal, literal descendants of those mythical characters. The implication is clear. Synge had sought out the Irish people least changed over time and had decided that he could legitimately represent even the kings and queens of the indefinite past as being similar. Sadly, he died before the first production, and we are forever denied his commentary on the result.

The opposite of truth is confusion, and in a society whose people worship a foreign god and speak a foreign language, the truth lies hidden — the real hidden Ireland — while confusion reigns. Ireland always baffled me, through success and failure, in business and personal life, to the point that I eventually left. And I believe that, if I had not left, I would have self-destructed completely. Even in Silicon Valley I cannot really re-invent myself, since I am always rearranging the same pieces. But, gradually, I am dealing with the past, the voices from out of that Irish childhood, no longer crushed by the weight of it all. The cacophony all around me was just too loud ever to sift through it for whatever few grains of that precious substance can ever be found in one lifetime.

This is why Synge is a hero to me. He was able to listen and to hear the meaning in every phrase. Just as surely as if he had discovered the source of the Nile, he found out what the Irish think about life and death, ideas laid bare on a tiny microcosm of the bigger island. And, by whatever insight it is that separates the artist from the rest of humanity, he knew he was the last person who would have the opportunity to look so clearly at the origins of the Irish mind. Had he gone a year later, old Pat Dirane would already have been dead and Synge would never have heard the story on which *The Shadow of the Glen* is based, and his metamorphosis would have gone no further. And, as if he wants us all to know that he was aware that the timeless ways of the island were passing, Synge himself sent the first clock, as a gift to his hosts, and comments at length on this and the islanders' sense of time in his Aran journal.

A major change in Irish demographics shaped me and my genera-tion. This was a chaotic social transformation, unanticipated by any political leadership, whose major parties remained as mired in the past as its clerics, to the point where, now that the successful new Irish economy has emerged, no person, no ideology, no movement, no activists and no momentous event can claim credit for the outcome.

Ireland today is a wealthy nation. The transformation to a modern nation, where time is all-important, is complete. Emigration has been replaced with immigration. Those of us who live abroad can increasingly choose to be expatriates rather than permanent exiles. But this great journey, this migration to an urban high-tech economy, has been at enormous spiritual expense.

Ireland, over the past decade, has been preoccupied with scandals within the Catholic Church and is steadily dragging the politicians of the whole late-twentieth-century era through the courts as more and more evidence of corruption is discovered. Beneath the achievements of the recent past lies, not brilliant planning and selfless patriotism, but a sordid swamp of duplicity and perversion. This then is the conundrum of this essay, and much of this book. What is the true nature of the Irish spirit? Is it the ability of the people to endure poverty and hardship? Is it their desire to do so rather than leave? And how can we avoid the idea that this is grounded in some hidden or unconscious beliefs far beyond the grasp of its religious or political leaders?

That elusive spirit is more valuable than all the grants and loans and roads and jobs and soaring house prices of Ireland's new economy. It is the essence of who we are, and in the end it is all we can point to as the basis for the country's recent successes and, even more importantly, draw on for the success of future generations, unless, of course, we choose to become yet another amorphous city-statelet on the edge of world culture and dismiss these ideas as no more than romantic idealism. But that is the point of this essay, and this book: to show that Ireland's spiritual heritage is richer than we ever imagined, and that within it we can find our way forward into the future if only we do not allow ourselves to be blinded by the pain of the Irish past or dazzled by the speed of the Irish present.

For further discussion on the topics raised in this book,
log on to the *Irish Spirit* interactive website:
www.irishspirit.org